Third Sector Performance

Third Sector Performance

Management and Finance in Not-for-profit and Social Enterprises

EDITED BY

GRAHAM MANVILLE
University of Southampton, UK

RICHARD GREATBANKS
University of Otago, New Zealand

Taylor & Francis Group

LONDON AND NEW YORK

First published 2013 by Gower Publishing

2 Park Square, Milton Park, Abingdon, Oxon OX14 4RN
711 Third Avenue, New York, NY 10017, USA

Routledge is an imprint of the Taylor & Francis Group, an informa business

First issued in paperback 2016

Gower Applied Business Research
Our programme provides leaders, practitioners, scholars and researchers with thought provoking, cutting edge books that combine conceptual insights, interdisciplinary rigour and practical relevance in key areas of business and management.

British Library Cataloguing in Publication Data
Third sector performance : management and finance in
    not-for-profit and social enterprises.
    1. Nonprofit organizations--Management. 2. Nonprofit
    organizations--Finance. 3. Nonprofit organizations--
    Political activity. 4. Civil society.
    I. Manville, Graham. II. Greatbanks, Richard.
    658'.046-dc23

Library of Congress Cataloging-in-Publication Data
Manville, Graham.
    Third sector performance : management and finance in not-for-profit and social enterprises /
    by Graham Manville and Richard Greatbanks.
        p. cm.
    Includes bibliographical references and index.
    ISBN 978-1-4094-2961-6 (hbk.)
      1. Nonprofit organizations. 2. Public-private sector cooperation. 3. Financial institutions--
    Social aspects. 4. Social responsibility in banking. I. Greatbanks, Richard. II. Title.

    HD62.6.M3678 2012
    658'.048--dc23

                                          2012022805

ISBN 978-1-4094-2961-6 (hbk)
ISBN 978-1-138-25119-9 (pbk)

Contents

List of Figures

List of Tables

Notes on Contributors

Pratima Dattani has twenty-five years' experience of working in local government and has managed community development and community regeneration programmes. She has also managed equality and community safety programmes and has led significant partnership work between statutory and non-statutory partners. Pratima has experience of working closely with the voluntary and community sector, leading key infrastructure developments. She is a founder member and Chair of Gharana Housing Association, a black and ethnic minority housing association providing housing and support services for older Asian people. Pratima's research is part of her Master's in Public Administration (MPA) from Warwick Business School (2010) and is based on consideration of the role of public value and performance management in the third sector. This offers the third sector a means of maintaining its independence while operating within a political economy that continues to be based on neo-liberal market economy principles which prefer competition to collaboration.

Patrizia Garengo is an assistant professor at the Department of Industrial Innovation and Management at the University of Padua, Italy. She holds a degree in business economics from Ca' Foscari University in Venice and a PhD in industrial engineering from the University of Padua. For over ten years she has taught economics and business administration at the University of Padua and carried out research and advisory work in the field of organizational development, performance management and management systems in SMEs. She continues to make a significant contribution to this research field; to date she has published an edited book and over fifty papers in international journals and for conferences.

Richard Greatbanks is a senior lecturer within the School of Business, University of Otago, Dunedin, New Zealand. He is a Chartered Manufacturing Engineer, a Member of the New Zealand Institute of Directors, and has acted as a consultant to both UK and New Zealand organizations. His PhD explored the use of operational performance with UK SME organizations, and his subsequent academic research interests include the application of quality and performance improvement approaches within manufacturing, healthcare, the public sector and not-for-profit organizations. Richard is Associate Director of the Centre for Health Systems within the Dunedin School of Medicine, and of the Centre for Organisational Performance Measurement and Management with the Otago School of Business. He has also been involved in establishing the Performance Measurement Association (PMA) Australasia. Richard teaches operations and quality management to undergraduate, post-graduate and doctoral levels, and also has a part-time academic leadership role within the Otago MBA programme.

Brett Knowles is a long-time thought leader in the performance measurement field. Over the last twenty years he has worked with Doctors Kaplan and Norton and has had clients referenced in each of their books. Brett has assisted over 3,000 organizations from around the world and in all sectors, from AT&T to Zeneca, and from the IRS to the City of Kingston. His clients have had as many as 250,000 employees and as few as 5. He is the co-founder of the first Balanced Scorecard application, has developed numerous measurement concepts around intangible assets, and has served on countless editorial boards and conference constructs. Brett's clients have been profiled in *Harvard Business Review*, *Fortune* and *Forbes*. There are over twenty business school cases covering the success of his clients. Three of Brett's clients have been placed on the Balanced Scorecard Hall of Fame by Doctors Kaplan and Norton.

Iain Lucas is Managing Director of RISE Community Development Ltd and RISE Computers. RISE is a social enterprise based in a area of deprivation in west Southampton that includes the wards of Millbrook, Redbridge, Coxford and Shirley Warren. Iain has worked in community development for over twenty years and has been developing social enterprises for 18 years. During this time he has developed extensive knowledge and experience of managing community projects and social enterprises. This has given Iain a unique understanding of the challenges faced when creating and sustaining a social enterprise. Iain is qualified at Master's level in business administration, which includes extensive study of SME development, and is currently studying part-time for a PhD at the University of Southampton in the subject area of social enterprise.

Rita S. Mano is a senior lecturer in the Department of Human Services at Haifa University, Israel. She received her DSc from the Faculty of Industrial Engineering and Management, Polytechnic Institute – Technion ITT in 1995. She teaches organizational theories, organizational behaviour and management as well as sociology and interdisciplinary approaches to employment and work (including turnover, managerial behaviour, performance and work policy). She teaches on both undergraduate and MA programmes. She engages in the study of management in non-profit organizations and recently published on non-profit management and performance, covering a great range of issues such as theories, funding, structure, goals, strategic choices, accountability, networking, volunteer recruitment and management, and change and crisis management in non-profit organizations. She currently serves as Chair of the Department of Human Services, University of Haifa. She publishes regularly in journals promoting the research and study of non-profit management and human services such as *Administration in Social Work, Journal of Technology in Human Services* and *Journal of Human Services* as well as in sociological and interdisciplinary journals such as *Human Relations, Journal of Workplace Learning, Sociological Focus*, etc.

Graham Manville is a senior fellow and formerly the Assistant Dean for Enterprise for the Faculty of Law, Arts and Social Sciences at the University of Southampton. Graham teaches strategic management and operations management and his current research area is organizational performance management. In 2008 his research was honoured with two awards including Best KTP Partnership for the South West of England and an Emerald Literati Award for Excellence for an 'outstanding paper'. He has published in international journals and in 2010 he guest-edited a special issue of the *International Journal of Productivity and Performance Management* with the theme of third sector performance. He co-hosted a workshop on third sector performance in May 2010 which was sponsored by the British Academy of Management (BAM) and the Higher Education Entrepreneurial Group (HEEG). Graham is also a management consultant and director of Longview Consulting Ltd and has worked with many sectors, including multinational organizations as well as small charities. Graham is currently studying for his PhD at the University of Southampton and should complete it in 2012. His profile is listed in Marquis *Who's Who in the World 2011*.

John Merritt is a graduate of the University of Southampton, with a BSc in politics and sociology and later an MPhil (with his thesis titled 'Marx and the Moderns: democratic and artistic contributions of social humanism'). Writings and inter-university seminar presentations included unpublished essays on topics such as friendship, internationalism or cosmopolitanism, aesthetics and the fifth dimension, as well as work on faith, gender, environment and socialist humanist contributions. He has worked in the voluntary sector for many years, helping set up and acting as President of Coastal Credit Union and acting as a director for the Association of British Credit Unions. Since 2010 John has been involved with setting up Social Enterprise Link (Wessex) CIC (SEL), a social enterprise infrastructure organization, and with it (so far), nine new cooperatives, social enterprises, mutuals (fourth sector) and charities.

Tila Morris is a partner in Catch the Light, a consultancy service to the public and non-profit sector in Scotland that she co-founded in 2007 after graduating with her MBA from Glasgow Caledonian University, where she was awarded IBM prize for outstanding performance throughout the MBA and the Palman Memorial Award for the best dissertation. Catch the Light offers a range of consultancy services to support organizations, networks and partnerships to make a positive impact on young people and communities in Scotland. Tila's specialisms include the third sector, quality management, planning and evaluation. She has worked with a range of clients including SCVO, Scottish Training Foundation, Scottish Youth Dance, Lifelong Learning UK, Boys' Brigade Scotland, YouthLink Scotland and a wide range of Scottish public agencies and third sector organizations. Particular highlights include developing a programme to enable young people not in education or employment to gain SQA accreditation by researching and populating an online directory of local youth services. Prior to joining Catch the Light, Tila was the managing director of Voluntary Action East Renfrewshire, a third sector infrastructure organization. She led this from its inception through to achieving its ambition of creating 'under COVER', an innovative one-stop-shop concept providing office rental, learning facilities and meeting spaces for communities, organizations and volunteers. Through raising £1.3 million through a cocktail of European, Lottery and other funds, a derelict retail space within a deprived part of the local authority was transformed to create this facility.

David Newton became the Community Affairs Manager for The Body Shop International after an early career in community affairs and fundraising. In this role he worked to promote, support and monitor corporate community involvement through the company's stores across more than forty countries. David left The Body Shop to accept a position as Fellow of Stakeholder Engagement and Communications at the Office for Public Management (OPM), furthering his work on corporate social responsibility and cross-sector partnerships. For almost a decade after that he worked at a very local level, running and advising community enterprises. Most recently David was Chief Executive of West Itchen Community Trust Ltd, an innovative charity which financed its community work in inner-city Southampton through running a commercial property business. Through this work he became a founding director of the Social Enterprise Foundation.

John O'Byrne is the principal of Katalis, a business and IT consulting and delivery company based in Dublin. John has over twenty-five years in IT and business change in small, medium and large organizations in Ireland, UK and the US. As a keen technologist John has been involved in many innovative and appropriate IT solutions to business problems. In the past ten years he has worked with a number of small companies introducing business and IT solutions from a large company origin that have been tailored specifically for SME needs.

Susan Ogden is a senior lecturer in strategic and operations management at Glasgow Caledonian University in Scotland. Her PhD focused on the HR implications of outsourcing and competitive tendering in the public sector. Currently Susan's teaching and research interests lie mainly in strategic and operations management, specializing in business excellence, continuous improvement and performance management. She also has a research interest in management career development and previously ran a successful ESF-funded project on improving gender balance in management. She also co-authored a report for the Scottish Executive comparing gender balance in management issues across the public and private sector in Scotland. Susan has over twenty publications in a wide range of journals and books, including *Public Money and Management* and the *International Journal of Public Sector Management*, on topics that include quality management, supplier relationship management, benchmarking and performance management. In addition she has presented papers at many academic conferences such as the British Academy of Management and the TQM World Congress. Susan provides external consultancy and training in the area of strategic performance management, project evaluation and strategy development for public, non-profit and private sector organizations. She has also worked on various Glasgow Caledonian University's bespoke business education programmes by Learning Contract for clients that include Scottish and Southern Energy, Clyde Union, Community Learning Development and various Scottish local authorities. She is a member of the Chartered Management Institute as well as the Institute of Operations Management and the Scottish Research Group for Industrial Management.

Tuuli Pärenson is a director of development in a small Estonian bank. She started her career in the field of auditing, including both internal and external audit, accounting and performance evaluation. To create synergy of theory and practice, she is active in both. She completed her doctoral studies in the Faculty of Economics of the University of Tartu in 2011: her thesis concerned social impact evaluation in social enterprises. Her research issues concern social enterprises, social entrepreneurship, effectiveness of not-for-profits and impact evaluation. She has been a volunteer for the Good Deed Foundation, which was the first investor for social enterprises in Estonia, since its establishment in 2003. Currently her attention is focused on the establishment of an umbrella organization for social enterprises in Estonia.

Gareth Rees has been involved with third sector organizations for over fifteen years. He is a former third sector CEO and has been a management adviser for organizations working in economic development, education and health. A former VSA volunteer and ODA Technical Adviser, Gareth has worked in developing countries and now lives in Lima in Peru, working as a researcher at Universidad ESAN. Gareth holds MBA and MCom degrees from the University of Otago.

Aonghus Sammin is the principal of Bradán Consulting based in Galway City. The firm acts as a CFO (Chief Financial Officer) for a number of companies as well as specializing in strategic business planning, fundraising, business performance management and risk management. Aonghus is a qualified accountant with 18 years' business experience, ranging from small practice clients to multinational companies. He completed his training in Galway in the 1990s before working overseas for several years, most notably with Diageo where he was responsible for implementing systems and organizational change programmes. He is a board member of two charities, COPE Galway and SpunOut.

Zachary Sheaffer is a senior lecturer in the Department of Economics and Business Administration at the Ariel University Centre, Israel. He received his DPhil in management at the University of Waikato, Hamilton, New Zealand. His research interests include organizational crisis, crisis management, organizational change, downsizing and organizational decline. Sheaffer is the co-author of two books and he has published in such journals as *The Journal of Organizational Behavior, Journal of Management Studies, Entrepreneurship: Theory and Practice, Journal of Applied Behavioural Science, European Management Journal, Journal of Business Ethics, Journal of Homeland Security and Emergency Management, The Journal of Contingencies and Crisis Management* and others.

Richard A. Werner is Chair in International Banking at the University of Southampton and founding Director of the Centre for Banking, Finance and Sustainable Development. After a BSc in Economics at the London School of Economics and a DPhil at the University of Oxford, Professor Werner has accrued two decades of experience in the financial sector: his posts included that of chief economist at Jardine Fleming Securities (Asia) Ltd, Senior

Managing Director at Bear Stearns Asset Management, and senior consultant/ visiting researcher at the Asian Development Bank, the Japanese Ministry of Finance, the Bank of Japan, the Japan Development Bank and the Nomura Research Institute. Professor Werner is also known for coining the concept of 'quantitative easing', which he popularized during his time as Japan's leading monetary economist and central bank critic. The World Economic Forum, Davos, selected him as 'Global Leader for Tomorrow' in 2003.

Cáthál Wilson is a researcher in the area of performance measurement for SMEs. He graduated with a degree in manufacturing engineering in 2005 and is currently completing his PhD which is titled 'Dominant operational performance measures for SME owner managers'. He also has a number of contacts with industry, acting as a productivity improvement specialist. He currently works as a project manager in his family company, Ceramicx Ireland. Cáthál has presented papers at various conferences and has had a number of publications in journals, including *Technology Ireland*, an Enterprise Ireland publication.

Foreword

As I write at the end of 2012, when major world economies are still coming to terms with the after-effects of the 2008 global financial crisis (GFC), we are aware that the long-term consequences from this event are far from over, let alone fully understood. In this new landscape, voluntary and community sector organizations and social enterprises are being encouraged to take a much greater role in the provision of services and functions previously provided by public sector organizations.

The role and value provided by the third sector is increasingly the subject of political debate. This is partly because of the huge responsibilities now being outsourced to the third sector and partly because of the untapped potential available in the third sector. The GFC has fuelled this debate to the point of influencing and changing government policy. I expect to see real change in the size, funding and business models of voluntary organizations and social enterprises.

The book's primary purpose is to draw attention to the academic and practitioner debates and issues facing this long-undervalued eclectic mix of organizations, which often work untiringly at a local grassroots level in our communities. Such organizations have historically emerged to fulfil a valued community need or purpose, and are often staffed by volunteers, run by altruistic executives, and funded largely by philanthropic means. But many such organizations have developed into providers of social and community services, and thus have become partly or entirely funded by central government as a mainstay of state social and economic policy. The GFC has upset the funding balance which enabled state governments to effectively sub-contract out of these social and community services. Thus the third sector, as it is generically referred to, is set to change more in the next five years than it has in the last fifty. Therefore this book is timely, as it considers the development and repositioning of the third sector with a more central role in the provision of local and community public services. I value this book, as it provides a wide and holistic perspective on the likely changes and potential opportunities to third sector organizations as a consequence of the GFC.

Drawing on international insights from both academic and practitioner-based cases, the book provides a view of third sector organizational performance from several unique and valuable standpoints. It offers contrasting views of how performance management and measurement is being used within organizations in this sector, and clearly illustrates some of the unique challenges which the third sector organizations face.

The real value of this book is the balanced mix of international, academic and practitioner commentaries across a wide range of third sector themes. The early chapters, set against the backdrop of rapid socioeconomic change, take a financial standpoint and explore both the causes and the potential effects of the GFC on third sector organizations, as couched in the UK 'Big Society' movement. From this starting point the book provides a series of academic position pieces which inform and illuminate much of the current thinking around the changing roles of performance management and measurement in this sector. The final section presents several noteworthy practitioner pieces which provide examples of third sector organizational responses to the challenges of this changing position.

This text will appeal as much to the academic searching for new insights as the practitioner looking for examples of third sector best practice and latest thinking. So I think this book is a timely contribution, informing the academic and practitioner discussion on the future contribution and repositioning of this highly important economic sector.

Mike Bourne
Professor of Business Performance
School of Management
Cranfield University

Acknowledgements

The editors would like to thank the following people for making this book possible: the contributors for their insightful chapters and their diligence in the editing process; Dr Paul Jones, Professors Mike Bourne and Andy Neely for their support in raising the profile of performance management in third sector and charitable organisations; and Commissioning Editor Martin West and the rest of the team at Gower for their invaluable input in formatting the book. Finally we would also like to pay tribute to our partners Rhodora (Jojie) and Joanne for their unwavering support and patience.

Graham Manville,
University of Southampton, UK

Richard Greatbanks,
University of Otago, Dunedin, New Zealand

List of Abbreviations

BACS	Bankers' Automated Clearing System Ltd
BCUL	Association of British Credit Union Ltd
BIS	Bank for International Settlements
BLF	Big Lottery Fund
BSC	Balanced Scorecard
CC	crisis containment
CCCC	Cheque and Credit Clearing Company Ltd
CES	Charity Evaluation Service
CHAPS	Clearing House Automated Payments Scheme
CM	crisis management
CP	crisis preparedness
CPM	corporate performance measurement
CRED	Credit Unions Sourcebook of the FSA
CSR	corporate social responsibility
CVS	Council for Voluntary Services
DTA	Development Trust Association
ECB	European Central Bank
EFQM	European Foundation for Quality Management
FSA	Financial Services Authority
FSB	Financial Stability Board
GDP	gross national product
GNI	gross national income

IIP	Investors in People
KPI	key performance indicator
LEAP	Learning Evaluation And Planning
NFP	not-for-profit
NGO	non-governmental organization
NPM	new public management
NPO	non-profit service organization
ODA	Official Development Assistance
PMM	performance measurement and management
PMS	performance management system
PQASSO	Practical Quality Assurance System for Small Organisations
PR	public relations
QM	quality management
RBM	results-based management
SCVO	Scottish Council of Voluntary Organisations
SITF	Social Investment Task Force
SMEs	small and medium-sized enterprises
SMSEs	small and medium-sized social enterprises
SQMS	Scottish Quality Management System
SWIFT	Society for Worldwide Interbank Financial Telecommunications
TSO	third sector organization

Introduction

The chapters in this book provide a series of critical perspectives on the third sector from around the world and in a variety of contexts. The contributions have been written by established specialists in their field who have published in academic or professional journals.

This book was born from a passion and enthusiasm of the editors on the subject of third sector public service delivery which began in 2004. For the past twelve years, the third sector or civil society has been encouraged to offer a more active role in public service delivery, particularly in social and community contexts. Despite encouragement from the UK government and the establishment of an Office of the Third Sector in May 2006, the third sector's social role has been rather understated.

However, the global financial crisis (GFC) of 2007 and 2008 and the subsequent bailing out of the banking industry by governments across the Western world has led to a banking liability which has been transferred to a government liability. To quote Andrew Haldane from the Bank of England, 'the taxpayer has become the lender of last resort'. This has meant that taxpayers now shoulder the burden of addressing the largesse of an expanded economy built into an unsustainable banking and economic model.

Taking a Habermasian philosophical lens (Habermas 1987), the third sector (TS) can be viewed as the lifeworld, and the individual organizations such as charities, voluntary organizations and social enterprises which form the TS can be considered the system. The steering media, in the form of power, money and law, have, until the financial crisis of 2008, been relatively incremental in their drive for change within the third sector. However, since 2008, those steering media, driven by the rhetoric of the age of austerity, have accelerated the need for a repositioned third sector to provide a greater role within the social and community structure.

The full implications of this change in stance are still to emerge, but significant reductions in the public spending of countries exposed in the financial crisis is already taking place. In terms of impact on the third sector, services traditionally carried out by the public sector may eventually be carried out by third sector organizations, the private sector or a tripartite combination of public/private/third sectors.

Performance measurement and management, involving both financial and non-financial measures as well as quantitative and qualitative analysis, have grown exponentially during the past twenty-five years. The measurement revolution emerged in the public sector during the early 1990s and has developed into an explosion of performance metrics and benchmarking. Extensive performance measurement has not always equated to effective performance management, which belies the maxim of 'what gets measured gets managed'. In many instances what gets measured simply gets measured, and an unintended consequence of form-filling and box-ticking has manifested itself which some say has diverted organizations away from their core business processes. With regard to public service delivery and the constraints now being placed on funding and execution of these vital services, it is of paramount importance that the third sector does not make the same mistakes regarding performance measurement and management.

Performance management in the third sector is subtly different from that of the public sector for a number of reasons. Firstly, the third sector is made up of a broad constituency of volunteers and paid employees. Secondly, there are multiple stakeholders to contend with, such as the usual internal organizational stakeholders through to government, regulators, governors, and most importantly service users. However, this does not mean to say that lessons cannot be learned from the public or private sectors.

This edited book has called upon the expertise of subject matter experts who are academics, policy-makers and practitioners in the third sector. It is intended to appeal to academics teaching performance management, strategy and social enterprise within business schools, the social sciences and the humanities. In addition it will be an invaluable volume for policy-makers in developing policy and strategy around the third sector.

Both editors have been at the forefront of performance management in the third sector: their relationship was cemented during the editing of a special issue on performance measurement and management in the third sector for the *International Journal of Productivity and Performance Management* in July

2010. Although some of the contributions to this book were written after the GFC, between 2009 and 2011, we felt ready to draw them together in early 2012.

The editors believe that if the third sector is to play a more pivotal role in public service delivery, then the respective third sector organizations need to have not only a sustainable business model but the ability to manage themselves efficiently and effectively. The research into this area is scant and much more research is required. It is intended that this book, with its international perspective on performance measurement and management, will provide inspiration to other academics, policy-makers and students to join the debate and to help the third sector to successfully make the transition and play a greater part in the delivery of public services in an age of global austerity.

Reference

Habermas, J. 1987. *The Theory of Communicative Action: Volume 2: The Critique of Functionalist Realism*. Cambridge: Polity Press.

PART I:

FINANCING THE THIRD SECTOR

Overview of Part I:
Financing the Third Sector

The global financial crises of 2007 and 2008 have given rise to what Habermas describes as 'steering media', in the form of power, law and money which are hastening the reform of public service delivery. This is likely to result in significant cuts to funding budgets, and public services no longer being delivered by the state. However, there is a compelling case for the financial services sector to play a more pivotal role than they are currently playing. The future sustainability of the financial services, in particular the banking industry, was secured after governments around the world took on colossal sovereign debt to provide the liquidity for the global banking system. Due to a lack of global regulation and a very strong banking lobby, the pace of reform in the sector is now out of alignment with the reforms currently proposed in the state and civil society sector. A healthy, ethical and sustainable banking system is vital for the future prosperity of the world as the well-being of the banking sector is inextricably linked to the sustainability of public service provision. Nevertheless, many commentators still believe further reform is needed in the banking industry, and more research on possible solutions is required from academia. Such an approach may guard against the charge of epistemic arrogance which the author and academic Dr Nassim Taleb levelled against the banking industry in his best-seller, *Black Swan*.

This section considers the financial environment within which the third sector now finds itself, and offers three contributions which specifically explore the dynamic financial issues facing the third sector. The first chapter is a position piece, originally authored by Greg Pytel and submitted in 2009 to the House of Commons Treasury Select Committee as evidence in support of the enquiry into the banking crisis. This essay provides a provocative but credible argument to the lack of insight into the parlous state of the financial system, and is reproduced with permission of the UK National Archives. It provides a layperson's introduction to the intricacies and potential deficiencies of the global banking and finance system, and explores the root causes of the 2007–08 global financial crisis against which this book is set.

The second chapter is written by the editors, Graham Manville and Richard Greatbanks, and develops the thinking presented in the first chapter to the creation of a social investment bank or 'Big Society Bank' in the UK. The idea was conceived by the previous Labour government and has been continued by the current Conservative/Liberal coalition government. The Big Society Bank will be a fully serviced wholesale lending bank for the third sector. It is an important first step for third sector financial services and its aim is to supplement the role of the state.

The third contribution to this section is written by Richard Werner, who provides a compelling justification for expanding the role of credit unions in financial services. He argues that currently credit unions cannot compete on a level playing field with commercial banks, who are able to effectively create money using the principle of fractional reserve banking. Werner calls for credit unions to have the same powers as commercial banks, which would give them the scale necessary to compete effectively. This view of credit unions becoming larger entities is not universally accepted by credit union policy-makers, but is offered as a thought-provoking position piece.

These three pieces explore the recent changes, and the subsequent potential opportunities or challenges, which have increasingly placed third sector organizations at the centre of social and economic change with many societies throughout the world.

1

The Financial Context for an Expanded Third Sector

Graham Manville and Richard Greatbanks

Since the GFC of 2008, the world economy has been experiencing a great deal of uncertainty and many governments, predominantly North American and European, have stepped in to become the lenders of last resort, providing both direct and indirect financial support and guarantees to prop up the banking industry which came close to collapse. Three years after the initial crisis, there is still a high degree of uncertainty and general reluctance for banks to reform. The report into UK banking (arguably the global financial centre) by the Independent Banking Commission chaired by Sir John Vickers published its findings in November 2011 (Vickers 2011). Among its recommendations were a series of eye-catching headlines, such as the separation of retail banking from investment banking, but no real reform until 2015 at the earliest and more likely 2019 when Basel 3 global regulation takes effect (International Law Office 2010). However, what the Vickers Report did not even begin to address was the issues resulting from 'shadow banking' (which includes collateralized debt obligations, credit default swaps, special purpose vehicles and hedge funds), and herein lies the problem, like an iceberg beneath the water.

In 2010 the Federal Reserve Bank of New York published a report explaining how the opaque world of shadow banking operates (Pozsar et al. 2010). Within the report is a flowchart which shows the sheer complexity of shadow banking (it has to be viewed on poster size, 36 × 48 inches/92 × 122cm, in order to read the text). Shadow banking has insidiously swelled the balance sheets of the world banks and despite the banking reforms post-2007 and -2008, it remains largely unregulated. The banking sector in the UK has risen from the stable levels of 50 per cent of GDP in the 1960s to over 450 per cent at the end of the first decade of the twenty-first century (King 2010). In addition, the key ratio of the loan to deposit ratio (a function of fractional reserve banking) has betrayed the fragility of the banking sector, having risen appreciably in recent years. As a result of securitization and other shadow banking activities, the loan to deposit ratios of many of the UK banks have risen beyond 100 per cent (Davies 2008, Pytel, 2009).

To illustrate how fractional reserve banking works we have reproduced, with permission, the essay by Greg Pytel, submitted to the House of Commons Treasury Select Committee (Pytel, 2009).

> *It is the most rudimentary money creation mechanism for banks, which if administered properly serves the economy and public at large very well. In the deposit creation process a bank accepts deposits and lends them out. But almost every lending returns soon to the bank as a deposit and is lent out again. In essence, when people borrow money they do not keep it at home as cash, but spend it, so this money finds its way back to a bank quite quickly. It is not necessarily the same bank, but as the number of banks is limited (indeed very small) and there is – or was – a very active interbank lending, in terms of deposit creation, the system works like one large bank.*

> *Therefore, the same money is re-lent over and over again, however if all depositors of all banks turned up at the same time there would not be enough cash to pay them out. Such a situation is highly unlikely. Every borrower repays his loan and pays interest on it. In principle, the difference between a loan and a deposit interest rate is a source of the banks' profit. Naturally, banks have to account for some creditors that will default and reflect it in the lending interest rate, or all the creditors who repay cover the costs of defaults. On top of it, the banks possess their own capital to provide security.*

> *Fundamental to this deposit creation principle is the percentage of deposits that a bank lends out. The description above used a 100 per cent loan-deposit ratio, meaning that all deposits are lent out. In traditional banking this ratio was always below 100 per cent. For example, years ago, Westminster Bank (before it merged into National Westminster Bank), intended to lend out 86.5 per cent of every deposit. For every £100 deposited, the bank lent out £86.50, while the remaining £13.50 was retained in the bank's reserve with a small portion of it kept in the Bank of England. In practice, this ratio was the bank's control tool on deposit creation process, ensuring that the amount of money supplied to the market was limited. According to this principle, for every £1*

deposited, a bank lends out £0.865. After only five cycles the amount is reduced to below £0.50 and after 32 cycles it is below 1 penny (£0.01). If this process continued forever the total amount of money lent out of a pound would be less than £6.41. With every cycle of deposit creation, a bank builds up its reserves, ultimately collecting almost entire £1 for every £1 initial deposit. Added to capital repayments, interest payments on loans and the bank's own capital base this system ensured that that there was always enough money in the bank for every depositor. For years banks worked as a confidence trick, in that the notional value of deposits and liabilities to be paid by the bank exceeded the value of money on the market. Since only a very small number of depositors demand cash withdrawals at the same time and almost all these paid-out deposits are deposited in a bank again quickly the banks ensured that every depositor got his money while circulating money in the economy and stimulating growth. The loan-deposit ratio was a self-regulating tool. As with every cycle it multiplies, the reduction of amounts created decreases exponentially and quickly. The faster the deposit creation cycles occur the faster the reduction progresses, thus accelerating with every cycle. The total 'created' from the original £1 deposited in a bank is a finite, not more than £6.41 at the 86.5 per cent loan-deposit ratio, backed by nearly £1 reserve. It is effectively an inverted pyramid scheme starting from a fixed initial deposit base and quickly reducing through deposit creation cycle to zero.

The deposit creation process is at the heart of the banking system servicing the public and stimulating economic growth. The modern banking instruments of securitisation, hedging, leveraging, derivatives and so on turned this process on its head. They enabled banks to lend more out than they took in deposits. According to Morgan Stanley Research, in 2007 UK banks loan-deposit ratio was 137 per cent (Davies 2008). In other words the banks were lending out on average £137.00 for every £100 paid in as a deposit. Another conservative estimate shows that this indicator for major UK banks was at least 174 per cent. For others like Northern Rock it was a massive 322 per cent (Shaw 2008). Banks were 'borrowing on the international markets' and lending money they did not have but assuming they would have in the future. Likewise, 'international markets' were doing exactly the same. At first sight it might not seem so much different than deposit creation. Deposit creation is lending money by the banks they do not have on the assumption that they will get enough back in sufficient time in the future from borrowers.

On closer examination there is a remarkable difference. With every cycle of the 86.5 per cent loan-deposit ratio every £1 deposited is reduced becoming less than £0.50 after five cycles and less than 1 penny after 32. With a loan-deposit ratio of 137 per cent – lending £137 for every £100 – not to mention 174 per cent or indeed 322 per cent, the story is drastically the opposite. Assume a banker gets the first £1 deposit in the first week of a new year and lends it out. Assume that twice every week in that year the amount lent out comes back to him as a deposit and he sustains such deposit creation process with a ratio of 137 per cent twice every week for the year. This is a perfectly plausible, in fact a conservative scenario on the current electronic financial markets. By the following New Year's Eve, the final amount he finally lends out from the original £1 is over £165 trillion (165 with 12 zeros, or over 16 times the amount governments have so far injected into economy, or more than 3 times the world's GDP). The total amount lent out in a year by a banker is over £447 trillion. Significantly with a loan-deposit ratio 100 per cent or above no cash reserve is generated.

It is an acknowledged monetary principle that the lending interest rate cannot be below 0 per cent. This would allow borrowers to borrow money and banks would keep paying them for doing so. Indeed, there would be no incentive to lend and borrowing would have become a source of income for a borrower. Ultimately, lending would have stopped completely. It is a very similar principle that the loan-deposit ratio cannot be sustained at 100 per cent or above, as in such circumstances an amount of money coming from economic activities into deposit creation cycle would be multiplied very rapidly to infinity. Economic growth and inflation would not be able to catch up with it, which happens if the loan-deposit ratio is below 100 per cent.

The loan-deposit ratio below 100 per cent that traditionally served as a very strict self-regulating mechanism of money supply stimulating the economy becomes unsustainable above 100 per cent. The banking system then behaves in a similar manner to the classic pyramid scheme. But as with every pyramid scheme, as long as people and institutions are happy not to demand cash withdrawals from the banks it is sustainable. Any bank can always print an impressive account statement or issue a new deposit certificate. The problem is whether the cash is there.

The qualitative and quantitative difference between loan-deposit ratio of 0 per cent and 99 per cent is infinitely smaller than between 99 per cent and 100 per cent or 101 per cent. With ratios between 0 per cent and 99 per cent, we always end up with a money-making machine that creates a finite amount of money out of the initial deposit with a reserve nearly equal to the original deposit. If a ratio climbs to 100 per cent or above the amount of money created spirals to infinity, if above 100 per cent with exponential speed and no cash reserve is generated in this process. It is little wonder that Northern Rock which used the ratio of not less than 322 per cent collapsed before any of the other banks. HBOS with a ratio of around 175 per cent ended up in a meltdown scenario later, while HSBC that used the ratio of not more than 91 per cent was relatively safe (being a part of the global banking system, however, it has been at a risk stemming from the actions of other banks) (Shaw 2008).

Facing the inevitable

For years the impressive-looking British-based banks' results brought a lot of confidence. The City was hailed as a beacon of the British economy. Bank executives, traders and financiers collected huge bonuses – not surprisingly, a lot of it in cash, rather than financial instruments. Influential economists and politicians alike justified stratospheric bonuses and hailed the City as the workhorse of the economy. Government strategic decisions were quite often subordinate to the objective of keeping the City strong. To quote a classic: 'irrational exuberance' triumphed. Ultimately, City executives, traders and financiers proved to be pyramid purveyors operating the same scheme, in terms of its mechanism design, as the fraudsters who bankrupted Albania with their innovative financial products in 1996–97 (Jarvis 2000).

The problem with the banks is that credit creation was out of control because of the warping of fractional reserve banking (loan to deposit ratios greater than 100 per cent). The complexity and opacity of 'shadow banking' has hidden the risks and caused the balance sheets of banks to swell to unsustainable levels. This has led to the need for taxpayer money to be pumped into the system to maintain the economy and this has been achieved through direct support, guarantees, credit lines and quantitative easing. The taxpayer has now become the lender of last resort (Haldane

2009). Despite the need to radically reform the banking sector there are still several UK banks with respective balance sheets greater than the sum total of the UK economy, that is, £1,300,000,000,000 (King 2010). The reforms that have been proffered have been the Basel 3 reform package which seeks to reinforce banking sector supervision and hopefully prevent another crash. The reforms include larger capital requirements, but the Basel 3 capital requirements will not be fully implemented until 2019 (International Law Office 2010). Another reform put forward by Kotlikoff (2010) is limited purpose banking which is a development of narrow banking and is a concept pioneered by Fisher (1936), Friedman (1959) and more recently Kay (2009).

At present banking reform is being hampered by the majority of banking post mortems being carried out by either banking insiders or academics with a banking background (Williams et al. 2009). Williams came to prominence for his surgical dissection of the lean claims made in the ground-breaking book by Womack et al. (1990), *The Machine that Changed the World* (Wickens 1995). Williams's work is compelling, well thought through as well as being backed up by rigorous qualitative and quantitative analysis. Nevertheless a caveat should be added that his research group includes a member from the Unite trade union, so it could be perceived, rightly or wrongly, as a vested interest piece. This research should be welcomed, as current closed-loop thinking of banking enquiries by bankers may not lead to a paradigm-shifting outcome. To paraphrase the late Professor Abraham Maslow, when all you have is a hammer, every problem is viewed as a nail. For this reason it is vitally important that more non-banking academics are encouraged to contribute to this research area. The rush to regulate will not solve the problem as there is a revolving-door phenomenon of banking and politics and powerful vested interests will ensure there is plenty of 'wiggle room' in the regulations. This was brought to light when Lord Oakeshott resigned from his role as Treasury spokesperson in the House of Lords because of the apparent political compromise with the banking lobby (BBC News, Politics 2011). This is hampered further by former leading politicians from all political parties taking up prominent roles in leading banks.

Banking reform is not an easy solution and is in fact a complexity akin to the Gordian Knot, an intractable problem only cured by a swift cut by the sword. In some quarters there is a call for draconian regulation of the banking industry but this would be difficult to implement. John Varley, the former CEO of a leading global bank, argued that financial services constitute 10 per cent of UK GDP and 15 per cent of the corporate tax take, and are of high social value (BBC 2009). If this is true then the banking industry holds a loaded gun to the taxpayer's head and will implicitly argue that 'if you over-regulate us we will move our operations offshore and the UK GDP will shrink'. A counter-argument put forward by Williams et al. (2009) takes issue with this assertion of the finance industry's value to the economy, arguing that, rather than banks being net contributors to the economy, the direct and indirect taxpayer bailout has negated the tax take.

Another factor to consider is the sustainability and shareholder value of the banking industry in its current form: this affects the majority of the UK working population as pension funds have equity stakes in most of the leading FTSE100 companies, which happen to be banks.

Like it or loathe it, the banking system needs government help to sustain itself in the long term, yet such government help has resulted in national debt rising exponentially over the past four years (Porter and Conway 2008, HM Treasury 2011, Peston 2011). Since 2010, there has been a drive to reduce the government debt by cutting spending on public services. Such actions have had an immediate impact on both the public sector and indeed the third sector, which relied implicitly on public sector contracts. The current path of austerity cuts is forcing a game change in the provision of public service delivery which may ultimately lead to a more balanced delivery by public, private and third sector organizations. There will still be funding available from government sources but the sector may need to look to other sources of revenue generation beyond grants, donations and renewable local government contracts. The hope is that it will lead to more imaginative thinking of public service delivery through third sector organizations. However, for the third sector to have a fighting chance of sustainability in this new economic landscape, the banking industry will need to provide a more holistic and pluralistic lead. Examples such as the creation of a state bank which could create credit without interest (not to be confused with lending without interest) has been postulated by senior members from within Goldman Sachs (O'Neill 2008). This option is credible as it was suggested by the Chief Economist of Goldman Sachs, and yet, in the time since he wrote this article at the height of the crisis, nobody in academia, the business media or the banking industry has followed this up. Other initiatives that the banking industry could lead on are the establishment of a social investment bank and the expansion of credit unions. These options will be discussed in more detail in the next two chapters.

Acknowledgement

The authors would like to thank Greg Pytel, an independent consultant, for his permission and support in developing this opening chapter which considers the global financial crisis (GFC) and its impact on the third sector.

References

BBC News. 2009. London 'damaged' by bonus tax, Barclays chief says [Online]. Available at: http://news.bbc.co.uk/1/hi/8421312.stm [accessed: 7 September 2011].

BBC News, Politics. 2011. Lib Dem Lord Oakeshott stands by criticism of bank deal [Online]. Available at: http://www.bbc.co.uk/news/uk-politics-12414700 [accessed: 7 September 2011].

Davies, H. 2008. *Banking and the State: Changing the Social Contract* [Online]. Available at: http://www2.lse.ac.uk/aboutLSE/meetTheDirector/pdf/ speechesAndLecturesPDFs/Banking%20and%20the%20State%20 Barclays%20021008%20SLIDES.pdf [accessed: 22 January 2012].

Fisher, I. 1936. *100% Money*, rev. edn. New York: Adelphi.

Friedman, M. 1960. *A Program for Monetary Stability*. New York: Fordham University Press.

Haldane, A. 2009. Banking on the state [Online]. Available at: http://www.bis. org/review/r091111e.pdf [accessed: 23 May 2011].

HM Treasury. 2011. *Autumn Statement 2011* [Online]. Available at: http:// cdn.hm-treasury.gov.uk/autumn_statement.pdf [accessed: 22 January 2012].

International Law Office. 2010. *Basel 3: Higher Capital Requirements, Liquidity Rules and Transitional Arrangements* [Online]. Available at: http://www. internationallawoffice.com/newsletters/detail.aspx?g=69944d6e-884d-468f-8e01-a1a7e2f9a13f [accessed: 7 September 2011].

Jarvis, C. 2000. The rise and fall of Albania's pyramid schemes. *Finance and Development*, March, 37(1), 46–9.

Kay, J. 2009. *Narrow Banking: The Reform of Banking Regulation*. CSFI report. London: Centre for the Study of Financial Innovation.

King, M. 2010. *Banking: from Bagehot to Basel, and Back Again* [Online]. Available at: http://www.bankofengland.co.uk/publications/speeches/2010/speech455. pdf [accessed: 7 September 2011].

Kotlikoff, L.J. 2010. *Jimmy Stewart is Dead: Ending the World's Ongoing Financial Plague with Limited Purpose Banking*. Hoboken NJ: Wiley.

O'Neill, J. 2008. There is one simple way out of the mess, Gordon: a state bank [Online]. Available at: http://www.thisislondon.co.uk/standard/article-23601662-there-is-one-simple-way-out-of-the-mess-gordon-a-state-bank.do [accessed: 22 January 2012].

Peston, R. 2011. UK's debts biggest in the world [Online]. Available at: http://www.bbc.co.uk/news/business-15820601 [accessed: 7 September 2012].

Porter, A. and Conway, E. 2008. Nation hit with another £100bn Northern Rock debts [Online]. Available at: http://www.telegraph.co.uk/finance/newsbysector/banksandfinance/2784076/Nation-hit-with-100bn-Northern-Rock-debts.html [accessed: 22 January 2012].

Pozsar, Z., Adrian, T., Ashcraft, A. and Boesky, H. 2010. *Federal Reserve Bank of New York Staff Reports: Shadow Banking* [Online]. Available at: http://www.ny.frb.org/research/staff_reports/sr458.pdf [accessed: 6 September 2011].

Pytel, G. 2009. *The Greatest Heist in Corporate History* [Online]. Available at: http://www.publications.parliament.uk/pa/cm200809/cmselect/cmtreasy/144/144w254.htm [accessed: 7 September 2011].

Shaw, A. 2008. Adam Shaw's week in business [Online]. Available at: http://news.bbc.co.uk/today/hi/today/newsid_7648000/7648508.stm [accessed: 22 January 2012].

Vickers, J. 2011. *Independent Commission on Banking, Final Report, September 2011* [Online]. Available at: http://bankingcommission.s3.amazonaws.com/wp-content/uploads/2010/07/ICB-Final-Report.pdf [accessed: 22 January 2012].

Wickens, P. 1995. *The Ascendant Organisation*. Basingstoke: Macmillan.

Williams, K., Caulkin, S., Folkman, P., Francis, S., McDougal, A., MacGregor, R., Engelen, E., Erturk, I., Froud, J., Johal, S., Leaver, A., Moran, M. and Nilsson, A. 2009. *An Alternative Report on UK Banking Reform* [Online]. Available at: http://www.cresc.ac.uk [accessed: 10 December 2010].

Womack, J., Jones, D. and Roos, D. 1990. *The Machine that Changed the World: The Story of Lean Production*. New York: HarperCollins.

2

Third Sector Funding Streams: The Big Society Bank

Graham Manville and Richard Greatbanks

Third sector organizations, according to Anheier and Siebel (1990), are those organizations that lie between profit-making and government organizations. They include charities, trade associations, credit unions, social enterprises and voluntary organizations (Moxham and Boaden 2007, Doherty et al. 2009, Manville and Broad 2011). For the past dozen years the UK government has been promoting a wider role of third sector organizations in public service delivery. It began under a guiding set of principles known as compacts (Kendall 2000). 'The compact idea is completely without precedent, representing an unparalleled step in the positioning of the third sector in public service delivery' (Kendall 2000: 2). Since then, third sector bodies have relied on direct or indirect government funding in the form of grants, awards and packages of work secured by commissioning agents, usually public sector bodies. Members of the third sector have traditionally had an ethical stance that is rooted in the desire to shape society as a result of their ideology and their reliance on a partial or full volunteer workforce (Manville and Broad 2011). In recent years there has been a growing shift to encourage third sector organizations to become more focused on performance management and corporate sustainability. Yet the limited research on these organizations reveals that they have little knowledge of performance management and limited sustainability beyond existing revenue streams (Moxham and Boaden 2007, Manville and Broad 2011). The post-GFC environment has threatened the sustainability of such organizations as governments around the Western world embark on austerity cuts to address the economic challenges, and the economic and competitive landscape emerging in the second decade of the new millennium provides a little hope of greater certainty for this sector. We feel this situation will lead to both opportunities and threats for the third sector. What is certain, however, is that third sector organizations will require ongoing support to navigate these uncharted waters.

The parlous state of the banking system of many Western sovereign states, as outlined in the first chapter, has led to austerity cuts which have resulted in government spending on public services being cut, and in an economic environment of needing to do more with less: some services previously carried out by the state will either be offered out to tender to non-public sector bodies in a drive to gain more efficiency for taxpayers' money, or the service will no longer be provided. Whilst the banking system is global, governments are national in their respective reach and influence. The possibility of the much-needed reform in banking is unlikely to occur until countries around the world agree on a global solution for banking and financial services. It is not feasible for governments to wait around until a solution is found, and as a result more imaginative means of squaring the circle will need to be sought. This could be an opportunity for third sector organizations to rise to the new social challenges and, rather than the age of austerity being a threat, it could be an opportunity for organizations to really make a difference. The third sector is an eclectic mix of unrelated organizations that fall outside the classification of public and private sector: this mix has often been referred to as a 'loose and baggy monster' (Kendall 2000). The current UK government has launched its flagship policy of the 'Big Society' to rebalance the economy from a predominantly state provision of public services to a more mixed solution of public, private and third sector participation (Big Society 2010). 'The Big Society' is both a nebulous and a divisive term. It is nebulous in the sense that it is unclear what the Big Society is trying to achieve, and how it intends to deliver these objectives. There have been several policy documents in the last three years but it has so far failed to capture the imagination of the wider public. The definition of the Big Society is 'a society with much higher levels of personal, professional, civic and corporate responsibility; a society where people come together to solve problems and improve life for themselves and their communities; a society where the leading force for progress is social responsibility, not state control' (Big Society 2010: 1). These are laudable aims but there are concerns that there can be an unrealistic expectation of what voluntary action can achieve. Mohan (2011) believes that it can result in a polarized effect, where the Home Counties have well-funded and -resourced volunteer networks comprising professional people with time on their hands which will bear little resemblance to disadvantaged inner city areas blighted by generations of structural unemployment.

It can be viewed as divisive because it can be interpreted in polarized views by differing stakeholder groups and opinion formers.

> *The neo-liberal interpretation of 'The Big Society' is an empowering agenda to free up social capital to deliver public services in more*

imaginative and efficient ways without the constraints of the dead hand of the state. However, a contradictory interpretation is that it is a cynical ploy to fulfil a free market dogmatic agenda of a smaller state provision which would have been unthinkable prior to the financial crisis of 2008. (Manville and Broad 2011: 28)

Notwithstanding these different interpretations the Big Society does have support, but for it to succeed it will need the enrolment of all sections of society in order to turn this dream into a reality.

Financial services are inextricably linked to the health of the economy and our ability to fund public services. King (2010: 16) stated that 'Of all the many ways of organising banking, the worst is the one we have today'. This provides a case for Schumpeterian 'creative destruction' in the banking industry, where governments are proactive rather than being continuously reactive to global economic events. One of the first salvos of creative destruction could be to introduce more third sector competition into banking. This would have to be a significant commitment and not simply a gesture. The corporate governance models of banking have been called into question, and laissez-faire free market financial services with an out-of-touch compensation model to its senior non-board (and unaccountable) bankers should not be the blueprint for the twenty-first century (Williams et al. 2009, Kotlikoff 2010). The social justice of awarding billions in bonuses to employees even before taxpayers and free market shareholders who have borne the risk seems absurd and, with the rise in the 'Occupy Wall Street Movement', this appears to be tolerated less as time goes by. This is not just a topical response to corporate banker behaviour; in an age of austerity, the banking industry should be leading from the front in finding a third sector solution and not being dragged into social reforms kicking and screaming.

The Big Society bank or social investment bank will be a wholesale funding body whose aims are to provide funding for social enterprises in the UK, and could arguably be the engine that will drive the expansion of the third sector. For several years third sector organizations have been encouraged to become more business-like (Dart 2004, Little 2005). The third sector's response to this has been lukewarm at best as they have traditionally secured funding from donations and community funding bodies. Academics have been arguing for several years that third sector organizations need to develop more sustainable business models and not be reliant on donations and grants (Loidl-Keil 2002, Chell 2007). The financial crisis has provided a tipping point in awareness of the need for the third sector to change. In addition it has also provided the

Conservative-led UK coalition government with a compelling narrative to argue the case for wholesale reform in the public sector and third sector in order to fulfil its ideological beliefs of a smaller state provision. The traditional Labour Party argument, that state provision is good and private sector provision bad, has been neutralized by the arrival of social enterprises. These are social businesses run for profit with an ethical stance of reinvesting their profits back into society (Dart 2004).

The concept of a social investment bank or Big Society bank does not belong in any political ideology, as it was first conceived by the last Labour government who established the Social Investment Task Force (SITF) (Kneiding and Tracey 2009). This led to legislation in 2008 to liberate unclaimed assets from dormant bank and building society accounts to provide liquid finance (Social Investment Task Force 2010). This legislation would facilitate the release of £250 million of funding to initiate the bank and £20 million per annum thereafter for a period of four years. This has now been revised up as of May 2011 to £400 million in dormant accounts plus another committed £200 million in long-term loans agreed under the Merlin Agreement (Project Merlin 2011, Cabinet Office 2011).

In 2010 it was envisaged that the creation of a social investment bank would unlock up to £14.2 billion per annum of capital to devote to social investment projects. This would be comprised of the following: £5.5 billion from philanthropic foundations and institutionally managed assets, £4.4 billion from government grants and £4.3 billion from Individual Savings Accounts (ISAs) (Social Investment Task Force 2010). The Big Society bank (BSB) would then fund social enterprises that provided compelling business plans with superior triple bottom-line potential. The loans would be made at 'much more attractive rates' than high street banks according to Nick O'Donohoe, former head of Global Research at JP Morgan at the Voice 11 Conference on Social Enterprise (Barrett 2011).

The financial crisis which began in 2007 has arguably cost the UK taxpayer colossal amounts of money and has witnessed the debt as a percentage of GDP rise from around 40 per cent to over 70 per cent. The direct and indirect government bailouts and guarantees to wholesale banks has led to a collapse in the confidence of the general public. O'Donohoe added: 'Three years ago it was impossible to get anyone interested in social investment. But the credit crisis has changed that – globally, not just in the UK.' This provides a more convincing argument for the realization of the aims of the SITF objective of marshalling up to £14.2 billion of investment to social enterprises.

In July 2011, the Big Society bank was formally launched under the name Big Society Capital (Cabinet Office 2011). Its twin aims are to provide capital to help third sector organizations become sustainable and to act as a champion for social investment. The rhetoric is compelling but the reality is that there has been no emergence of the critical mass necessary for this to be the driving vehicle for mobilizing this untapped sector. The latest press release by Big Society Capital has revealed the release of £3.1 million of funding for social enterprise (Big Society Capital 2011). On face value it seems a large sum but compared to the aspirations of the SITF, it is relatively small-scale and much more is needed in the coming years.

At the time of writing, the terms of the Big Society Capital are still being worked out as the banking lobby and the coalition government have yet to reach a satisfactory compromise with respect to interest payments on the £200 million investment. This may mean that they restructure the 'loans' and classify them as charitable donations to offset against tax (Jenkins and Timmins 2011). It is clear though that the Big Society bank would be a very positive step forward in providing much-needed funding to third sector organizations which are being asked to take on a greater role in our communities and society as a whole.

References

Anheier, H. and Siebel, W. 1990. *The Third Sector: Comparative Studies of Nonprofit Organizations*. Berlin and New York: Walter de Gruyter.

Barrett, H. 2011. Plan for Big Society Bank is almost ready [Online]. Available at: http://www.guardian.co.uk/social-enterprise-network/2011/mar/30/big-society-bank-nick-donohue [accessed: 7 September 2011].

Big Society. 2010. *Big Society not Big Government* [Online]. Available at: http://www.conservatives.com/News/News_stories/2010/03/~/media/Files/Downloadable%20Files/Building-a-Big-Society.ashx [accessed: 24 February 2012].

Big Society Capital. 2011. *£3.1 Million from Dormant Bank Accounts Invested in Big Society Projects* [Online]. Available at: http://www.bigsocietycapital.com/pdfs/Press%20Release%2028-12-11.pdf [accessed: 24 January 2012].

Cabinet Office. 2011. *Big Society Bank Outline Proposal* [Online]. Available at: http://www.cabinetoffice.gov.uk/resource-library/big-society-bank-outline-proposal [accessed: 7 September 2011].

Chell, E. 2007. Social enterprise and social entrepreneurship: towards a convergent theory of entrepreneurship. *International Small Business Journal*, 25(1), 5–26.

Dart, R. 2004. Being 'business-like' in a non-profit organization: a grounded and inductive typology. *Non-Profit and Voluntary Sector Quarterly*, 33(2), 290–310.

Doherty, B., Foster, G., Mason, C., Meehan, J., Meehan, K., Rotheroe, N. and Royce, M. 2009. *Management for Social Enterprise*. London: Sage.

Haldane, A. 2009. Banking on the state [Online]. Available at: http://www.bis.org/review/r091111e.pdf [accessed: 23 May 2011].

HM Treasury. 2011. *Autumn Statement 2011* [Online]. Available at: http://cdn.hm-treasury.gov.uk/autumn_statement.pdf [accessed: 22 January 2012].

Jenkins, P. and Timmins, N. 2011. FT lenders may cry foul of Big Society loan [Online]. Available at: http://www.ft.com/cms/s/0/6a1c929c-84bb-11e0-afcb-00144feabdc0.html#axzz1NABRaRRL [accessed: 23 May 2011].

Kendall, J. 2000. The mainstreaming of the third sector into public policy in England in the late 1990s: whys and wherefores. *Policy and Politics*, 28(4), 541–62.

King, M. 2010. *Banking: From Bagehot to Basel, and Back Again* [Online]. Available at: http://www.bankofengland.co.uk/publications/speeches/2010/speech455.pdf [accessed: 7 September 2011].

Kneiding, C. and Tracey, P. 2009. Towards a performance measurement framework for community development finance institutions in the UK. *Journal of Business Ethics*, 86(3), 327–45.

Kotlikoff, L.J. 2010. *Jimmy Stewart is Dead: Ending the World's Ongoing Financial Plague with Limited Purpose Banking*. Hoboken NJ: Wiley.

Little, W. 2005. Charities ready to play with the big boys but say 'Let's be fair'. *Health Service Journal*, 27 January, 14–15.

Loidl-Keil, R. 2002. Juggling with paradoxes in social enterprise? Characteristics of organisation and management in social enterprises: findings and conclusions from an Austrian study. *Euram Conference proceedings*, Stockholm, 8–11 May 2002.

Manville, G. and Broad, M. 2011. Changing Times for Charities: Performance Management in a Third Sector Housing Association. European Institute for Advanced Skills in Management, 8th Workshop on the challenges of managing the third sector, Galway, Ireland, 9–10 June 2011.

Mohan, J. 2011. *Mapping the Big Society: Perspectives from the Third Sector Research Centre*, TSRC Working Paper 62. Available at: www.tsrc.ac.uk.

Moxham, C. and Boaden, R. 2007. The impact of performance measurement in the voluntary sector: identification of contextual and processual factors. *International Journal of Operations and Production Management*, 27(8), 826–45.

Porter, A. and Conway, E. 2008. Nation hit with another £100bn Northern Rock debts [Online]. Available at: http://www.telegraph.co.uk/finance/newsbysector/banksandfinance/2784076/Nation-hit-with-100bn-Northern-Rock-debts.html [accessed: 22 January 2012].

Project Merlin. 2011. *Project Merlin – Banks' Statement 9 February 2011 – Revised* [Online]. Available at: http://www.hm-treasury.gov.uk/d/bank_agreement_090211.pdf [accessed: 7 September 2011].

Social Investment Task Force. 2010. *Social Investment Ten Years On* [Online]. Available at: http://www.socialinvestmenttaskforce.org/downloads/SITF_10_year_review.pdf [accessed: 7 September 2011].

Williams, K., Caulkin, S., Folkman, P., Francis, S., McDougal, A., MacGregor, R., Engelen, E., Erturk, I., Froud, J., Johal, S., Leaver. A., Moran, M. and Nilsson, A. 2009. *An Alternative Report on UK Banking Reform* [Online]. Available at: http://www.cresc.ac.uk [accessed: 10 December 2010].

3

Can Credit Unions Create Credit? An Analytical Evaluation of a Potential Obstacle to Enhanced Performance by Credit Unions

Richard A. Werner

Introduction

The global financial crisis has prompted a high-level reconsideration of the role of banks in the economy. Lord Adair Turner, the chairman of the British Financial Services Authority (the financial sector regulator), who is also a member of the new international Financial Stability Board (FSB), a group of regulators appointed by the G20 to design a more stable financial system, has argued that the banking sector in Britain had become 'too big' to be 'socially useful' (Turner 2009). Specifically, Lord Turner named proprietary trading and the derivatives sector as areas in banking that had 'grown beyond socially optimal levels'. He argued that pay in the financial sector was too high and that too many of Britain's brightest graduates were attracted to the financial services sector, so that the economy had become unbalanced. Meanwhile the German and French governments have recently called for new joint measures at the G20 level to 'prevent banks from becoming "too big to fail" and holding governments to ransom in future financial crises' (Benoit and Bryant 2009).

Regulators, governments and commentators have focused on the travails of large financial institutions, many of which failed, were kept alive through significant public sector capital injections, or were integrated into other financial institutions with public financial support. Meanwhile, small financial institutions appear to have fared better during the turbulent times of 2008. One type of small financial institution in the UK, as well as other countries, appears to have experienced very few, if any, problems during the global financial crisis: credit unions.

At a time when bankers' large bonuses, excessive speculative investments by banks and lack of support for local communities by banks is being discussed, it would seem that there is a bright future for financial institutions that pay no bonuses to their staff, engage in no speculative investments, focus on helping local communities and, finally, redistribute all of their proceeds to the local community. These are some of the core features of credit unions. Yet, surprisingly few members of the financial community, policy-makers or opinion-makers have focused on credit unions as being part of a reformed financial system. It was left up to a religious leader to highlight the already existing business model of credit unions as a role model for the financial sector: Pope Benedict XVI, commenting on the wider implications of the global banking crisis in his encyclical *Caritas in veritate* (Benedict 2009) named the expansion of the 'third sector' as the main recommendation for concrete changes in economic policy and singled out credit unions for their deep experience in delivering long-term and just economic results.[1]

> *Profit is useful if it serves as a means towards an end that provides a sense both of how to produce it and how to make good use of it. Once profit becomes the exclusive goal, if it is produced by improper means and without the common good as its ultimate end, it risks destroying wealth and creating poverty. (Ibid.: 21)*

> *Financiers must rediscover the genuinely ethical foundation of their activity, so as not to abuse the sophisticated instruments which can serve to betray the interests of savers. Right intention, transparency, and the search for positive results are mutually compatible and must never be detached from one another. If love is wise, it can find ways of working in accordance with provident and just expediency, as is illustrated in a significant way by much of the experience of credit unions. (Ibid.: 65)*

---

1   As will be seen, Benedict's (2009) emphasis on concepts such as 'solidarity', 'community', 'freedom', 'independence', 'fraternity', 'reciprocity' and 'fraternal cooperation' in their role in generating true human development, as well as his scepticism about profits as main motivation appear reminiscent of the key concepts of cooperative societies and credit unions, namely solidarity, autonomy and free local choice and decision-making.

Whether credit unions may represent a viable – or even preferable – alternative to the main banking services providers that have failed spectacularly is contingent on credit unions being institutionally and legally able to perform well or better than banks. A minimum requirement is that they are able to act as substitutes for banks and thus can play the major roles in the economy that banks perform. It is the purpose of this chapter to examine this question, with a particular emphasis on one fundamental role of banks, namely that of creators of credit and the money supply. Macroeconomically, this is a pivotal function of banks (and building societies, included in the bank definition in this chapter), which, however, has not been addressed in previous literature. While filling this gap in the literature, the chapter also delivers a new hypothesis about why credit unions have failed to grow significantly in the UK, namely their inability to create credit (meaningfully) during previous decades. It is also found that recent and pending regulatory changes are opening some, albeit limited, new opportunities for the 'third sector' which had not been identified in the literature: credit unions' ability to create credit has improved since 2002 and should be further enhanced with the new regulatory regime scheduled for April 2010. However, it will be found that major obstacles remain and thus even after the implementation of the pending reforms credit unions are handicapped in their competition with banks. Meanwhile, it seems neither regulators nor law-makers nor credit unions are fully aware of the issues involved with credit creation; none seems aware of the need for further reform should one wish to meaningfully enhance the role of credit unions in the economy. While this chapter remains analytical, it is hoped that it can provide insights and hypotheses for future empirical research.

The chapter is organized as follows. The subsequent section briefly introduces relevant facts about credit unions and compares them to banks. The third section introduces the concept and macroeconomic role of credit creation. The fourth section analyses whether credit unions have the ability to create credit in the same way as banks. The discussion is divided into the time period from 1979 to about 2002, the subsequent period until April 2010, and the likely future regime. The fifth and final section concludes by pointing out policy implications, including opportunities and issues for the future development of credit unions, and directions for future research.

What We Know about Credit Unions

Credit unions were first introduced in Germany in the middle of the nineteenth century by Hermann Schulze-Delitzsch and Friedrich Wilhelm

Raiffeisen.[2] They spread rapidly in Germany, Austria, Italy and the Netherlands, among others. The credit union organizations that were developed thanks to the contributions of these pioneers are known as People's Banks (such as Volksbanken, Banque Populaires, etc.), which centred more on urban members, and Raiffeisen Banks (Dahrlehnskassen, Savings & Loans), located mainly in rural areas.

The founding activists produced a theoretical concept and practical blueprint for this type of financial institution (Raiffeisen 1866). The goal was to provide banking services for people not well covered by commercial banks, such as those living in rural areas or those too poor to be of interest to commercially oriented financial service providers, and to prevent them from falling prey to predatory lending, 'loan sharks', or what is today referred to as 'sub-prime loans'. Credit unions can thus be seen as the cooperative answer to the problems of sub-prime lending. Further, credit unions are the direct antecedents of today's microfinance movements. However, the credit union concept goes further, because it is designed to distribute the returns derived from the provision of financial services among the community members, and it has other attractive features.

Credit unions are not-for-profit firms (different from non-profit organizations) embedded in the local community and centred on the principles of solidarity, self-help and autonomy. They are owned by their members, who share a common bond. This can be the area they live in, the employer they work for, the religious belief they share, or other commonality. In the UK, only members can use the financial services of credit unions. There are no shareholders who might demand growing returns on equity capital. Instead, any operating profits can be shared with members, such as in the form of lower interest charges on loans or higher interest rates on deposits (the latter referred to as a 'dividend').[3] The staff of credit unions in the UK are to a large extent volunteers or part-timers working for modest remuneration. Since the credit union business model does not include lending for speculative purposes, speculative trading activities or fee-generation through product sales campaigns, there are no excess returns that are distributed between

---

2   The cooperative principle is far older, however. The founding of Germany's first Sparkasse (savings bank) in the eighteenth century was the result of cooperative activities. The cooperative sharing of communal resources has been documented for centuries in Germany, with some records reaching back to the era of the Germanic tribes (Kluge 1991).

3   'The interest from loans is used to pay expenses; to build up reserves (capital) and the remainder may be returned to the members by way of dividend.' See http://www.creditunion.co.uk/ savings.htm, accessed via the website of Southwark Credit Union on 3 September 2009.

dividend-maximizing owners and bonus-maximizing bankers. Indeed, their business model does not aim at the maximization of short-term profits, but explicitly aims at sustainability and long-term mutual support.[4] Further, the credit union concept aimed at mitigating asymmetric information problems (recognized in economics only much later, see Stiglitz and Weiss 1981) through the existence of a common bond.

Credit unions have grown to significant proportions and are important financial service providers in the world. Of the global working-age population, 18.5 per cent are members of credit unions (Bauer et al. 2009). McKillop (in Ward and McKillop 2005) estimated credit unions to make up 16 per cent of the banking market share in Germany, 29 per cent in Italy, 32 per cent in Austria, 40 per cent in France and 45 per cent in the Canadian province of Quebec. These figures are remarkable if one remembers that in many countries credit unions remain small, local and legally independent entities that control their own destiny and are not under instructions from a nationwide or regional headquarters. In Germany, for instance, the 16 per cent market share is the collective result of the work of more than 1,200 independent credit unions.

Their relative importance is illustrated by considering the situation in Germany. There are 1,200 independent Volksbanken and Raiffeisenbanken (not the only but the most important types of credit union in Germany) as at the end of 2008. These had over 12,000 branches and 16.2 million members. Their total assets amounted to €668.4 billion and they employed over 186,000 staff at the end of 2008. If one included their central organizations, total assets exceeded €1 trillion at the end of 2008.

In the UK, the worldwide credit union movement cannot be said to have been successful by international comparison. There are currently close to 700 credit unions in the UK, with close to 300,000 members.[5] While only about 0.5 per cent of the adult population in the UK are members of a credit union, the equivalent figures for Ireland, the US, Australia and Canada are 45 per cent, 30 per cent, 20 per cent and 16 per cent respectively (HM Treasury 1999). Northern Ireland, on the other hand, boasts nearly as

---

4   'Unser auf Foerderung und Nachhaltigkeit und eben nicht auf kurzfristige Gewinnmaximierung basierendes Geschaeftsmodell ueberzeugt.'

5   476 credit unions are members of the Association of British Credit Unions Ltd (ABCUL), with approximately 250,000 members. In addition, about 200 credit unions with 20,000 members have not joined ABCUL: see Bank of England 2000b: 31, citing HM Treasury 1999. However, Bank of England 1999: 31 cites 'over 700 credit unions' with 'over 400,000 members'.

many members as there are in the rest of the UK.[6] Compare the Volksbank
Frankfurt, one of Germany's largest Volksbanks, with Leeds City Credit
Union, of the largest credit unions in Britain: while Volksbank Frankfurt
has approximately 500,000 customers, about 170,000 members (owners) and
total assets at the end of 2007 of €6.7 billion, LCCU has 24,000 members and
total assets of £30 million.

There is a growing body of literature on the growth and performance
of credit unions, particularly in the US, Ireland, and, to a lesser extent, in
the UK. Black and Dugger (1981) analyse credit union growth, structure and
regulatory issues in the US. Goddard et al. (2002 and 2008) analyse growth,
diversification and financial performance of US credit unions. Hannafin and
McKillop (2007) as well as Karels and McClatchey (1999) discuss the role of
deposit insurance in the context of credit unions. Bauer (2008) analyses credit
union performance.

A number of hypotheses have been formulated concerning this relative
lack of growth by credit unions in the UK. Gerwyn et al. (1990) argue that the
lack of a specific statutory framework prior to the Credit Union Act 1979 was
a major factor in their slow growth. The Bank of England (2000b) suggests
that a key factor has been the lack of a central services organization, such as
exists in other countries (an example of which is the Raiffeisen Zentralbank
in Austria). Another suggested reason is that legislation 'restricts very
severely the range of services credit unions can provide to their members
and how they can fund themselves' (Fitchew 1998, as cited by Fuller and
Jonas 2002). A fourth reason may be that UK credit unions, unlike their
equivalents (for instance) in Germany, only cater to individuals and not to
businesses (such as small businesses) (Bank of England 2000b). Additional
reasons have been postulated by researchers, including the social context of
their members, ethos and ideology of their decision-makers or reliance on
unpaid volunteers (Ward and McKillop 2002, see also 2005).

A potential additional reason for their weak growth performance in the
UK that has so far not been cited is the possibly impeded ability of credit
unions to create credit. Should credit unions in the UK (and countries with
a similar regulatory environment) not be able to create credit in the same
way as banks, it would constitute a severe handicap in their competition with
banks and a significant hindrance to their expansion. On the other hand,

---

6   'Most of these are from the Catholic community, where membership levels are closer to those
    in the Irish Republic' (Bank of England 2000b: 31).

should credit unions be able to create credit, they could potentially offer an alternative to commercial banking, if the expectation can be confirmed that their business model is more sustainable than that of banks.

Credit Creation

There is a recent and growing literature on credit creation. The concept had been relatively widely understood among economists in the pre-war and early post-war era. It seems to have fallen out of fashion since about the 1960s, approximately following the time of James Tobin's (1963) article downplaying the role of bank credit creation and the subsequent apparent reluctance by leading journals to publish articles that make reference to it.

This does not mean that the concept of credit creation has disappeared from academic economics. Some widely used university textbooks regularly mention credit creation at introductory undergraduate level (such as Begg et al. 2005, Stiglitz 1997). However, credit creation does not feature at all in more advanced textbooks, such as Blanchard and Fisher (1989), Walsh (2003) or Woodford (2003). This disappearance of credit creation from advanced textbooks may be due to the fact that a banking system does not feature in their more stylized models of the macro or monetary economy. Financial instruments and financial service providers are assumed to be homogeneous and perfectly substitutable with those aspects of financial markets that do appear in the monetary models (such as a bond market, or a rate of time preference, standing in for a bond market, which in turn is assumed to be substitutable with all other financial instruments and intermediaries).

The recent global banking crisis suggests, on the other hand, that the institutional reality represented by banks cannot be ignored without a loss of information concerning the monetary transmission mechanism and the functioning of the economy in general, and financial markets and the banking system in particular. It is not the purpose of this chapter to reiterate the debate concerning commercial banks' ability to create credit.[7] For the purposes of this

---

7   Werner (2005) explains the process of credit creation. See also, for instance, Macleod (1855), Hahn (1920) and Mayer (1979). Werner (2009) reviews the arguments and presents empirical work on the operational details of bank credit creation, demonstrating banks' ability to create credit, deposits and thus the bulk of the money supply. For an example, see the Federal Reserve's PDF on 'the principle of multiple deposit creation', available at: http://www.federalreserveeducation.org/fed101_html/policy/frtoday_depositCreation.pdf [accessed: 3 September 2009].

chapter, the view of major central banks (albeit a not widely publicized one), namely of the Federal Reserve, the ECB and the BIS, is adopted. In this view, which is widely shared by academics and professionals familiar with banking, banks are the primary creators of money.[8] In line with it, private-sector commercial banks can be seen to provide a non-trivial public goods function as the originators and allocators of the money supply.

Somewhat stylized and applied to a standard fractional reserve system, the process works as follows (following the description in Werner 2005): when Bank A receives a new deposit of £100 and a 1 per cent reserve requirement is applied by the central bank, the bank will not deposit £1 with the central bank and lend £99 to borrowers (as many textbooks still state), but instead deposit the entire £100 with the central bank, thus being able to extend credit amounting to £9,900 (illustrated in Figure 3.1).

This is possible because the loan is granted in the form of a numerical entry into the borrower's deposit account (or, alternatively, appears as a deposit in the banking system upon first use of the money). In others words, bank credit is extended by banks by recording a credit in the borrower's deposit account in the amount of the loan. Observers are unable to distinguish such 'fictional' deposits from actual deposits, as banks combine their financial service function with the provision of transactions settlement and clearing services.

In general, the joint necessary requirements for credit creation by a privately owned financial institution are as follows (Werner 2009):

1.   The financial institution must engage in both taking deposits and extending loans.

---

8   'The actual process of money creation takes place primarily in banks' (Federal Reserve Bank of Chicago 1961: 3). 'At the beginning of the 20th century almost the totality of retail payments were made in central bank money. Over time, this monopoly came to be shared with commercial banks, when deposits and their transfer via checks and giros became widely accepted. Banknotes and commercial bank money became fully interchangeable payment media that customers could use according to their needs. While transaction costs in commercial bank money were shrinking, cashless payment instruments became increasingly used, at the expense of banknotes' (ECB 2000). 'Contemporary monetary systems are based on the mutually reinforcing roles of central bank money and commercial bank monies. What makes a currency unique in character and distinct from other currencies is that its different forms (central bank money and commercial bank monies) are used interchangeably by the public in making payments, not least because they are convertible at par' (BIS 2003).

Balance Sheet of Bank A

Step 1   Deposit of £100 by customer at Bank A

Assets	Liabilities
	£100

Step 2   £100 used to increase the reserve of Bank A

Assets	Liabilities
£100	£100

Step 3   Loan of £9,900 granted, by crediting borrower's bank account with deposit

Assets	Liabilities
£100	£100
+	+
£9,900	£9,900

The original deposit of £100 becomes the 1% reserve on the basis of which loans 99 times as large can be granted by the same bank. Credit creation has 'lengthened' the bank's balance sheet.

Figure 3.1   Illustration of credit creation

2.   It must either have an account with the central bank or be part of a settlement system of which the central bank is a member, or be able to use the services of a member of such a settlement system.

3.   It must be able to lend to or borrow from other credit creating financial institutions on commercial terms.

4.   The reserve required to be held at the central bank (usually non-interest bearing and calculated as a percentage of deposited funds) must be smaller than 100 per cent (hence the name 'fractional reserve banking system').

5.   The capital required as a percentage of assets must be smaller than 100 per cent.

6.   There must not be quantitative restrictions on the volume of loans extended, such as to limit their size to the amount of deposits received by individuals, or a figure negligibly above this.

Do Credit Unions Create Credit?

The literature seems in agreement that credit unions are able to fulfil most of the major functions of commercial banks. The Association of British Credit Unions Ltd (ABCUL) maintains that credit unions are identical to banks, except for their common bond: 'It is the common bond which makes credit unions unique and different to banks and building societies' (ABCUL 2008). However, ABCUL does not directly address the issue of credit creation. Indeed, there is no literature explicitly analysing the question of whether credit unions can create credit. This question is of importance to understand credit unions better (including some recent research issues on credit unions in the UK, such as their relative growth). It also requires an answer, if one is to assess and compare the sustainability qualities of banks and credit unions, and whether a potentially greater role for credit unions is desirable and feasible. Should they not have the ability to create credit, this would constitute an important and new explanation for their lack of growth in the UK in the past. At the same time, they could not, in this case, act as substitutes for the commercial banking sector and thus offer a viable 'third sector' alternative to banking.

THE OFFICIAL VIEW

Our analysis of this question should start with the 'official' view, as described by credit unions and the regulatory authorities. The following description is taken from Southwark Credit Union, one of England's largest credit unions, catering to those who live and work in the southern London Borough of Southwark, with 8,500 members and £8.4 million in deposits.[9] Like many credit unions, it offers an explanation of the function of credit unions on its website:

> *The members* are *the credit union. They provide services to themselves.*[10]

> *A credit union is a group of people who save together and lend to each other at a reasonable rate of interest.*[11]

---

9 Southwark Credit Union statistics as of December 2008, according to their website, accessed at http://www.creditunion.co.uk/news.htm on 3 September 2009.

10 http://www.creditunion.co.uk/details_home.htm accessed via the website of Southwark Credit Union on 3 September 2009.

11 http://www.creditunion.co.uk/britain.htm, accessed via the website of Southwark Credit Union on 3 September 2009.

Savings are used to make loans to members.[12]

Another, similar definition of credit unions comes from the Financial Services Authority (FSA). In its information pamphlet on credit unions, it defines them as follows:

They are community savings and loan cooperatives, where members pool their savings to lend to one another and help to run the credit union. (FSA 2009: 2)

How much a credit union can lend you depends on how much its members have saved and how good the members are at repaying loans and interest on time. (FSA 2009: 6)

This view is also reflected in the literature. Concerning US credit unions, Bauer (2008) states: 'Credit unions are cooperative credit institutions, borrowing funds from one set of members/owners and lending those funds to others, seeking to benefit both sets of owners by offering below market loan rates and above market deposit rates.' These descriptions assert that credit unions take deposits from members and lend out the deposited money to other members. However, this does not mean that they also have the ability to *create* credit. To the contrary, if credit unions' activities are limited to lending out the money actually deposited by members, then credit unions – in contrast to what banks do – would act as mere financial intermediaries that channel savings from the depositors to borrowers, and would not (could not) create credit.

The FSA goes further and argues that credit unions cannot even lend out as much as has been deposited by their members: 'Credit unions can't lend all their members' savings or invest the remaining money in risky ventures. Instead they must put it into bank deposit accounts and the most reliable investments, such as government bonds. This ensures they can get the money back if they need to' (FSA 2009: 3). Finally, we cite the Bank of England on this issue. The Bank of England Act of 1998 defines its client institutions ('eligible institutions') as 'deposit-takers'. This is in line with the textbook definition of banks as being deposit-taking financial institutions that are clients of the central bank. It is often also used as the definition of financial institutions that have the ability to create credit. However, the Bank of England excludes credit unions from this definition: Schedule 2

---

12 http://www.creditunion.co.uk/savings.htm, accessed via the website of Southwark Credit Union on 3 September 2009.

of the Bank of England Act 1998, citing cash ratio deposits, specifies when listing eligible institutions, 'Deposit-taker has the meaning given in section 17, except that it does not include a credit union; a friendly society; ...' (Houses of Parliament 1998). In line with this, the Bank of England does not include credit union statistics in its national deposit or banking statistics.[13] It would appear, therefore, that the Bank of England does not treat credit unions even as full-blown deposit-taking financial institutions. This is consistent with the FSA's view that credit unions cannot create credit.

The ability to create credit is dependent on legal and institutional arrangements. In Germany, where the credit union movement started, credit unions have bank status, are subject to central bank monetary policy and their deposit and credit statistics are aggregated by the authorities. Furthermore, they are recognized as being able to create credit. So our question could be reformulated: what makes UK credit unions so different from German credit unions? In the sections below we employ an analytical evaluation of the legal and institutional framework determining the relevant actions of credit unions in the UK in order to assess the question whether credit unions can and do create credit.

INSTITUTIONAL EVALUATION 1979–2002

Until 1 July 2002, credit unions were supervised by the Registry of Friendly Societies. In 1979, the Credit Unions Act was passed, which defined the scope for activities by credit unions.[14] This act prevented credit unions from granting unsecured loans for longer than two years, restricted loans to a maximum total of £5,000 above the amount a member had deposited at the credit union, and limited total membership to 5,000 people. Applying the conditions for the ability to create credit cited above, we find that condition 6 is violated. Under this regulatory regime credit unions thus did not have the power to create credit.

---

13 'The statistical framework covered by these instructions involves all institutions authorised to carry out deposit taking in the UK (and certain former banks). These are defined for the purposes of these instructions as: (1) firms with a permission under Part IV of the Financial Services and Markets Act 2000 to accept deposits other than (i) credit unions; (ii) firms whose permission to accept deposits is only for the purpose of carrying on insurance business; and (iii) friendly societies; ...' (see http://www.bankofengland.co.uk/statistics/reporters/defs/def_gene.pdf).

14 Prior to this, credit unions were subject to the Industrial and Provident Societies Act 1965. Allowable investments were defined by the Credit Unions (Authorised Investments) Order 1979, which was replaced by the Credit Unions (Authorised Investments) Order 1993 in reflection of EU directives.

In the words of the Bank of England, the act 'proved to be a constraint on the development of credit unions' (Bank of England 1999: 31). Since it quantitatively restricted the extension of loans, it also severely restricted the ability of credit unions to create credit, to the extent that it is a reasonable approximation to conclude that they did not create credit. Credit extension beyond deposit contribution was limited to £5,000 per person, extended to a maximum of 5,000 people, thus limiting it to a total maximum of £25 million per credit union at any one time. With 700 credit unions, this implies a maximum one-off credit creation ability at any one time of £17.5 billion. With actual membership of about 300,000, the actual maximum one-off credit creation that could theoretically be reached was only £1.5 billion. This represents 0.09 per cent of outstanding credit in the UK, or 0.5 per cent of total credit creation.[15] However, credit creation is a flow-concept: loans get repaid and new loans are extended. Credit creation is the difference in outstanding credit balances in the observation period compared to the reference period (for example, the same month or quarter in the previous year). Thus credit creation is measured by the increase in net credit balances. This is likely to be a much smaller figure each year. To illustrate, if we assume credit unions get all 'loaned up' in the first time period, and maintain this state of affairs, their credit creation in the following periods would be zero (assuming the same number of credit unions). The only way to expand credit creation by credit unions further would then be to establish more credit unions. But since each credit union could only account for a maximum one-off credit creation of £25 million, the number of credit unions would have to grow dramatically for this to become significant in the economy. We conclude that maximum potential allowed one-off credit creation by credit unions was miniscule under the 1979 regulatory regime.

This, however, was not the only obstacle to the smooth creation of credit by credit unions. Another obstacle was the restriction of depositors to members. German credit unions, for instance, allow both individuals and legal persons to become customers, and customers do not need to become members. In the UK, only members can be customers, and membership is restricted to natural persons.[16] Everything else being equal, this restriction means that credit unions

---

15 A handy approximation of credit creation is the annual difference of the difference between M4 and M0. According to the Bank of England, at the end of December 2007, M4 stood at £1,675.4 billion. Subtracting cash in circulation, amounting to £43.6 billion, we obtain £1,631.8 billion (since the abolition of reserve requirements in the UK, high-powered money has no longer been represented by cash and reserves, but cash alone). For the end of December 2008, the figures are, respectively, £1,995.4 billion minus £46.8 billion = £1,948.6 billion. Hence, credit creation over the year to December 2008 was £316.8 billion.

16 With the exception of minors who cannot become full members and are thus categorized as non-associated members.

would suffer from an outflow of deposits upon credit creation, as loaned money tends to be spent with legal persons, who, however, were barred from having deposit accounts with the credit unions. There could be no natural reflux of created deposits to the credit unions, as is the case with banks.[17] This situation does not disable credit creation per se, but renders it more costly and less attractive. Credit unions would consistently have to borrow deposits from other banks. Unfortunately, this was not possible: the legislation also forbade credit unions to borrow money from banks or other credit unions. As a result, even if the loan limits did not exist, credit unions were limited in their ability to create credit by the inability to balance their balance sheets upon credit creation.

RESULT

The verdict on credit creation by credit unions while under the Credit Unions Act 1979 is that the combination of regulatory restrictions effectively disabled credit unions' capacity to create credit. Their credit creation was so limited as to be irrelevant, rendering them in status equal to non-bank financial institutions without the power to create credit. Credit unions could not contribute to the task of producing part of the money supply. Even if larger in scale, they could therefore not be considered an alternative to the banking system. Given this finding, a new hypothesis for the failure of growth by credit unions in the UK can be formulated: they are likely to have failed in the UK in their competition with banks and building societies due to the severe handicap of not being allowed to create credit.

INSTITUTIONAL EVALUATION SINCE 2002

Since then the legal situation has changed to some extent. Partly because the government believed that 'credit unions have a vital role to play in tackling financial exclusion in deprived neighbourhoods' (Bank of England 1999: 31), the Credit Unions Act 1979 was amended by the Deregulation Order of 1 September 1996. Further, since 2 July 2002, credit unions have become regulated under the provisions of the Financial Markets and Services Act 2000.[18] This included the transfer of authorization and regulation of credit unions to the FSA.

---

17 Banks can capture a proportion of such outflows due to the fact that sellers often use the same bank as the buyers/borrowers. Hence, there is a reflux of funds. Should insufficient funds flow back, they must accumulate in other banks. Banks would thus borrow in the interbank market from those banks with excess deposits.
18 Under the Financial Services and Markets Act 2000 (Consequential Amendments and Transitional Provisions) (Credit Unions) Order 2002. This also repealed the Credit Unions (Authorised Investments) Order 1993, among others.

These legal changes scrapped many of the above restrictions on credit unions. The 5,000-member limit was rescinded, longer repayment periods for loans were allowed and the absolute loan limit was tripled to £15,000. Furthermore, credit unions are now allowed to borrow from non-member external sources, including banks, other credit unions and market participants in general.[19] They are now also allowed to offer fee-earning additional services, such as bill payments. The definition of common bond was also broadened, allowing credit unions to combine association-type common bonds with other types of common bonds (Band of England 2000b). However, businesses still could not become credit union customers. The FSA wrote in 2009: 'You can't save or borrow in the name of a business you run. Only members can borrow from a credit union and the loan must be in your name even if you want to use the money for a business you run' (FSA 2009: 4).[20] Furthermore, a limit on the maximum amount of deposits that can be accepted by any one member remains in place, restricted to £10,000.

This new legal status, within the post-FSA regulatory and institutional framework, requires a renewed analysis of the ability of credit unions to create credit. We proceed by confirming in turn whether credit unions meet all of the criteria necessary for the ability to create credit, detailed at the end of the section headed 'Credit Creation' above.

Credit unions meet condition 1, as their main activity is deposit-taking and loan extension. Criterion 2 is not quite as quickly ascertained. In the UK, monetary transactions are settled through one of three settlement companies: (a) CHAPS Clearing Company; (b) BACS Ltd.; and (c) Cheque and Credit Clearing Company Ltd (CCCC). These focus on different types of transactions. CHAPS (Clearing House Automated Payment System) has 13 direct clearing members and settles on the same day. It operates on a SWIFT technical platform (enabling fast international settlement) and is the most expensive form of clearing. Most of its transaction volume comes from high-value wholesale payments. The average daily value of CHAPS sterling payments was £195 billion in 2000.[21] The remaining two payment clearing companies are retail-oriented and thus likely

---

19 In addition to the ability to borrow from other sources, the government has also provided public funds to increase available liquidity at credit unions, mainly in the form of the Community Finance Initiative, which provides loans to credit unions and various growth funds.

20 On the other hand, already in 2000 the Bank of England acknowledged that some credit unions do lend to businesses: 'While there are only a small number of credit unions which specialise in lending to businesses, individual members do use such finance to support their business ventures' (Bank of England 2000b: v).

21 BIS 2003: 407.

to be the relevant channels for credit unions. BACS has 13 direct members, and focuses on electronic (giro) transactions. The Cheque and Credit Clearing Company has 12 direct members and processes chapter instructions, such as cheques and credit vouchers.[22] The Bank of England is a full (direct) member of all three clearing companies. Further, it is accounts held at the Bank that are used to effect settlement between full members. Full members of CHAPS additionally benefit from the Bank of England's intraday liquidity provision via repo agreements. The Bank of England 'is responsible for the oversight of UK payment systems and as such for ensuring that sufficient weight is given to risk reduction and management in such systems' design and operation' (BIS 2003: 397; see also Bank of England 2000b).

Credit unions are not direct members of any of these three payment structures. CHAPS would be too expensive and not in line with the low transaction value relevant for credit unions. BACS and CCCC require their members to be either banks or building societies, and therefore explicitly exclude credit unions.[23] However, both BACS and CCCC employ a two-tier access structure consisting of direct settlement members and 'indirect' participants. CCCC currently has about 400 indirect settlement members,

---

22 As of September 2009, the members were: the Bank of England, Abbey, Alliance & Leicester, Bank of Scotland, Barclays Bank, Clydesdale Bank, the Cooperative Bank, HSBC Bank, Lloyds TSB Bank, National Westminster Bank, the Royal Bank of Scotland and Nationwide Building Society.

23 'To be eligible to become and remain a settlement member of the Cheque and Credit Clearing System, an entity must fulfil a number of criteria. It must be: 1. be a bank or building society, a public authority or publicly guaranteed undertaking; 2. have an appropriate settlement account at each relevant settlement service provider for the relevant currency; 3. carry out business and operate an office within the EEA; 4. provide a cheque and/or credit clearing service (for sterling cheques and/or sterling credits and/or euro cheques) to its customers through the clearing systems operated by the Cheque and Credit Clearing Company; 5. have the ability to comply on a continuous basis with the technical and operational requirements of each clearing system in which it participates; 6. pay the membership charges; 7. sign legal agreements in respect of membership and of the settlement arrangements; 8. have a minimum credit rating of: (a) a prime short-term credit rating of A-3 or higher by S&P, F-3 or higher by Fitch and P-3 or higher by Moody's; and (b) an investment grade long-term credit rating of BBB- or higher by S&P, BBB- or higher by Fitch and Baa3 or higher by Moody's; 9. become a shareholder of the Cheque and Credit Clearing Company Ltd' (CCCC 2009). 'To become a member of Bacs a number of criteria need to be met. Each member of Bacs must: – have a settlement account at the Bank of England; – be based in the European economic area; – meet agreed technical and operational requirements, including having an agreement in place with Voca (or another provider of approved clearing services), and having an approved trust service; – be a bank or building society; – have a minimum credit rating of (a) a prime short-term credit rating of A-3 or higher by S&P, F-3 or higher by Fitch and P-3 or higher by Moody's; and (b) an investment grade long-term credit rating of BBB- or higher by S&P, BBB- or higher by Fitch and Baa3 or higher by Moody's; – sign a legal document in respect of membership, and of the settlement arrangements; – pay a share of Bacs costs' (BACS 2009).

which consist of many smaller banks and building societies which have settlement arrangements with member banks (CCCC 2009). The indirect membership does not seem formally limited to banks and building societies, but credit unions are currently not among them. Crucially, 'Members of BACS are also able to sponsor other organizations as users of the service. Users are allocated a BACS user number by their sponsor and are able to submit payment instructions directly to the system' (BIS 2003: 410). Such 'other organizations' submit payment instructions through an intermediary who is a member. They are not restricted to banks and building societies and, given the large total number of about 60,000, are likely to include all credit unions. Most credit unions thus are likely to meet criterion 2.

Criterion 3, concerning the ability to borrow funds from other sources, is met by credit unions thanks to the recent regulatory changes (CRED 7.3.2.A R). Like banks, they are allowed to borrow wholesale funds. The new regulatory framework established in 2002 created two types of credit unions in the UK. The so-called 'version 1 credit unions' must not borrow more than 20 per cent of share capital (that is, members' deposits). This limits their ability to create credit significantly, compared to commercial banks. 'Version 2 credit unions' can borrow up to 50 per cent of the 'total shareholding in the credit union' (CRED 7 .3.5 R). Thus the ability of version 2 credit unions to create credit is less hampered by this restriction, since shareholding in this case means total deposits in the credit union by members. However, it remains a significant handicap compared to banks.

By way of comparison, at the end of 2008, Lloyds TSB Group plc recorded customer accounts (that is, deposits from corporate and individual depositors) amounting to £162.13 billion. If the remainder of non-equity liabilities are considered a form of borrowing from non-customer sources, external borrowing amounts to close to 100 per cent of deposits in the case of Lloyds TSB.[24]

Criterion 4 is met, as the reserve requirement in the UK has been zero in the observation period.

We thus turn to a discussion of criterion 5, the capital adequacy requirement. This is administered by the FSA and has been in place since the beginning of the observation period. It is detailed in the FSA's Credit Unions Source Book ('CRED'). According to CRED, credit unions must at all times maintain a liquidity reserve of 5 per cent of total liabilities.

---

24 Total liabilities (excluding equity) amounted to £356.7 billion.

The so-called 'version 1 credit unions' must have initial capital of at least £1,000. What formerly was a restriction on the maximum amount of loan extended has been raised to £7,500 and changed into a threshold: it can be exceeded if the credit union maintains a capital to total assets ratio of at least 5 per cent. In addition, version 1 credit unions must maintain a general reserve of at least 10 per cent of total assets. Further, they must ensure that their liquid assets to total liability ratio does not fall below 10 per cent on two consecutive quarter ends. If a version 1 credit union has either assets larger than £5 million or more than 5,000 members, it is classified as a 'large version 1 credit union' and must maintain a 5 per cent capital to total assets ratio at all times. Large version 1 credit unions with either more than 10,000 members or more than £10 million in deposits must maintain at least an 8 per cent risk-weighted capital to total assets ratio. For version 2 credit unions, the regulatory regime is simpler: there are no member, deposit or loan-size thresholds. Version 2 credit unions must have initial capital of at least £5,000 and they must maintain at all times a risk-adjusted capital to total assets ratio of at least 8 per cent (or £5,000, whichever is larger).[25] These capital adequacy rules are comparable to the BIS capital ratios required for banks – though more onerous than the 4 per cent risk-weighted requirement for banks that do not engage in international business. It is somewhat puzzling that regulators have chosen the 8 per cent risk-weighted capital adequacy rule, which applies to banks engaging in international business, although credit unions virtually never engage in international business.

Finally, we come to criterion 6. The quantitative restriction on loans has been lifted to some extent, but continues to exist and, by comparison to banks, continues to limit loans to any one customer to micro-credit. In addition, the limits on maximum deposits that can be accepted by any one customer remain in place.

RESULT

The regulatory changes since 2002 have enabled credit unions to create credit. However, they can do so only in a modest and still severely restricted fashion, when compared with commercial banks. Their growth thus remains artificially restricted and they remain unable to perform in aggregate the macroeconomic functions of the banking system.

---

25 CRED 8.4.1 R (2) defines risk-adjusted capital as Capital + (provisions – balance of the net liability of borrowers where their loans are 12 months or more in arrears – 35 per cent of the net liability of borrowers where their loans are 3–12 months in arrears).

EVALUATION OF 2010 REGULATORY CHANGES

A further amendment to the Credit Unions Act 1979 has been under consideration and consultation. The changes are outlined in the Legislative Reform Order (LRO), coming before Parliament in October 2009 (HM Treasury 2008). The changes are likely to become effective in April 2010. With respect to the present inquiry, one major obstacle to the normal process of credit creation will to some extend be cleared by the new legislation: credit unions will be allowed to accept legal persons as members. However, the government proposes to cap the proportion of corporate membership to 10 per cent and to limit the proportion of total assets, and of lending, accounted for by corporate members. As the reason for this continued restriction, the government cites fears about the 'a risk that corporate membership could crowd out individual member involvement' (HM Treasury 2009: 16). According to the LRO, these restrictions are considered necessary and proportionate to ensure that corporate members do not

> *exercise more than 10 per cent of the voting rights in a credit union; that they do not exert a disproportionate influence through holding a large proportion of the credit union's allotted shares; and that loans to corporate members are limited and only allowed if the rules so provide. Restricting bodies corporate to deferred shares ensures that they do not exert undue influence by being able to withdraw (or threaten to withdraw) their share capital. (HM Treasury 2008: 41)*

While the restrictions on corporate membership are one method to ensure that corporate members 'do not exert a disproportionate influence' on credit unions, it is incorrect to state, as LRO does, that they are 'necessary' to achieve this goal. In Germany, credit unions have long addressed this problem while maximizing growth potential of credit unions, through distinguishing between members and customers, and through limiting each member to one vote. Thus anyone can become a customer of a credit union – thereby supporting the aims and goals of the credit union – while not having any voting or influence. Customers can make virtually unlimited amounts of deposits, though not receive loans. By contrast, UK legislation continues to impose artificial limits on who can deposit money with credit unions and how much. While these restrictions remain in place, credit unions are not able to create credit in the same way as commercial banks are. The fundamental cooperative principles of solidarity, self-help and autonomy are more easily represented by a one-member one-vote system, not a system where the votes are proportional to investments made, as is the case with profit-oriented joint stock companies. Thus the latest UK legislative changes continue to restrict the growth potential and performance of credit unions artificially, and they fail to recognize the cooperative character of credit unions.

If one is interested in allowing credit unions to grow and benefit society, the principle should be to allow everyone, including legal persons, to deposit unlimited amounts of money with credit unions. It would appear that the important issue of the ability to create credit had not been considered either by the government or credit union representatives in their efforts to reform legislation. This may explain why the above problems have not been highlighted in the discussions and consultations of the present LRO.

Conclusions and Policy Implications

Credit unions in the past were not able to create credit. This is likely to have been a key reason for their failure to grow in the UK. However, the legal situation changed in 2002. Credit unions are now able to create credit to a modest extent. But present and pending legislation continues to restrict their ability to create credit so severely that they cannot compete on level grounds with banks, let alone pose a potential alternative to commercial banking in a macroeconomic sense. It would appear that the regulators (FSA) are not aware of this fact, nor are the leadership of credit unions.

While financial institutions aiming at private short-term profits, paying out high bonuses, engaging in unrestricted speculative activities and investments face no restrictions on their loan-taking, deposit-taking or indeed their speculative investments in the UK, financial institutions that explicitly focus on long-term benefits to the local community, do not pay high bonuses and do not engage in speculative credit extension or churning activities, are severely restricted by regulations in their ability to take deposits, grant loans or indeed grow their business to become of a size that might make their positive role felt in the UK economy. Furthermore, commercial banks, which are explicitly oriented towards maximizing the short-term profits of their shareholders, are being utilized as the main source of credit creation in the UK economy and thus given the privilege to create the money supply and select who should receive newly created purchasing power. Meanwhile, not-for-profit financial institutions that aim at supporting the local community are largely prevented from enjoying this privilege or participating in this macroeconomically important resource-allocation process.

Why has regulation been so much more restrictive of credit union activities in the UK than in other countries? Asking the question *'cui bono?'* may provide the answer. The UK banking sector has enjoyed a monopoly on the creation of the majority of the money supply and this has for decades been a most lucrative activity – both for the bank owners and the senior bank staff. This appears to have created a powerful lobby group that has been influential in the creation of legislation. Unfortunately what is good for the bankers is not necessary good for the rest of the economy, as both Lord Turner and Pope Benedict have recently pointed out. Thus society must be allowed to consider and test alternative models of financial intermediation. Credit unions appear to offer a tested, realistic and viable answer. However, before they can be utilized in a more meaningful scale, they need to be given that public goods privilege that banks have enjoyed and have frequently misused for their own private gains: the ability to create credit.

In the words of Pope Benedict:

> *What is needed, therefore, is a market that permits the free operation, in conditions of equal opportunity, of enterprises in pursuit of different institutional ends. Alongside profit-oriented private enterprise and the various types of public enterprise, there must be room for commercial entities based on mutualist principles and pursuing social ends to take root and express themselves. It is from their reciprocal encounter in the marketplace that one may expect hybrid forms of commercial behaviour to emerge, and hence an attentiveness to ways of civilizing the economy. Charity in truth, in this case, requires that shape and structure be given to those types of economic initiative which, without rejecting profit, aim at a higher goal than the mere logic of the exchange of equivalents, of profit as an end in itself ... The exclusively binary model of market-plus-State is corrosive of society, while economic forms based on solidarity, which find their natural home in civil society without being restricted to it, build up society.* (Benedict 2009: 38)

References

ABCUL. 2008. *A to Z of Credit Union Terminology, ABCUL Information* [Online]. Manchester: ABCUL. Available at: http://www.abcul.org/lib/liDownload/919/A%20to%20Z%20of%20Credit%20Union%20Terminology%20Apr08.pdf [accessed: 13 September 2009].

BACS. 2009. *Criteria for Membership, BACS Ltd* [Online]. Available at: http://www.
bacs.co.uk/Bacs/Banks/BecomeABacsMember/Pages/CriteriaForMembership.
aspx [accessed: 3 September 2009].

Bank of England. 1999. *The Financing of Ethnic Minority Firms in the United
Kingdom: A Special Report.* London: Bank of England. Available at: http://
www.bankofengland.co.uk/publications/financeforsmallfirms/ethnic.pdf
[accessed 3 September 2009].

Bank of England. 2000a. *Oversight and Payment Systems.* London: Bank of
England.

Bank of England. 2000b. *Finance for Small Businesses in Deprived Communities.*
London: Bank of England, November.

Bauer, Keldon J. 2008. Detecting abnormal credit union performance. *Journal of
Banking and Finance*, 32(4), 573–86.

Bauer, Keldon J., Miles, Linda L., and Nishikawa, Takeshi. 2009. The effect of
mergers on credit union performance. *Journal of Banking and Finance*, 33(12),
2267–74.

Begg, David, Fischer, Stanley, and Dornbusch, Ruediger. 2005, *Economics*, 8th
edn. London: McGraw-Hill Higher Education.

Benedict XVI, Pope. 2009. *Caritas in veritate*, Encyclical Letter, 29 June, Acta
Sanctae Sedis (ASS) 101 [Online]. Available at: http://www.vatican.va/
holy_father/benedict_xvi/encyclicals/documents/hf_ben-xvi_enc_20090629_
caritas-in-veritate_en.html [accessed: 20 September 2009].

Benoit, Bertrand, and Bryant, Chris. 2009. Berlin bids to halt 'too big to fail'
banking. *Financial Times*, 31 August.

BIS (Bank for International Settlements). 2003. *The Role of Central Bank Money
in Payments Systems.* Basel: Bank for International Settlements. Available at:
http://www.bis.org/publ/cpss55.pdf.

Black, H., and Dugger, R. 1981. Credit union structure, growth and regulatory
problems. *Journal of Finance*, 36(2), 529–38.

Blanchard, Olivier, and Fisher, Stanley. 1989 *Lectures on Macroeconomics.*
Cambridge MA: MIT Press.

CCCC (Cheque and Credit Clearing Company Ltd). 2009. *Eligibility, Cheque
and Credit Clearing Company Ltd* [Online]. Available at: http://www.
chequeandcredit.co.uk/membership/-/page/eligibility/ [accessed: 3
September 2009].

ECB (European Central Bank). 2000. *Domestic Payments in Euroland: Commercial
and Central Bank Money.* Speech by Tommaso Padoa-Schioppa, Member of the
Executive Board of the European Central Bank, at the European Commission
Round Table 'Establishing a Single Payment Area: State of Play and Next
Steps', Brussels, 9 November 2000.

Federal Reserve Bank of Chicago. 1961. *Modern Money Mechanics: A Workbook on Deposits, Currency and Bank Reserves*. Chicago: Federal Reserve Bank of Chicago.

FSA (Financial Services Authority). 2009. *Just the Facts about Credit Unions, Money Made Clear Guide*. London: FSA, June. Available at: http://www. moneymadeclear.fsa.gov.uk/pdfs/credit_unions.pdf.

Fitchew, G. 1998. Address by the Chief Registrar of Friendly Societies to the World Council of Credit Unions conference, Glasgow, 26 May 1998.

Fuller, Duncan, and Jonas, Andrew. 2002. Capacity-building and British credit union development. *Local Economy*, 17(2), 157–63.

Gerwyn, LL., Griffiths, H., and Howells, G.G. 1990. Britain's best kept secret? An analysis of the credit union as an alternative source of credit. *Journal of Consumer Policy*, 13(4), 447–66, DOI: 10.1007/BF00412339.

Goddard, John, McKillop, Donal G., and Wilson, J.O.S. 2002. The growth of US credit unions. *Journal of Banking and Finance*, 22(12), 2327–56.

Goddard, John, McKillop, Donal G., and Wilson, J.O.S. 2008. The diversification and financial performance of US credit unions. *Journal of Banking and Finance*, 32(9), 1836–49.

Hahn, L. Albert. 1920. *Volkswirtschaftliche Theorie des Bankkredits*. Tuebingen: J.C.B. Mohr.

Hannafin, K., and McKillop, Donal G. 2007. Deposit insurance and credit unions: an international perspective. *Journal of Financial Regulation and Compliance*, 15(1), 42–62.

HM Treasury. 1999. Credit Unions of the Future, Credit Unions Taskforce [Online].

HM Treasury. 2008. Proposals for a Legislative Reform Order for Credit Unions and Industrial & Provident Societies in Great Britain, July [Online].

HM Treasury. 2009. Proposals for a Legislative Reform Order for Credit Unions and Industrial & Provident Societies in Great Britain: response to consultation, April [Online].

Houses of Parliament. 1998. Bank of England Act 1998. Available at: http://www. bankofengland.co.uk/about/legislation/1998act.pdf [accessed 3 September 2009].

Karels, G., and McClatchey, C. 1999. Deposit insurance and risk taking behaviour in the credit union industry. *Journal of Banking and Finance*, 23, 105–34.

Kluge, Holger Arnd. 1991. *Geschichte der deutschen Bankgenossenschaften*. Schriftenreihe des bankhistorischen Instituts. Frankfurt am Main: F. Knapp.

Macleod, Henry Dunning. 1855. *The Theory and Practice of Banking: With the Elementary Principles of Currency, Prices, Credit and Exchanges*. London: Longmans.

Mayer, Helmut. 1979. *Credit and Liquidity Creation in the International Banking zSector.* BIS Economic Papers no. 1. Basel: Bank for International Settlements, Monetary and Economic Department.

Raiffeisen, Friedrich Wilhelm. 1866. *Die Darlehnskassen-Vereine als Mittel zur Abhilfe der Noth der ländlichen Bevölkerung, sowie auch der städtischen Handwerker und Arbeiter: praktische Anleitung zur Bildung solcher Vereine, gestützt auf sechszehnjährige Erfahrung als Gründer derselben.* Neuwied: Strüder.

Stiglitz, Joseph E. 1997. *Economics,* 2nd rev. edn. New York: Norton.

Stiglitz, Joseph E., and Weiss, A. 1981. Credit rationing in markets with imperfect information. *American Economic Review,* 71(3), 393–410.

Tobin, J. 1963. Commercial banks as creators of 'money'. Cowles Foundation Discussion Papers, no. 159. Published in Dean Carson, ed., *Banking and Monetary Studies,* for the Comptroller of the Currency, US Treasury. Homewood IL: Richard D. Irwin, 408–419.

Turner, Adair. 2009. How to tame global finance. *Prospect,* 162, 27 August.

Walsh, Carl E. 2003. *Monetary Theory and Policy,* 2nd edn. Cambridge MA: MIT Press.

Ward, Ann-Marie, and McKillop, Donal G. 2002. *Emergence of the Credit Union Movement in the United Kingdom: Comparisons with the United States and the Republic of Ireland.* Working Paper [Online]. Available at: http://www.creditunionresearch.com/uploads/Working paper2.PDF [accessed 13 September 2009].

Ward, Ann-Marie, and McKillop, Donal G. 2005. The law of proportionate effect: the growth of the UK credit union movement at national and regional level. *Journal of Business, Finance and Accounting,* 32(9), 1827–1859.

Werner, R.A. 2005. *The New Paradigm in Macroeconomics: Solving the Riddle of Japanese Macroeconomic Performance.* Basingstoke: Palgrave Macmillan.

Werner, R.A. 2009. *The Accounting Mechanics of Credit Creation.* Discussion Paper. Southampton: Centre for Banking, Finance and Sustainable Development, School of Management, University of Southampton.

Woodford, Michael. 2003. *Interest and Prices: Foundations of a Theory of Monetary Policy.* Princeton: Princeton University Press.

PART II:

ACADEMIC RESEARCH IN THIRD

SECTOR ORGANIZATIONS

Overview of Part II: Academic Research in Third Sector Organizations

From a scholarly perspective organizational performance measurement and management have gained considerable popularity over the last two decades. From this academic interest many different models of performance management implementation have developed. Predictably, most have been developed from the large corporate for-profit perspective, and have slowly transitioned through public sector adoption to sectors such as healthcare and local government environments. Only recently has the academic community begun to focus on the non-for-profit sector and the subtle but important distinctions that it offers.

The following section offers contributions which address this specific area of third sector performance measurement. This section comprises five chapters which explore and consider the various academic perspectives of performance measurement and management with a third sector context.

The first chapter, by Tila Morris and Susan Ogden, considers the role of quality management in non-profit networks in Scotland, UK. It highlights issues from the perspective of the Scottish Council of Voluntary Organisations (SCVO) as it faces increasing pressure to develop a quality framework for its network of constituent organizations. This discussion serves to highlight the changing nature of the third sector and the greater need for more developed managerial processes to manage third sector organizations.

The second contribution to this section, by Tuuli Pärenson, is a research piece which focuses on the relationship between the strategic objectives of not-for-profit organizations and the stakeholder evaluations. The goals of the not-for-profit sector organization are often less quantifiable and not as readily defined as in the for-profit sector, which makes impact evaluation more problematic and less standardized. This chapter therefore offers a step toward standardization of impact evaluation.

The third chapter is by Rita Mano and Zachary Sheaffer, who consider how organizational competence is influenced by past experience. It presents research that considers which factors are likely to influence the preparedness of a third sector for crisis. This work further considers whether the historical experience of the organization, and of its management team, influence its future ability to respond to crisis.

The fourth contribution, by Richard Greatbanks and Graham Manville, draws attention to the issues and problems of third sector funding, and explores the typical funding model dynamics from both the funded organization's and funding body's perspectives. This work highlights the potential tensions and opposing objectives which are not often visible or considered in third sector funding, and considers yet another structural change that third sector organizations will have to contend with in the immediate future.

The final contribution to in this academic research section is by Pratima Dattani and reviews the changing role of the UK's third sector and the consequent shift in the performance management requirements which result. This work considers if a public value scorecard approach, reflecting the current political and economic climate, can provide an alternative performance management framework.

This section therefore draws together just a few of the many academic research avenues currently being considered within the field of performance measurement and management in the third sector.

4

Quality Management in Non-Profit Networks in Scotland: Cynical, Committed or Reflective?

Tila Morris and Susan Ogden

Introduction

Data on Scotland's non-profit sector has been consistently catalogued since 1991 by the Scottish Council for Voluntary Organisations (SCVO), the national body representing Scotland's voluntary sector. SCVO (2009a) estimated that Scotland has 45,000 non-profit organizations with a collective annual income of £4.1 billion and 130,000 paid employees (5 per cent of Scotland's workforce) as well as around 1.3 million volunteers. Of these, however, over 40 per cent are registered charities regulated by the Office of the Scottish Charity Regulator (OSCR) (SCVO 2008). The regulated subset is dominated by social care and development organizations and the wider unregulated subsector is predominantly made up of arts and sports organizations. Inequality within the sector is vast when considering the distribution of wealth. SCVO's research shows that 2 per cent of this subset receives 62 per cent of the overall share of the income (SCVO 2007). By contrast 64 per cent of regulated organizations survive on less than £25,000 per annum (ibid.). Scotland's non-profit context can therefore be summarized as a 'loose' but extremely diverse, and rapidly changing sector; one which is tasked with a 'monster' challenge of creating economic, social and political change. For the vast majority this is achieved with limited resources relying on voluntary effort and commitment.

Scottish non-profit organizations are reported to be more likely than their English counterparts to be dependent on central government funding yet Scottish funding is less likely to be secured over a longer term (Vincent and

Harrow 2005). A further challenge is that grant income fell from 39 per cent to 28 per cent between 2004 and 2006 while contract income increased from 8 per cent to 18 per cent (SCVO 2007). This reflects Cairns's (2005a) observation that there is a shift away from 'arm's-length' grants to contractual relationships between government and non-profits. As a consequence of these contractual relationships the sector is experiencing 'increasing pressures from governmental funders to improve their management and organisational systems' (Cairns et al. 2005a: 869). One way of doing this is to put in place quality systems that are recognized externally as likely to lead to more consistent use of policies and procedures and instil a continuous improvement culture. This chapter sets out to explore the responses to such pressures within the non-profit intermediary organizations that are challenged to both provide a voice and management/organizational support for a myriad of small non-profit organizations. A key question is the extent to which quality management solutions are adopted cynically, leading to little positive cultural change, or whether they are adopted in a committed but reflective manner.

Supporting Scotland's Non-Profit Sector

Whilst the non-profit sector has been accused of being 'loose and baggy' the intermediary support-service infrastructure in Scotland was described as 'cluttered and muddled' in the most recent investigation into its nature (Rocket Science 2007). Yet there is little published on the capacity of intermediaries or their potential to support performance management and continuous improvement across the sector. Despite this it is recognized that intermediaries can serve as 'a catalytic function that includes elements of encouragement, support, cajoling and mandate' (Lowery 2001: 75). Over 200 support service providers known as 'infrastructure organizations' have evolved to support the regulated, predominantly social care, non-profit sector in Scotland (Rocket Science 2007). These are organized within a number of national networks. The largest of these, the Scottish Council for Voluntary Organisations (SCVO), is a membership body responsible for representing the sector in Scotland. Its objectives include promoting stronger governance, promoting civic action and civic engagement, building capacity within the sector and increasing the effectiveness of the sector's infrastructure (SCVO 2009b). One of the main mechanisms used to deliver these objectives is a network of 56 Councils for Voluntary Services (CVSs) (see Figure 4.1). In turn each CVS provides a range of developmental and support services directly to 'front-line' service delivery organizations, usually within a certain geographical locale.

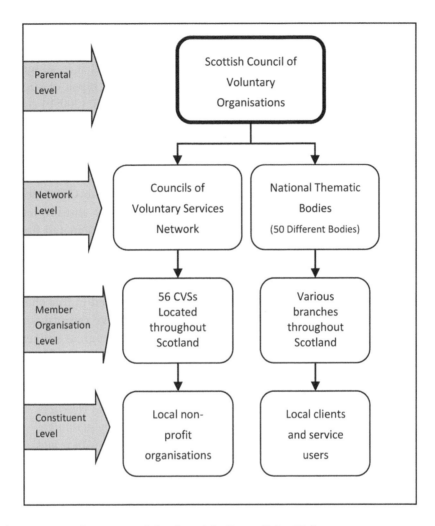

Figure 4.1   Structure of the Scottish Council for Voluntary Organisations (SCVO)

The CVS network has an important role to play in helping the many small non-profit organizations across Scotland to deliver high-quality services to communities and to engage them in policy and decision-making processes. For example, one service provided relates to 'the provision of start-up support, including advice on legal structures, governance and recruitment – as well as on securing much needed funding' (SCVO 2009b: 1). They also provide ongoing training and advice and support services. Other core activities include promoting good practice, growing the sector and representing the interests of their members (SCVO 2007).

The Scottish government allocates around £4 million each year to SCVO to ensure CVS network members fulfil their role of supporting the development of the non-profit sector in each locality. Yet it is suggested that the CVS network lacks the capacity to provide the types of support which are now needed (Rocket Science 2007). Cairns et al. (2005b) concur that infrastructure organizations themselves require support to intervene effectively. It is therefore to be welcomed that the Big Lottery Fund (BLF) has decided to make a one-off investment of £20 million for improving non-profit infrastructure in Scotland (Big Lottery Fund 2007a), of which the SCVO secured £8.4 million to fund development activity for the CVS network over 2008–11. A requirement of the funding is to develop and implement a suitable quality framework for the CVS network. The anticipated flavour of the framework is that it will be a self-assessment framework which will aid the development of improvement action plans by CVS members, followed possibly by network validation or accreditation (SCVO 2008). It is the implications of this development which are explored in this chapter. Myers and Sacks (2001) suggest that attempts to improve performance in an over-centralized fashion can prove counteractive to progress suggesting that:

> Inhibitors for strategic thinking and development become more likely when organisations are too closely tied to funders aims and objectives or ... where attempts are made to control new initiatives by subsuming their activities under a centralised and regulated umbrella. (Myers and Sacks 2001: 456)

The challenge for any network lies in satisfying the requirements of stakeholders at network and organizational levels 'while building a cooperative network of interorganizational relationships that collectively provides services more effectively and efficiently than a system based on fragmented funding and services' (Provan and Milward 2001: 422). This could involve reflectively improvising an opportunity by negotiating for approval to develop self-assessment tools that enable ongoing learning and evaluation (Wilford 2007).

The chapter continues with a discussion of literature on the challenges of implementing quality management frameworks and tools within the non-profit sector, paying particular attention to the influence of external stakeholders. It then proceeds to explore how the demand from the BLF for a CVS network-wide quality framework is influencing attitudes to quality management.

Quality Management in the Non-Profit Sector

The view that quality management is universal and should be context-free is in direct conflict with emphasis on emergent approaches and their political dimensions to management. The reality is that even within an industrial context, managers' perceptions of how to manage quality improvement are evidently influenced by the external environment and expectations (Benson et al. 1991). External stakeholder pressures have much higher strategic importance in public and non-profit services than in the private sector and these pressures potentially influence quality management practice in this sector (Fletcher et al. 2003, Lewis et al. 2001, Wisniewski and Stewart 2004). Within non-profits, stakeholders such as service users, staff and the general public have interests which are seldom the same yet can exert power and influence to satisfy those interests (Hudson 1995).

In general, quality management and its performance measurement tools are often perceived as either essential to performance or a distraction (Jackson 2005), yet the race to gain quality management credentials carries on regardless. There are an increasing range of industry bespoke frameworks as well as generic and bespoke self-assessment frameworks based partially on self-assessment based on adaptations of the EFQM (European Foundation for Quality Management) Business Excellence model (see Ogden and Grigg 2003). However, failure rates of up to 70 per cent at the implementation stage of a change programme are allegedly linked to problems of ensuring internal management commitment and maintaining a quality orientation throughout (Pfeifer et al. 2005). Thus, although quality management has 'spread from its industrial origins to health care organizations, public bureaucracies, non-profit organizations, and educational institutions … [it] has become controversial – something whose worth and impact people argue about' (Hackman and Wageman 1995: 309). Disillusioned managers across sectors grow increasingly sceptical of the effectiveness of QM tools and techniques:

> There still appears to be no one panacea which will guarantee immediate and long-lasting success to improving quality and it is no wonder that many busy managers just do not have the time nor patience to try to grapple with the array of initiatives which have been actively promoted over the past decade. (Kaye and Anderson 1999: 485)

Different interpretations of excellence, internal and external influences and the costs versus benefits of striving for improved performance are all identified in literature as factors contributing to growing cynicism (Wilford 2007). Contrary to quality management philosophies many organizations across sectors seek a quick fix and are disappointed when it is not delivered (Hendricks and Singhal 2000). Regardless of the reasons, researchers remain puzzled by the 'improvement paradox' where even successful efforts have been difficult to sustain and in some cases led to declining performance (Keating et al. 1999). Whilst acknowledging the downward trend Conti (2004: 1) asserts that quality management is not a fad but 'a unique opportunity to rethink organizations from new perspectives: quality, value, systems thinking'.

Quality and performance management among non-profits is gaining an increasing amount of attention in literature (see for example: Baruch and Ramalho 2006, Cairns et al. 2005b, Davenport and Gardiner 2007, Kaplan 2001, Kearns 1994, Macpherson 2001, Paton and Foot 2000, Crittenden et al. 2004, Myers and Sacks 2001, Speckbacher 2003, Van Slyke and Johnson 2006, Moxham 2009). Many of these studies tend to focus on analysis of larger and well-resourced organizations, while there is sparse research relating to the development of quality management among the vast majority of small to medium-sized local organizations which dominate the non-profit landscape. A study by the Aston Centre for Voluntary Action Research produced in 2004 did present an overview of both the quality systems in use and drivers for the adoption of quality systems that included the views of some voluntary sector infrastructure bodies as well as a wide range of non-profit organizations, although the views of the former are not highlighted separately (CVAR 2004, Cairns et al. 2005b). A key finding from 165 respondents to a survey of English non-profit organizations found that 'respondents generally rated increased efficiency, effectiveness, improved quality of services and enhanced organisational image higher than securing funding' (CVAR 2004: 2). However, the choice of system used was generally influenced by guidance from statutory funders, with the most commonly used systems being PQASSO, Investors in People, the Excellence Model and Chartermark. While accountability was therefore accepted to be a key driver in the use of quality systems, the need for fit between the selected quality system and the organizational characteristics were recognized as vital for benefits to be forthcoming. This finding is important given Paton's (2003: 162) concern that 'managers and funders need to beware the spurious certainties and simplicities of methods that are frequently over-sold, and to avoid pressuring adoption of particular methods and then rushing the implementation process.' This warning arose from Paton's (2003) research of non-profits' quality management approaches based on case studies of 13 organizations (12 English, 1 US). The different responses to pressures for improved performance management, including quality management, in non-profits was characterized by Paton as the committed, the cynical and the reflective approach (see Table 4.1). A key indicator of each

Table 4.1   Approaches to methods of performance measurement and improvement

	The committed approach	The cynical approach	The reflective approach
Philosophical position	Positivist, rationalist	Sceptic	Constructivist
Attitude to measurement	Generally positive	Generally negative	Interested but cautious
Where measures come from	Goals	Someone's agenda	Problems and issues
Expected use of measurement	For learning and accountability	For control	Various – for dialogue, to clarify expectations; for challenge, check and conformity
What matters in performance reporting	The facts	Creative accounting	A grounded narrative and analysis tailored to the concerns of the stakeholders in question
Proper relationship between institutional, managerial and professional levels	Close alignment	Close alignment with own view – failing which, de-coupling	Loose coupling (to accommodate differences, and change, in concepts of performance)
Attitude to new improvement methods	Useful tools	Fads, waste of time	Depends on use and context
Way of applying new methods	Follow the rules, do it properly	Tactically, perhaps collusively, with a view to appearances	Open-minded, willing to improvise, adapt, collude, depending on context
Internal/external orientation	Internal orientation (integration or emulation)	External orientation (bearing or badging)	If possible, a dual orientation (creative integration)
Benefits sought	Improve performance	Maintain confidence of external bodies; preserve autonomy	Develop relationship with external bodies and make some improvements (while accepting one or other may not be achievable)

Source: Paton 2003: 166.

approach is the nature of the internal/external orientation motives for introducing quality and performance management systems or frameworks. He suggests that motives adapt and change over time and shift between four main 'territories':

1. 'bearing', where the quality or performance framework imposes behaviours perceived as burdensome by the majority;

2. 'badging' where organizations with well-developed systems seek the external recognition for what they already do;

3. 'integration', where the framework or award is 'lived and breathed' by the organization seeking to continuously improve; and

4. 'emulation', where the framework is implemented and standards are met without external awards or recognition.

Paton leaned towards the conclusion that a reflective attitude of sceptical curiosity and interest might serve non-profits better than a cynical/bearing approach or an over-committed approach which can result in failure to filter inconsistent external expectations (ibid.). Where managers exhibit a reflective approach, self-assessment is used for dialogue, clarifying expectations and challenging the status quo. This approach is also described as featuring a dual orientation (internal and external) whereby management of external stakeholder demands are grounded in analysis of what can realistically be achieved and systems are adapted to the context.

Studies of quality management within the Scottish non-profit context are extremely scarce, with only one published article being sourced which examines service quality attributes rather than quality systems and continuous improvement (Vaughan and Shiu 2001). Research of quality management in relation to infrastructure organizations is equally limited: only one piece of research was sourced on a case study of how an intermediary had fostered quality management in its member organizations by introducing quality principles and practices using a 'circumspect' approach that recognized that their non-profit members had 'varying degrees of organisational capacity and that a one-size-fits-all approach' would not succeed (Lowery 2001: 5). This implies that the role of QM in non-profit intermediaries in Scotland, and in the UK, is fairly uncharted research territory in published academic work and it is hoped that this chapter goes part of the way in filling this gap.

Research Design

The research findings presented are based on a three-pronged approach to data collection employing survey, interviews and focus group methods. First, a survey of all members of the CVS network was undertaken to establish a baseline of the quality and performance management approaches used throughout the network, an overview of perceptions of both barriers and motives to uptake, as well as an insight into whether expectations of benefits have been fulfilled. The survey gathered information on the variety of performance and quality management solutions prevalent among non-profits (Cairns 2005b). These included generic self-assessment frameworks and quality standards such ISO 9000, Investors in People (IIP), social audit (a way of measuring and reporting on social and ethical performance) and the EFQM Business Excellence Models well as sector-specific frameworks such as PQASSO (a self-assessment guide on implementing a quality assurance system for small non-profits) and the Big Picture (SCVO's framework for quality improvement in non-profit organizations). Also included were SQMS (the Scottish Quality Management System, for vocational education and training) and outcome models such as LEAP (Learning Evaluation And Planning), an outcome-based framework created by the Scottish Community Development Centre (see SCDC 2007). Survey respondents were also invited to comment on expected benefits sought from pursuit of any frameworks or tools they had adopted and to offer a view on the extent to which internal and external expectations were met. The survey was distributed electronically to chief officers of all 58 members of Scotland's CVS network, with returns from 48 members, a response rate of 83 per cent. Although the number of survey responses is small, the response rate is good in relation to the size of the network particularly when compared to other research in this area. For example, Cairns et al. (2005b) received a 30 per cent response rate from a survey of 410 voluntary and community organizations. On the other hand the Rocket Science *Review of Support Services Needs* in Scotland achieved a two-thirds (170 returns, around 67 per cent) response to a widely publicized online and chapter survey distribution (Rocket Science 2007). The CVS survey respondents were fairly evenly distributed in terms of regional coverage and representative of the total network population: North (15, 100 per cent); South (8, 89 per cent); East (12, 67 per cent) and West (13, 81 per cent). Most CVSs are small, with the largest employing around 60 full-time equivalents (FTE) and only 10 CVSs have more than 10 employees. For the purpose of this study the CVSs are categorized into small (<10 FTEs) and medium (>10 FTEs).

The survey was followed by in-depth qualitative interviews with seven CVSs and three focus groups. Interviewees were selected from the survey

Table 4.2   Summary of data collection

Methods	Code	Organizational characteristics
7 CVS interviews (Chief Officers)	CVS1	Small, semi-rural; no formal quality frameworks used
	CVS2	Medium, rural; IIP
	CVS3	Medium, semi-urban; PQASSO, Big Picture, LEAP
	CVS4	Medium, semi-urban; PQASSO, LEAP
	CVS5	Medium, urban; IIP
	CVS6	Small, rural; LEAP, Big Picture, IIP – ended in 2006
	CVS7	Small, semi-rural; IIP
2 Big Lottery interviews (1 telephone and one face-to-face interview)	BLF1, BLF2	Scottish Office of the largest UK lottery fund distributor
2 CVS focus groups	Service User 1; Board Member 1	Small volunteer-led youth arts organization
	Service User 1; Board Member 2	Branch of large national charity – with a Disability Remit
1 SCVO focus group (2 representatives)	SCVO1; SCVO2	Parent body for Scotland's non-profit sector and CVS network
Documentation	SD	Solicitation Document – internal document that sets out the Big Lottery Fund's requirements of SCVO in relation to the funding

Source: SD: 2.

respondents mainly to represent differences in the size of their organization and level of uptake of quality management frameworks or standards. The follow-up CVS interviews explored motives for choice of frameworks or standards, perceptions of the extent of stakeholder influence and views on the development of a framework for the whole CVS network. Two of the focus groups investigated the role and expectations of a CVS network in relation to use of quality frameworks from both user and board member perspectives. One of the focus groups comprised representatives of SCVO's network management section. The interview and focus group data was used to triangulate views of quality management imperatives from the different stakeholders at interconnected levels of the network system (see Table 4.2).

Discussion of Results

USE OF STANDARDS AND FRAMEWORKS

The survey revealed that very few CVSs are using formal quality standards or self-assessment frameworks. For example, only one had used EFQM self-assessment and only one was using Chartermark. The only standard with a real presence in this network is Investors in People (IIP), in use by just under half of respondents (21, 44 per cent). One significant divergence between Scotland and England relates to use of PQASSO, a model designed by the Charity Evaluation Service (CES) in England for small non-profits. According to the Aston Business School it has widespread use in England but uptake is very low among Scotland's CVSs (2 CVSs, 4 per cent). SCVO has an equivalent framework for quality improvement called 'Big Picture' which is more commonly used in Scotland (13 CVSs, 27 per cent). Both interview and survey responses reveal that PQASSO and Big Picture are seen as similar tools useful for supporting local organizations rather than adopted internally by the CVSs.

Outcome models (usually LEAP, a planning and evaluation tool developed by the Scottish Community Development Centre) are reasonably well used (18 CVSs, 37.5 per cent) and is the second most common framework after IIP. Other cross-sectoral frameworks are seldom used, apart from the Scottish Quality Management System (SQMS) which is used by five respondents. This is due to a compulsory funding requirement for four out of the five respondents who provide accredited training. In the Scottish CVS network four organizations are using social audit tools which are a relatively recent integration of business ethics accounting methods to non-profits (see Raynard 1998). All CVSs (100 per cent) report using a national monitoring framework as a condition of Scottish Executive funding, which is monitored by SCVO. In addition to the frameworks mentioned above, respondents also offered that they were using annual customer surveys and customer feedback to help monitor quality (28 CVSs, 58 per cent and 28CVSs, 79 per cent respectively).

In summary, it can be seen that the use and adoption of off-the-shelf frameworks and tools within the CVS network in Scotland is in its infancy, with relatively few recognized frameworks or tools in use other than IIP. Strategic planning tools and informal tailor-made tools such as customer feedback are more embedded and used alongside the compulsory CVS Core Activities monitoring framework.

MOTIVATIONS, BENEFITS AND BARRIERS

Findings from the interviews and focus groups, as well an analysis of open-ended survey questions, provides insight into the motivations and experiences of those using quality frameworks and tools within the CVS network. In relation to IIP, the most frequently used framework, examples of both internal and external benefits experienced are described:

> We have found IIP, especially first time round, as a rewarding staff/ management team builder and organization development tool. (CVS survey respondent)

> [IIP] was renewable over 3 years and also involved review from a neutral independent party, someone not-connected was able to give you a reasonable assessment of where you stood in the areas it covered ... It emphasized that we had an ethos of training and development of our people whether volunteers or staff and that added to elements of our ability. If we were looking for money from funders it gives confidence that there's a sound organization behind it. Showing the world there's a credible organization here with a commitment to the people who work with us. (CVS2 interviewee)

However, another survey respondent had tried IIP and failed to see any real benefits, leading to this more cynical response:

> My big worry about any Quality Standard having been involved in IIP and SQMS is that they mostly concentrate on administrative procedures rather than customer outcomes. They are 'time intensive' in comparison to the benefits they achieve and they tend to be a 'one size fits all' approach. (CVS survey respondent)

There were also examples found of CVSs with experience of IIP displaying reflective tendencies when they recognized some benefits but had ceased to use it in order to save funds:

> We did not continue our IIP recognition at renewal as no funding was available and we felt there had been little benefit to the organization

> *[as] we gained the award without having to alter our procedures. (CVS survey respondent)*

Cynical-type attitudes in relation to the CVS monitoring framework were also found, as voiced below:

> *[The monitoring form] doesn't easily or necessarily fit into the language or into the way that the CVS core framework sits. We almost need to reinterpret what we're doing to fit the framework. There is an element of duplication and reinterpretation. It becomes drudgeful rather than being the best fit. (CVS2 interviewee)*

> *The CVS framework doesn't make us think about the quality of what we do. It is output led if anything. (CVS6 interviewee)*

FUNDER INFLUENCE – A CYNICAL RESPONSE?

The discussion of benefits and motives above displays signs of funder influence in orientation to quality systems in the network. For example, the CVS form was used to maintain confidence of the external fund manager rather than improve internal performance. Such cynical responses are not exclusive to the CVS monitoring form as this interviewee also expressed doubt about the worth of the LEAP framework:

> *I'm most cynical about LEAP. It's someone rolling out something that we've always done and calling it something else. Most people end up adapting it to suit the way that they're working. (CVS3 interviewee)*

The focus group and interviewee responses reiterated tensions relating to compliance with funders' requirements, comments included:

> *I get concerned about [the funders'] tendency to focus on the activities we do rather than its impact. (CVS7)*

> *We need to manage expectations too – the demands placed on CVS can often be unreasonable. (SCVO interviewee)*

> *Probably these days funding organizations are much more explicit about what they want to achieve and about measuring the benefits in terms of the impact for beneficiaries. To a large degree measuring those is becoming sharper … In a way it's almost taken as read by funders that*

> *you have some of the quality standards in place when you're awarded funding. (CVS2 interviewee)*

> *[The funding has] a disproportionate amount of compliance and control of small amounts of money. It doesn't relate in any way to continuous improvement. It causes particular problems. It is not relative to the amount of money received … I would think twice before applying for the money again. (CVS7 interviewee)*

However, one CVS that saw QM as 'gimmicky' actually demonstrated the 'creative integration' characteristic of a reflective approach:

> *I had a couple of conversations with SCVO about the monitoring and said really I'm already reporting on this through other monitoring. I was asked to add an additional column to show how that other monitoring fits with the CVS core framework. (CVS1 interviewee)*

This shows clear evidence of developing relationships and using dialogue to clarify expectations. Invariably the reflective approach emerges when external pressures are weighed up against organizational survival, as these interviewee comments show:

> *If asked to implement a framework I would not be enthusiastic. I think we'd look at how we could best use it to help the service here and that would probably involve tailoring it. If it came as an all or nothing … I'm not sure. (CVS1 interviewee)*

> *Personally I'm positive but also reflective in my approach to quality management. It's useful when we are submitting tenders for contracts. (CVS4 interviewee)*

Positive reactions to external influence was shown in one CVS where joint working and support from the local authority caused one CVS to switch from using Big Picture to PQASSO, as this interviewee explains:

> *We used Big Picture before PQASSO. Both work well together but we're working as part of a pilot group with the local authority, so we decided PQASSO would be the best tool. The Council is funding us to go to London to be trained in using it. We are going to roll it out to local voluntary organizations and this is going to be used to manage quality across the local sector. (CVS3 interviewee)*

This calls for a reflective response of maintaining a dual internal/external orientation. Occasionally the balance orients internally and there is less experience or awareness of stakeholder influence, as explained by these interviewees:

> *Externally our stakeholders are not aware or not that interested, to tell you the truth. What we do is totally internally driven. There is not huge pressure to use systems … If there is external pressure it couldn't be any greater than what we put on ourselves. (CVS5 interviewee)*

In relation specifically to pressure from the BLF, there was some acceptance of possible benefits related to improving the external relationships and reputation of the network, especially given concerns about failure to fully realize synergies. This is reflected in the following comments by a CVS interviewee:

> *As a network we are always told that the network is judged by the poorest members. We already attain standards in other quality systems. But for the network external recognition and validation is fundamental. (CVS5 interviewee)*

However, at the same time there was concern that compulsion would taint perceptions about any new framework introduced, as the interviewee further explained:

> *A framework would help people come together and align their work to the framework. Common understanding is lacking. There is a danger of incorporating this because it's something Big Lottery wants. We need to decide are we doing this defensively? Is it with a carrot or with a stick? (CVS5)*

Nonetheless there is apparent scope for accommodating a reflective response, as on the surface the specific but non-prescriptive requirements may provide clear parameters for the network to operate within, as explained by one BLF interviewee:

> *We're not looking at how the network manages quality as such. We're only interested in how the fund is managed – the money and the management of it. It's up to the CVS network and its users how it's done. (BLF interviewee)*

However, the document goes on to detail the minimum standards in a surprisingly prescriptive way and the tight timescales appear to remove any room for manoeuvre. Messages are therefore confusing and contradictory. While BLF representatives claimed to favour a two-way process of open communication between themselves and SCVO, during the research period BLF shifted emphasis from negotiating a loose QM framework with SCVO to issuing a 'Solicitation Document' which outlines more formal requirements:

> *The portfolio will enable and equip individual CVSs to ensure that their operations, initially in relation to organizational management, human resources management, analysis of community needs, service provision, partnership working and community engagement, are being delivered at a minimum standard as formally agreed ... so that ... the whole of the CVS network in Scotland is operating to at least this minimum quality standard across these six operational areas ... (SD: 2)*

Conclusion

Regardless of current experience, stakeholder demands look set to rise in relation to the non-profit infrastructure intermediaries as well as for non-profit service delivery organizations. This is not surprising if one accepts that 'establishing whether or not a network is effective is critical from the perspective of those organisations that make up the network, those who are served by the network, and those whose policy and funding actions affect the network' (Provan and Milward 2001: 422). The scenario discussed above provides further evidence that 'influence strategies', whereby stakeholders influence how quality is managed by making their priorities clear, are present (Fletcher et al. 2003). A previous review of lottery fund management advised distributors to 'encourage applicants to become more self-critical, and to assess honestly both their own positions prior to application and the learning process they will have to undertake in order to manage the grant' (McKinney and Kahn 2004: 17). Whilst funders seek the uniformity of a fully committed approach across the network, the research findings suggest approaches are more likely to be reflective. Individual CVSs will continue to shift positions as they grapple with new quality management frameworks and fluctuating internal and external stakeholder demands. In light of the recent BLF solicitation document, there are benefits to be gained from developing mechanisms for a more strategic approach, supported by a commitment to shared practice, cooperation and continuous learning and improvement. Ongoing dialogue with funders and other key stakeholders appears critical to funding success. It could therefore be argued that the network should avoid tactics of emphasizing the differences in approach between its members. As McKinney (in McKinney and Kahn 2004: 8) argues: 'The key to success lies not in "shared belief" or "shared reality" but rather in the mechanisms the organization develops for conflict resolution and the channelling of different beliefs and priorities into learning and cooperative practice.'

Reflective behaviours will allow network solutions to emerge that fit external and internal orientations. Improved network synergies and performance will gradually erode negative connotations of loose and baggy monsters. Paton's typology has therefore provided a useful theoretical guide for analysing QM approaches in a non-profit context rather. Essentially it is useful in understanding the reasons for varying responses to the imperative to introduce quality and performance management systems in organizations, particularly when there is an element of external stakeholder pressure. It lends further support to Lowery's (2001) view that a 'one-size-fits-all' solution should be avoided.

References

Baruch, Y., and Ramalho, N. 2006. Communalities and distinctions in the measurement of organizational performance and effectiveness across for-profit and non-profit sectors. *Non-Profit and Voluntary Sector Quarterly*, 35(1), 39–65.

Benson, P.G., Saraph, J.V., and Schroeder, R.G. 1991. The effects of organizational context on quality management: an empirical investigation. *Management Science*, 37(9), 1107–24.

Big Lottery Fund. 2007a. *Scotland Home Page* [Online]. Available at: http://www.biglotteryfund.org.uk/Scotland [accessed: 17 July 2007].

Big Lottery Fund. 2007b. *Dynamic, Inclusive Communities – Further Guidance Summary* [Online]. Available at: http://www.biglotteryfund.org.uk/ [accessed: 17 July 2007].

Cairns, B., Harris, M., and Young, P. 2005a. Building the capacity of the voluntary non-profit sector: challenges of theory and practice. *International Journal of Public Administration*, 28, 869–85.

Cairns, B., Harris, M., Hutchison, R., and Tricker, M. 2005b. Improving performance? The adoption and implementation of quality systems in UK non-profits. *Non-Profit Management and Leadership*, 16(2), 135–51.

Conti, T. 2004. From infancy to maturity: rethinking the role of ISO 9000 Standards, TQM and business excellence models. *ASQ, 58th Annual Quality Congress Proceedings* (24–26 May 2004, Toronto), 58, 1–8.

Crittenden, W.F., Crittenden, V.L., Stone, M.M., and Robertson, C.J. 2004. An uneasy alliance: planning and performance in non-profit organizations. *International Journal of Organization Theory and Behavior*, 7(1), 81–106.

CVAR. 2004. *The Adoption and Use of Quality Systems in the Voluntary Sector: Research Report*. Centre for Voluntary Action Research (CVAR), Aston Business School, UK [Online]. Available at: http://www.ivar.org.uk/documents/Quality_ExecSummary.pdf [accessed: 20 October 2009].

Davenport, J., and Gardiner, P.D. 2007. Performance management in the not-for-profit sector with reference to the National Trust for Scotland. *Total Quality Management and Business Excellence*, 18(3), 303–311.

Fletcher, A., Guthrie, J., Steane, P., Roos, G., and Pike, S. 2003. Mapping stakeholder perceptions for a third sector organization. *Journal of Intellectual Capital*, 4(4), 505–27.

Hackman, J.R., and Wageman, R. 1995. Total quality management: empirical, conceptual, and practical issues. *Administrative Science Quarterly*, 40(2), 309–42.

Hendricks, K.B., and Singhal, V.R. 2000. Firm characteristics, total quality management and financial performance. *Journal of Operations Management*, 238, 1–17.

Hudson, M. 1995. *Managing Without Profit*, 2nd edn. London: Directory of Social Change.

Jackson, A. 2005. Falling from a great height: principles of good practice in performance measurement and the perils of top down determination of performance indicators. *Local Government Studies*, 31(1), 21–38.

Kaplan, R.S. 2001. Strategic performance measurement and management in non-profit organizations. *Non-Profit Management and Leadership*, 11(3), 353–370.

Kaye, M., and Anderson, R. 1999. Continuous improvement: the ten essential criteria. *The International Journal of Quality and Reliability Management*, 16(5), 485–509.

Kearns, K.P. 1994. The strategic management of accountability in non-profit organizations: an analytical framework. *Public Administration Review*, 54(2), 185–92.

Keating, E., Olivia, R., Repenning, N., Rockart, S., and Sterman, J. 1999. Overcoming the improvement paradox. *European Management Journal*, 17(2), 120–134.

Lewis, L.K., Hamel, S.A., and Richardson, B.K. 2001. Communicating change to non-profit stakeholders. *Management Communication Quarterly: McQ*, 15(1), 5–41.

Lewis, L.K., Richardson, B.K., and Hamel, S.A. 2003. When the 'stakes' are communicative: the lamb's and the lion's share during non-profit planned change. *Human Communication Research*, 29(3), 400–430.

Lowery, D. 2001. Implementing quality programs in the not-for-profit sector. *Quality Progress*, 34(1), 75–80.

McKinney, R., and Kahn, H. 2004. Lottery funding and changing organizational identity in the UK voluntary sector. *Voluntas*, 15(1), 1–19.

Macpherson, M. 2001. Performance measurement in not-for-profit and public-sector organisations. *Measuring Business Excellence*, 5(2), 13–17.

Mook, L., Richmond, B.J., and Quarter, J. 2003. Integrated social accounting for non-profits: a case from Canada. *Voluntas*, 14(3), 283–97.

Moxham, C. 2009. Performance measurement: examining the applicability of the existing body of knowledge to non-profit organisations. *International Journal of Operations and Production Management*, 29(7), 740–763.

Myers, J., and Sacks, R. 2001. Harnessing the talents of a 'loose and baggy monster'. *Journal of European Industrial Training*, 25(9), 454–64.

Ogden, S.M., and Grigg, N.P. 2003. The development of sector-based quality assurance standards in the UK: diverging or dovetailing. *The TQM Magazine*, 15(1), 7–13.

Paton, R. 2003. *Managing and Measuring Social Enterprises*. London: Sage.

Paton, R., and Foot, J. 2000. Non-profit's use of awards to improve and demonstrate performance: valuable discipline or burdensome formalities? *Voluntas*, 11(4), 329–53.

Pfeifer, T., Schmitt, R., and Voigt, T. 2005. Managing change: quality-oriented design of strategic change processes. *The TQM Magazine*, 17(4), 297–308.

Provan, K.G., and Milward, H.B. 2001. Do networks really work? A framework for evaluating public-sector organizational networks. *Public Administration Review*, 61(4), 414–423.

Raynard, P. 1998, Coming together. A review of contemporary approaches to social accounting, auditing and reporting in non-profit organisations. *Journal of Business Ethics*, 17(13), 1471–9.

Rocket Science UK Ltd. 2007. *Review of Support Service Needs of Voluntary Organisations: Perceptions of Users and Providers*. Edinburgh: Scottish Executive Social Research.

SCDC. 2007. *The LEAP Framework*. Homepage of Scottish Community Development Centre/Glasgow University [Online]. Available at: http://leap.scdc.org.uk/leap-framework/?sess_scdc=5e7175201c3c2e09573cb0e721661e71 [accessed: 17 July 2007].

SCVO. 2007. *Scottish Voluntary Sector Statistics 2007* [Online]. Available at: http://www.workwithus.org [accessed: 28 July 2007].

SCVO. 2008. *Quality Matters: Quality within the Scottish CVS Network* [Online]. Available at: http://www.gcvs.org.uk/documents/352/352.pdf [accessed: 16 February 2009].

SCVO. 2009a. *Get to Know Scotland's Third Sector* [Online]. Available at: http://www.scvo.org.uk [accessed: 16 February 2009].

SCVO. 2009b. *Mission and Purpose* [Online]. Available at: http://www.scvo.org.uk [accessed: 20 January 2009].

Speckbacher, G. 2003. The economics of performance management in nonprofit organizations. *Nonprofit Management and Leadership*, 13(3), 267.

Van Slyke, D.M., and Johnson, J.L. 2006. Non-profit organizational performance and resource development strategies. *Public Performance and Management Review*, 29 (4), 467–96.

Vaughan, L., and Shiu, E. 2001. ARCHSECRET: a multi-item scale to measure service quality within the voluntary sector. *International Journal of Non-Profit and Voluntary Sector Marketing*, 6(2), 131–44.

Vincent, J., and Harrow, J. 2005. Comparing thistles and roses: the application of governmental–voluntary sector relations theory to Scotland and England. *Voluntas*, 16(4), 375–95.

Wilford, S. 2007. The limits of award incentives: the (non-)relationship between awards for quality and organisational performance. *Total Quality Management and Business Excellence*, 18(3), 333–49.

Wisniewski, M., and Stewart, D. 2004. Performance measurement for stakeholders: the case of Scottish local authorities. *The International Journal of Public Sector Management*, 17(2/3), 222–33.

5

Do the Strategic Objectives of Not-for-Profit Organizations Define the Criteria for Impact Evaluation?

Tuuli Pärenson

Introduction

The primary goal of not-for-profit organizations is not monetary success, but rather the achievement of sustainable and positive social impact for diverse stakeholders (Achleitner et al. 2009). A stakeholder is defined as a person, group, organization or system which affects or can be affected by an organization's actions. These goals can be assessed as social impact; a change in society resulting from an activity, project or organization.

The goals of the not-for-profit (NFP) sector organization are often less quantifiable and not as readily observable as in the private for-profit sector, which makes performance and impact measurement more problematic (Kober and Eggleton 2006). Within NFPs there is a lack of standardization that could be resolved by developing and implementing a generally accepted reporting standard, instructing social entrepreneurs how to assess and communicate their success, and the factors influencing it, to an external audience (Byrne 2002). More transparent and comparable information about social impact would lead to a lower cost of capital, and result in a more efficient capital allocation for social purposes (Achleitner et al. 2009, Meehan et al. 2004).

This chapter takes a first step forward to explore this area, by examining if the strategic objectives of not-for-profit organizations define the criteria for impact evaluation. The aim of this chapter is to analyse whether the stakeholder for whom the impact has to be evaluated differs from those in not-for-profit organizations, whose strategic objectives may well be different. Stakeholders and organizations' strategic objectives are analysed on two scales: firstly, that of the level of impact, which can be upon the individual, family, community, service or society; secondly, that of the internal and external view of the organization. The following propositions are made for analysing the relationship between strategic objectives and the stakeholders, impact to whom is evaluated.

Proposition 1: The level of social impact the organization expresses in its strategic objectives should correspond to the level of social impact on the most important stakeholder identified by the CEO.

Proposition 2: Internally focused organizations should evaluate the impact on the internal stakeholders while externally focused organizations should evaluate the impact on the external stakeholders.

These propositions are analysed using a qualitative research design. The strategic objectives of 33 not-for-profit organizations are considered in relation to these propositions, and the interviews are undertaken with the CEOs of these organizations.

The Term 'Social Impact'

The vocabulary of impact value chain used in this chapter is based on the Double Bottom Line Project Report (Clark et al. 2004), which is one of the first, if not the only, methods catalogue on assessing the social impact of social enterprises or not-for-profit organizations. The relationships between the terms which are used for analysing social impact are described in Figure 5.1.

'Inputs' are the resources that contribute to a programme or activity, including income, staff, volunteers and equipment (Wainwright 2003, Moxham and Boaden 2007). 'Activities' are what an organization does with its inputs in order to achieve its mission (Wainwright 2003, Moxham and Boaden 2007). 'Outputs' are results that a company, non-profit or project manager can measure or assess directly, for example direct products or activities (Buckmaster 1999). 'Outcomes' are the ultimate changes that one is trying to make in the world (Clark et al. 2004: 8).

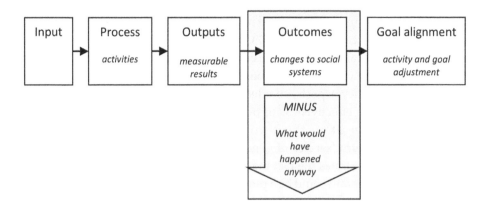

Figure 5.1   Social impact value chain

Source: Clark et al. 2004: 9.

The impact is the portion of the total outcome that happens as a result of the activity of the venture, above and beyond what would have happened anyway (Clark et al. 2004: 8). Impact therefore can be considered as all the changes resulting from an activity, project or organization. It includes effects which are intended as well as unintended, negative as well as positive, and long-term as well as short-term (Wainwright 2003, Moxham and Boaden 2007). A synonym for social impact might be value added or 'social benefit' (see, for example, Kober and Eggleton 2006). To measure the social impact, it is necessary to evaluate what would have happened or what is going to happen if the certain social enterprise (or not-for-profit organization in our case) did not exist. The idea of impact evaluation is to evaluate the impact of the specific organization only. All trends in people's behaviour should be discounted. Impact assessment and performance management are often used as synonyms. Performance management is the activity that managers perform in order to reach predefined goals that are derived from the company's strategic objectives (Lohman et al. 2004: 269). The term 'performance management' is used differently by many authors, but it mainly stands for managing the organization by its objectives.

The main differences in impact assessment and performance management come from different bases: (1) *what to measure*, and (2) *how to measure*. As the purpose of not-for-profit organizations is different from private for-profit companies, then the measurement and assessment has to be focused on different measurement subjects. The purpose of the for-profit companies, as it is known from microeconomics, is to maximize the value of the company, and ultimately to pass this back to the shareholders of that company. The purpose of not-for-profits is usually not based on gaining material income, but fulfilling public service objectives (Young 1997). The ultimate objectives of public sector operations are typically related to the enhancement of the usefulness of services to beneficiaries and citizens rather than the maximization of service provision (outputs) or efficiency aspects, so adequate measures of outcomes are pivotal for ascertaining the effectiveness of public sector organizations (Modell 2005, Kober and Eggleton 2006). The discussion at a European level, where some countries use the term 'service of general interest' while others prefer 'public services' (ibid.), illustrates the fact that social impact should be the purpose of public organizations and could be a purpose for all the other not-for-profits. The primary goal of not-for-profits should not be monetary success, but rather the achievement of sustainable and positive social impact for diverse stakeholders (Achleitner et al. 2009).

While there are readily observable performance measures in the for-profit sector (for example, profit, return on equity, return on assets, sales turnover, stock price, etc.), in the not-for-profit sector, goals of the agency are often less quantifiable and, as such, performance measurement is more problematic (Kober and Eggleton 2006). Performance management stands mainly for output and outcome measurement, but social impact assessment goes beyond that and estimates if the organization is achieving its long-term public goals (for example, improved public health, a higher employment rate). Assessing impact means that the trends in society are also part of the assessment.

Strategic Objectives as the Source for Defining the Purpose of a Specific Organization

It is said that it is impossible to manage something if you cannot measure it. Senior executives understand that their organization's measurement system strongly affects the behaviour of managers and employees (Kaplan and Norton 1992: 172). Although social impact assessment and performance measurement differ, there are things to learn from performance measurement systems about setting the measures.

Good performance management, like social impact evaluation, is based on setting appropriate measures. Irrespective of the multitude of the literature and articles written on the topic, the perpetual 'reliable criterion problem' and the creation of effective measurement system continues to receive considerable attention within the performance management literature (Fletcher 2001: 474).

Performance measures need to be positioned in a strategic context, as they influence what people do, and should be aligned to, and derived from, strategy; that is, they should be used to reinforce the importance of certain strategic variables (Neely et al. 2005: 1231).

For social impact assessment, as for performance management, the strategic objectives are taken as the best source for defining the purpose of a specific organization. Griggs (2003) found, while studying not-for-profit organizations in the disability sector, that strategic planning does have an effect on organizational performance. Though published empirical studies linking strategic planning and organizational performance for not-for-profit organizations are few, it is stated that success on a strategic level is evaluated by means of impact assessment (Achleitner et al. 2009).

Classification of Not-for-Profits according to their Strategic Objectives

As a debate is taking place, if not-for-profits should operate in the public interests or in the interests of the organization members, then it is presumed that organizations can be divided into two groups based on strategic objectives: organizations focused on the interests of *either* internal *or* external stakeholders. This chapter analyses whether organizational focus (that is, internal or external issues, according to its strategic objective) is aligned to the stakeholder whose impact is evaluated. In other words, internally focused organizations should evaluate the impact on the internal stakeholders while externally focused organizations should evaluate the impact on the external stakeholders (see Figure 5.2).

Not-for-profits could be divided by the level of social impact that they are trying to achieve according to their strategic objectives. Four levels are outlined by Lumley et al. (2005: 14): individual, the local community (including the individual's family), the services available to them, and society (state) level (see Figure 5.2).

Although many authors (Sud et al. 2008, Pearson 2001, Gray et al. 2003) agree that social entrepreneurs and not-for-profits may be able to address specific social problems more effectively, they are unlikely to bring about the broad and comprehensive reforms needed to provide widespread solutions to those problems. It might be sensible for a smaller organization to focus its efforts on achieving results at one particular level, but far-reaching and lasting

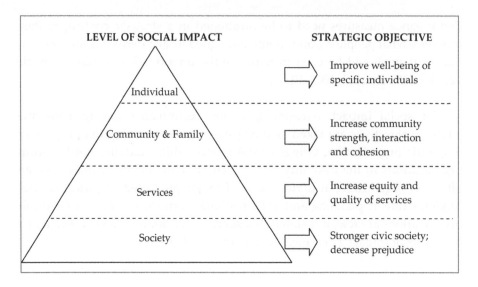

**Figure 5.2   Levels of social impact and their relationships
with strategic objectives**

Source: Lumley et al. 2005: 14.

change for a whole section of the population (such as older people or disabled children) is only likely to be brought about by the achievement of results at all levels, from the individual to the societal level (Lumley et al. 2005: 14).

What is measured, therefore, should be directly associated with the achievement sought (the measures should be linked to strategy), therefore the impact evaluation should be associated with the level of social impact that the organization is trying to achieve according to its strategic objectives. An educated guess is made – that the level of social impact and stakeholder group, which are most important for the organization, should be related. For example, if the organization's objective is to make the change in family and community level (such as social support for foster parents and foster children), then the impact of the organization has to be measured based on change of behaviour in the stakeholder level which also refers to the family level (here the foster family). If the objective is to make a change at the individual level, then the impact on the individuals has to be evaluated. In other words, if the organization is focused on achieving social impact on one particular level of social impact (such as society in general, see Figure 5.2), then the level of the stakeholder, the impact on whom is evaluated, should be the same (for example, government, state). For the same reasons, if the organization is trying to make the change for external stakeholders, then the impact on external stakeholders should be evaluated.

Methodology and Results

The strategic objectives of 33 organizations were examined. Organizations were chosen from public (23 organizations) and third sector (10 organizations, of which 7 were non-profits and 3 were foundations) acting in various capacities, starting with kindergartens, schools, court, libraries and organizations providing social services for orphans and disabled people and ending with entertainers, culture and interest centres and fellowship groups with similar hobbies. The strategic objectives of each organization were estimated based on the social impact level at which the organization is operating and whether it is focused on internal or external stakeholders (see Table 5.1).

Table 5.1   Allocation of examined organizations according to their strategic objectives

Strategic objectives	Individual	Community and family	Services	Society
Internal	2 non-profits, 2 public organizations; e.g. 'Discovering and developing the musical skills of the members of the organization'	2 non-profits; e.g. 'Uniting the breeders of one particular animal breed, who are members of the organization'	6 public organizations; e.g. 'Offering educational services for the students'	
External	1 foundation, 2 non-profits, 2 public organizations; e.g. 'Develop and retain the life quality of disabled'	1 foundation, 1 non-profit, 5 public organizations; e.g. 'Developing a positive image of certain area'	7 public organizations; e.g. 'Arranging concerts, etc.'	1 foundation, 1 public organization; e.g. 'Secure justice in the society'

Examination of the strategic objectives was based on the organization's strategic documents. If written strategic objectives did not exist then the strategic objectives were defined according to the CEO's statements. It was presumed that if the strategic objectives of the organization were documented then they are real and actual. If the strategic objectives were not documented then it was presumed that CEO knew what these strategic objectives are. In their study exploring agency theory principles in non-profits, Callen et al. (2003) found a positive relationship between major donors on the board and indicators of organizational efficiency (Mwenja and Lewis 2009). Although it can be said that the purpose of the not-for-profit organization (especially public organization) is to produce positive social impact, which is in accordance with board perceptions, then it is presumed that, if the CEO does not see this as a strategic objective, then this objective does not exist.

The scarcity of organizations focusing at the societal level, the total absence of organizations focusing on internal issues and the absence of organizations focusing on society level impact can be attributed to what Collis et al. (2003) observed while researching voluntary sector groups. Collis et al. (2003) suggest that some respondents were unable to describe the impact at societal level – suggesting that they were unaware of the potential for wider impact, or that this wider impact was not a priority to them (Reed et al. 2005).

It was mentioned that the primary goal of not-for-profits should be sustainable and positive social impact for diverse stakeholders. The contribution of the respective social entrepreneur to positive social change is determined by their specific strategic positioning or 'theory of change' (Scholten et al. 2006), and an 'impact map' is a way of systemizing and formalizing the theory of change.

For defining the stakeholders of the organization, impact maps were compiled for each organization in cooperation with the CEO. 'Theory of change' includes firstly the *beneficiaries and stakeholders (stakeholders)* of the organization and secondly, the *logic model* or cause-and-effect relationship; that is, how the social entrepreneur's activities will produce the objectives they have defined as their distinctive contribution (W.K. Kellogg Foundation 2004, Wei-Skillern et al. 2007, Achleitner et al. 2009).

Theory of change prescribes which stakeholders are concerned and why these stakeholders choose to focus on achieving these specific strategic objectives. An impact map describes the social impact of the organization on different stakeholders (stakeholders are given in the layers of the impact map). The column on the right side of the impact map is an impact value chain (Figure 5.2) responding to the specific stakeholder.

Defining the most important stakeholder, from the viewpoint of the impact evaluation, was a primary question in the CEO interviews: 'What are the most important stakeholders from the perspective of assessing the social impact of the organization?' The presumption was made that, if the CEO identified one or more particular stakeholders to be most important for the organization, then that is so. Although this may seem obvious, as based on current practices, it can be said that it is often not so. The goals that the organization pays attention to do not have to be in accordance with or at least not directly driven from the articles of association. After assessing the impact for all the stakeholders of the organization, the stakeholder who received the most positive social impact was identified. Which stakeholder received the most positive social impact is not particularly important from an impact assessment design viewpoint. However, which stakeholder the organization regards as the most important one is important as it defines who the organization thinks it is operating for.

The stakeholders can be divided in the same manner as for social impact (Figure 5.2). All the respondents chose a stakeholder that referred to the individual level of impact. The answers were different from the generalization level but still converged into two main classes (Table 5.2): members of the organization or employees, and service users or potential service users. Stakeholders who were classified as members of the organizations were named as: *employees, members, students*. Stakeholders who were classified as service users were named as: *children, residents of the region, visitors, users, students, scholars, teachers, academics, dancers, scientists, disabled people*, etc.

Some of the respondent organizations refused to name only one most important stakeholder and named two. As sometimes both groups did not classify under the same category, then the category where the members of the organizations or employees and service users were both mentioned was established.

There were two organizations that did not classify their stakeholders: these were the organizations that were dealing with children but who considered the parents of the children as the most important stakeholders. One of them was a public sector organization whose purpose was to provide shelter for children who are left without parental care. Although this organization focuses on working with problematic parents, this group does not appear in their strategic objectives. As this organization actually provides services for the parents, then parents as stakeholders were classified instead as 'service users'. The other non-profit, who found that parents are the most important stakeholders, explained it like this:

> The most important group is parents, as they are holding a wallet ... Active participants [are] not enough. We keep track of how many participants take part in our activities. The children of more active parents come more often and find more financial resources for making it possible to participate.

This could mean that the organization has to prove the value of its impact to the parents, meaning the parents want to be sure that the organization is having a good influence on their children, and not that the organization is trying to have an impact on parents. Therefore in this case the parents were left out, as they are actually not the ones upon whom the organization's impact should be evaluated.

Some examples of the stakeholders who were mentioned in the impact map but not described as the most important ones, and who needed to be classified on different levels are as follows: (1) *community and family*: citizens of the specific area, parents of the students, employers; (2) *services*: partner and competitor organizations, enterprises in the same area, owners/investors; (3) *society*: city, state (Estonia), media, society, (Estonian) economy. The stakeholders were divided into external or internal, based on the researcher's evaluation. The stakeholders who were categorized as 'members of the organization or employees' were estimated as internal groups. Surprisingly, stakeholders who were categorized as 'service users or potential service users' were not always estimated as external groups. The dissimilarities were caused by educational organizations. Scholars were taken as internal parties when they were accounted in organizations' members list (for example, students of secondary schools and kindergartens were considered as internal stakeholders). On the other hand the participants in educational programmes, who were not accounted for organizations' member lists, were classified as external stakeholders (for example, participants in skill conversion programmes). Also the members of the non-profit organization who used the services of the non-profit are evaluated as internal stakeholders. For nine organizations the service users were estimated as internal stakeholders.

Discussion

Proposition 1: The level of social impact the organization expresses in its strategic objectives should correspond to the level of social impact of the most important stakeholder identified by the CEO.

Surprisingly, there was little evidence to support Proposition 1, and so this was rejected. Although organizations were chosen from different levels (individual, community and family, services, society – see Table 5.2), the CEOs of all the organizations found that most important stakeholder, from the impact evaluation viewpoint, was the individual level stakeholder. Some examples are provided below regarding the responses CEOs gave for explaining their choice of most important stakeholder.

- A court, with a strategic objective to ensure peace and justice in society by giving judgement fairly, was classified as an organization operating at the societal level: 'If there were none participating in proceedings, then we would have nothing to do.'
- A library, with a strategic objective of offering library and information services and being a multi-cultural institution, classified to operate on service level: 'The most important stakeholder is children. I am sure that we cannot change the habits and interests of grown-ups, but it is possible to have an substantial impact on children, for deepening their interest for books and establishing a lasting reading habit.'
- A non-profit, with a strategic objective to unite those breeders and owners of a specific breed who live in Estonia into one organization: 'As there are only a few breeders, then the most important impact is for the owners.'

The focus on the individual level could be caused by the pressure of using business tools for evaluating social impact, where a lot of attention is given to the members, the clients and the owners. This also manifests in the explanations of several CEOs with small nuances: 'If there were no clients/members/public/children, then there would be no organization/ club'.

The fact, that all the organizations indicated individual level stakeholders were the most important for them, gives hope, and the same applies to the possibility for general acceptance of the standardization of impact evaluation.

It is therefore concluded that the level of impact an organization wants to achieve does not cause the difference in reporting of impact as there is always a need for estimating impact to individual level stakeholders.

Proposition 2: Internally focused organizations should evaluate the impact on the internal stakeholders while externally focused organizations should evaluate the impact to the external stakeholders.

If the strategic objectives of the organization relate to the internal stakeholder(s), then the stakeholder that the CEO considers to be the most important from the aspect of impact evaluation should also be internal and not an external stakeholder. If the strategic objectives of the organization refer to the goal related to the external stakeholder(s) then the stakeholder that CEO considers to be most important from the aspect of impact evaluation should also be external. The proposition holds for most of the sample organizations (Table 5.2).

Table 5.2   Stakeholders' focus and its relationship to the focus of the organization

Stakeholder/ organization	Internal	External
Internal	4 non-profits, 8 public organizations; e.g. 'Employees and service users in the organizations, whose purpose is to offer extracurricular activities for the members of the organization'	
External	1 foundation, 1 public organization	2 foundations, 3 non-profits, 14 public organizations, e.g. 'Children and visitors to the library'

However, there were two organizations that gave reason to doubt the proposition. The answers of the CEOs for the organizations for whom the proposition does not hold were as follows:

- A centre for culture and interests in a region of Estonia, whose purpose is to hold and develop cultural life in a specific city and county through offering cultural events and to attract and enlist the residents of that region (external objective, expected stakeholder is 'resident of that region'): 'We think that the most important stakeholders are managerial employees, the supervisors of hobby groups, administrative employees.'
- A higher education institution, whose purpose is to ensure sustainable coverage with specific specialists in Estonia (external objective, as the organization is relieving the external needs; the expected stakeholders are 'the people who need this specialist'): 'The knowledge of a student depends on how the teacher/lecturer teaches. The product of our job is a specific specialist. The lecturer through his/her practised activities motivates a student for independent work and life-long learning, which is important for this specific activity.'

Both organizations found that only the impact on stakeholders whom the organization directly influences should be evaluated. The CEO did not find it necessary to evaluate the impact on the indirectly influenced stakeholders although impacting these stakeholders was mentioned in their strategic objectives. It gives a hint that when constructing impact evaluation standards then most probably the impact on the indirectly influenced stakeholders can be left out of the evaluation. It is also in accordance with traditional performance measurement principles: the reporting must be as short as possible, and should evaluate the impacts as directly as possible. This study did not contain in-depth interviews that would explain why the impact on the individual level stakeholders was preferred. This aspect requires further research. The individual level impacts may be preferred because it is in the interests of organizations to measure the most immediate results, which are easier to measure, instead of the ones that are most in accordance with strategic goals.

Conclusions

The aim of this chapter was to analyse whether the stakeholders on whom the impact has to be evaluated differ in various not-for-profit organizations.

Stakeholders and organizations were analysed on two scales in 33 not-for-profit organizations, based on strategic objectives and interviews with the CEOs of these organizations.

Firstly, the level of impact (which can be individual, family and community, services or society) and its associations with impact evaluation were examined. It was tested whether the level of social impact the organization has expressed in its strategic objectives corresponds to the level of social impact of the stakeholder that the CEO finds to be most important from the aspect of impact evaluation of the organization. It was found that this proposition is not valid and there is always a need to evaluate the impact on the stakeholders on the individual level.

Secondly, the internal and external views of the organization and its correspondence with impact evaluation were analysed. It was found that for most cases (31 out of 33) the proposition is valid: the CEO of the organization that focuses on internal or external issues according to its strategic objectives should accordingly find the impact on the internal or external stakeholders to be most important. As a side-effect it was discovered that most probably the indirectly influenced stakeholders can be left out of the impact evaluation, which also gives a possibility for standardization of impact evaluation methods.

For overcoming the lack of generally accepted reporting standards for not-for-profits and the lack of standardization in impact evaluation the following points should be remembered: the impact on the individual level stakeholders has to be evaluated; the internally focused organizations should evaluate the impact on the internal stakeholders; externally focused organizations should evaluate the impact on the external stakeholders; and most probably the indirectly influenced stakeholders can be left out of the social impact evaluation.

As the current study is based on the 33 organizations in Estonia only and the interviews with their CEOs, then the results may not be valid in areas with different cultural backgrounds. As impact evaluation is not a natural part of non-profit organization management in Estonia, then the answers of the CEOs could change, if their knowledge and know-how about impact evaluation should increase. Additional analyses are needed to discover the reasons for preferring individual level stakeholders even if these are not in accordance with an organization's strategic goals.

References

Achleitner, A.-K., Bassen, A., and Roder, B. 2009. *An Integrative Framework for Reporting in Social Entrepreneurship* [Online]. Available at: http://ssrn.com/abstract=1325700 [accessed: 5 February 2010].

Buckmaster, N. 1999. Associations between outcome measurement, accountability and learning for non-profit organisations. *International Journal of Public Sector Management*, 12(2), 186–97.

Byrne, J.A. 2002. The new face of philanthropy – today's donors are more ambitious, get more involved, and demand results [Online]. Available at: http://www.businessweek.com/magazine/content/02_48/b3810001.htm [accessed: 16 February 2010].

Callen, J.L., Klein, A., and Tinkelman, D. 2003. Board composition, committee, and organisational efficiency: the case of nonprofits. *Nonprofit and Volunteer Sector Quarterly*, 32(4), 493–520.

Clark, C., Rosenzweig, W., Long, D., and Olsen, S. 2004. *Double Bottom Line Project Report: Assessing Social Impact in Double Bottom Line Ventures* [Online]. Available at: http://www.riseproject.org/DBL_Methods_Catalog.pdf [accessed: 21 February 2010].

Collis, B., Lacey, M., O'Hagan, S., Shah, R., Wainwright, S., and Wilding, K. 2003. *Measuring Impact: Case Studies of Small and Medium-Sized Voluntary Organisations*. London: National Council for Voluntary Organisations.

Fletcher, C. 2001. Performance appraisal and management: the developing research agenda. *The Journal of Occupational and Organisational Psychology*, 74, 473–87.

Gray, M., Healy, K.. and Crofts, P. 2003. Social enterprise: is it the business of social work? *Australian Social Work*, 56(2), 141–54.

Griggs, H. 2003. Corporatisation of the not-for-profit sector: strategic planning and organisational performance in disability-based organisations. *International Journal of Disability, Development and Education*, 50(2), 197–220.

Kaplan, R.S., and Norton, D.P. 1992. The Balanced Scorecard: measures that drive performance. *Harvard Business Review*, Jan–Feb, 172–180.

Kober, R., and Eggleton, I. 2006. Using quality of life to assess performance in the disability services sector. *Applied Research in Quality of Life*, 1(1), 63–77.

Lohman, C., Fortuin, L., and Wouters, M. 2004. Designing a performance measurement system: a case study. *European Journal of Operational Research*, 156(2), 267–86.

Lumley, T., Langerman, C., and Brookes, M. 2005. Funding success: NPC's approach to analysing charities. *New Philanthropy Capital* [Online]. Available at: http://www.philanthropycapital.org/tops/docs/Funding%20success.pdf [accessed: 24 January 2007].

Meehan, W.F., Kilmer, D., and O'Flanagan, M. 2004. Investing in society – why we need a more efficient social capital market and how we can get there. *Stanford Social Innovation Review*, 2, 33–43. Available at: ww.ssireview.org/articles/entry/investing in society [accessed: 24 January 2007].

Modell, S. 2005. Performance management in the public sector: past experiences, current practices and future challenges. *Australian Accounting Review*, 15(37), 56–66.

Moxham, C., and Boaden, R. 2007. The impact of performance measurement in the voluntary sector: identification of contextual and processual factors, *International Journal of Operations and Production Management*, 27(8), 826–45.

Mwenja, D., and Lewis, A. 2009. Exploring the impact of the board of directors on the performance of not-for-profit organisations. *Business Strategy Series*, 10(6), 359–65.

Neely, A., Platts, M.G., and Platts, K. 2005. Performance measurement system design: a literature review and research agenda. *International Journal of Operations and Production Management*, 25(12), 1228–63.

Pearson, N. 2001. Rebuilding indigenous communities, in *The Enabling State*, edited by P. Botsman and M. Latham. Annandale: Pluto.

Reed, J., Jones, D., and Irvine, J. 2005. Appreciating impact: evaluating small voluntary organisations in the United Kingdom. *Voluntas: International Journal of Voluntary and Nonprofit Organisations*, 16(2), 123–41.

Scholten, P., Nicholls, J., Olsen, S., and Galimidi, B. 2006. *Social Return on Investment. A Guide to SROI Analysis*. Amsterdam: Lenthe.

Sud, M., VanSandt, C.V., and Baugous, A.M. 2008. Social entrepreneurship: the role of institutions. *Journal of Business Ethics*, 85(1), 201–216.

W.K. Kellogg Foundation. 2004. *Logic Model Development Guide: W.K. Kellogg Foundation* [Online]. Available at: www.wkkf.org/~/media/475A9C21974D4 16C90877A268DF38A15.ashx [accessed: 21 February 2010].

Wainwright, S. 2003. *Measuring Impact – A Guide to Resources*. London: NCVO. Available at: http://www.nicva.org/sites/default/files/Research_measuring_Impact20012003.pdf [accessed: 21 February 2010].

Wei-Skillern, J., Austin, J.E., Leonard, H., and Stevenson, H. 2007. *Entrepreneurship in the Social Sector*. Thousand Oaks CA: Sage.

Young, D.R. 1997. The first seven years of 'Nonprofit Management and Leadership'. *Nonprofit Management and Leadership*, 8(2), 193–201.

6

Does the Past Matter? Exploring the Effect of Past Changes on Crisis Preparedness in Non-Profit Settings

Rita S. Mano and Zachary Sheaffer

Introduction

Crises in business firms often have far-reaching negative repercussions that generate detrimental exposure in terms of the involvement of external stakeholders (Elliott and Smith 2006, Ulmer 2001). These repercussions are relevant to the non-profit sector. Estes and Alford (1990: 173) heralded the role played by the non-profit sector with respect to crises. Key differences exist between these sectors concerning issues related to crisis or failure. Most importantly, failure is more difficult to gauge in the public and non-profit sectors (Mordaunt and Otto 2004). In this chapter we postulate that managerial evaluations of crisis containment (CC) and crisis predictability (CP) reflect the way managers perceived the influence of past radical changes in non-profit service organizations (hereafter NPOs).

Failure and the need to forego a radical change in NPOs means that certain stakeholders believe the organization is threatened in regard to its legitimacy, resource base or survival (Mone et al. 1998). Ongoing budgetary cutbacks and the introduction of profit-oriented approaches in non-profits have become institutionalized in an era typified by growing competition over scarcer resources and diminishing environmental munificence (Bryson et al. 2003). This era is characterized by pronounced tendencies to improve organizational processes and organizational coping mechanisms that enhance

NPOs' survivability (Herman and Renz 2004). Consequently, NPOs are forced to compete for access to scarcer resources by institutionalizing 'rational' perceptions reminiscent of for-profits (Eikenberry and Kluver 2004, Kettner and Martin 1996), often illustrated by the introduction of organizational change (Galaskiewicz and Bielefeld 2000, Stone et al. 1999, Durst and Newell 2001). As environmental changes in stakeholders' expectations increase, NPOs need to adjust to environmental turbulence (Durst and Newell 2001, Schmidt and Hasenfeld 1993). Changes involving greater rationalization of organizational processes as necessitated by the changing environmental circumstances and crises induce managers to increasingly rely on personal experiences and perceptions of past events.

While all organizational forms undergo change and strive for greater effectiveness, improved competitiveness and survival, few if any studies relate to the way these events affect managerial perceptions of crises. Although the reasons for these changes are addressed by various theoretical perspectives, such as selection, adaptation and structural models in NPOs (cf. Galaskiewicz and Bielefeld 1998, 2000), most models assume that the goal of change is to boost performance in terms of measurable outcomes. Adding on this line of thought we postulate here that managerial reliance on recollections of past changes may be used advantageously to evaluate the organizational ability to contain and prevent crises in NPOs (Dyck 1996). Accordingly we ask:

RQ1: Does the occurrence of significant changes affect crisis perceptions?

RQ2: Do organizational features mediate the relationship between past changes and present perceptions of crisis?

RQ3: How does managerial competence further shape the above link?

Theory

Organizations consist of people, structures and processes. Organizational behaviour and routines are firmly anchored to structure and organizational history: past experiences in the organization's life (Hambrick et al. 1998) and the link between them affect present organizational circumstances, including the development of future events. Organizational crises signify turning points separating past failures and future restructuring (Nathan 2000, Turner and Toft 2006). Various authors (Mitroff et al. 1989, Sheaffer and Mano-Negrin 2003) have shown that crisis-prepared and crisis-prone organizations differ in their activities and structures, and in their potential to avert or decrease damages inherent in crises. Crisis-prepared organizations are typified by effective audits, managerial competence, and actions and policies aimed at forecasting potential crisis occurrences (Greening and Johnson 1996, Thierry et al. 2006). Hence, these organizations feature well-established and practised crisis management designs characterized by transparency of information, flexibility and clearly identifiable work roles (Mitroff et al. 1996). They highlight crisis-sensing-and-diagnosis managerial and structural ingredients geared to averting escalation (Reilly 1993), and facilitate external and internal information flows (Pauchant and Mitroff 1992, Pearson and Mitroff 1993, Mitroff et al. 1989). As Towler (1990: 47) suggested, organizations should be aware of previous and similar situations that caused a re-evaluation and a reorganization of organizational values and principles. These processes are normally followed by change in organizational norms and action. Organizational change is deemed a painful outcome of past experience, but is likely to become a major organizational asset or competence (Slappendel 1996). Some studies have pointed out that the ability to change, while a less immediately visible capacity, may be described as an intangible organizational asset (Levinthal 1997, Zajak and Westphel 2005). Indeed, as globalization becomes widespread and dictates circumstances wherein change is a precondition for organizational survival (McKinley and Scherer 2000), theoretical treatises and research findings often address the processes of change and factors affecting organizational success. The literature considers almost every aspect of the origins, evolution and aftermath of organizational change. These aspects are discussed from the individual, managerial, group and organizational levels (for example, Haveman 1992, Hannan and Freeman 1984, Sastry 1997).

Central to management is the threat-rigidity theory (Staw et al. 1981). Threat-rigidity theory is most appropriate when considering organizations following fundamental changes. Organizational change aims to alert members to future environmental turbulence which has the potential to destabilize organizational and individual well-being. Although threat is conceived to have analogous effects on individuals, groups, and organizations, the managerial level of analysis is highly significant. The theory concerns situations of threat, defined as an external event or circumstance in which managers and employees perceive impending events that are negative or harmful to their vital interests (Ocasio 1993). The theory postulates that under adverse circumstances, such as those accompanying fundamental changes as opposed to incremental changes, managers tend to become inflexible and risk-averse. This led Barnett and Pratt (2000), following Drazin and Sanderlands (1992), to indicate that top managers may initiate strategic 'pre-adaptations' to future crises, thereby employing latent threat to engender organizational flexibility, learning and renewal.

Later, following a 'psychoanalytic' conceptualization of managerial responses to changes, Antonacopoulou and Gabriel (2001) discuss how change induces internal organizational stakeholders to experience different emotional states, from ambivalence about the process of change to strong reluctance to accept the actualized or forthcoming changes. Balancing fears of change with hopes of possible positive outcomes concerning their positions (Antonacopoulou and Gabriel 2001), employees become increasingly uncertain as to whether the enacted change affects them positively or negatively. Even if the endorsed change results in positive organizational outcomes, this does not necessarily lead to positive post-change attitudes among managers. Evaluating future crises in the present implies the acknowledgement that the current situation is probably related to past adverse situations. Changes raise such questions as management's confidence in addressing future crises. Managers previously involved in fundamental changes may experience a range of feelings regarding their ability or inability to come to grips with the consequences.

Furthermore, managers' predispositions in the present may draw upon such experiences. In such cases different outcomes to different emotional states can be generated that indirectly represent the organizational potential to cope with crisis in the future. Indeed, empirical treatises on crisis management highlight how advanced crisis-sensing-and-diagnosis managers geared towards averting escalation (Reilly 1993) and facilitating external and internal information flows (Meyer 1982, Pauchant and Mitroff 1992, Pearson and Miroff 1993, Mitroff et al. 1989). And as Towler (1990: 47) proposed, organizations need to have some degree of previous exposure to similar situations that induced the revaluation and reorganization of organizational values and principles, and that were followed by some type of organizational change in norms and action. When a change in the past has led to 'painful' experiences this may trigger the need to learn from previous 'mistakes' in order to maximize the gains and turn *past* changes into an organizational competence in the *present* to increase the organizational capability to prevent crises from happening in the *future*. We therefore hypothesize:

H1a: The effect of past changes on perceived crisis containment (CC) and crisis predictability (CP) will be positive.

By contrast, lacking concrete evidence in the way changes affect non-profit organizations (Spillan and Crandall 2002), it can be expected that the effect of past changes on crisis containment will be negative; that is, managers will perceive that crises cannot be contained. Accordingly:

H1b: The effect of past changes on perceived crisis containment (CC) and crisis predictability (CP) will be negative.

ORGANIZATIONAL AGE AND SIZE

Threat-rigidity theory also proposes a basic assumption about the way threatening conditions lead to organizational restructuring where organizations undergo a 'mechanistic shift' (Staw et al. 1981: 516) characterized by centralization of control, conservation of resources, restricted information flow and a tendency to escalate commitment to well-practised routines (Brockner 1992). This perspective has received extensive empirical support, principally from studies of organizational crisis (D'Aveni and MacMillan 1990, Tjosvold 1984), and studies of efficiency, centralization and resistance to change (Cameron et al. 1987, D'Aveni 1989, Walter 2003). However, change is viewed by contingency theorists (cf. Yasai-Ardekani and Nystrom 1996) as an inevitable step in response to the need for radical change aimed at halting diminishing resources. Structural changes aimed at accommodating environmental shifts (Daft 2004) often reflect institutional demands (Casciaro and Piskorski 2005, Davis and Marquis 2005, Schneiberg and Clemens 2006), and generate or increase organizational legitimacy and improved results, which in turn reinforce survivability (Aldrich and Ruef 2006).

Theoretical treatises and empirical findings reported in the organizational ecology literature (cf. Hannan and Freeman 1989, Baum and Amburgey 2005) suggest that larger firms tend to be inert and resistant to change, hence less likely to revamp corporate routines, culture and strategies. These features adversely affect openness and calculated risk-taking, stifle creativity and innovativeness (Tushman and O'Reilly 1996, Zajak and Westphel 2005), and enhance dysfunctional systems (Roberts 1994). Moreover, increased size-related complexity inhibits information processing (Walter 2003). Richardson (1994: 68) argued that older and renewal-reluctant organizations with a record of successful rather than deficient activities (Armenakis and Bedeian 1999) are inherently prone to crisis. Specifically, large and established organizations are often characterized by a 'tighter' configuration of strategy, culture and structure, and are therefore less consistent with variety and flexibility (Caldart and Ricart 2003, Rijpma 1997, Watkins and Bazerman 2003). Consequently, they often become crisis-prone (Miller 1990, Tushman and O'Reilly 1996). Accordingly,

H2a: Perceived CC and CP will be lower in larger organizations, and

H2b: Perceived CC and CP will be lower in older organizations.

A third variable associated with both age and size is geographical location. Successful NPOs are more likely to be located in and around major urban centres (Balser and McKlusky 2005). These locations are more likely to be conducive to greater social legitimacy owing to the proximity to potentially influential stakeholders. The ability to impact social and political constituents capable of affecting public opinion and policy is instrumental for NPOs (Dyck 1996). Accordingly:

H2c: Perceived CC and CP will be higher in organizations located in metropolitan areas.

STRUCTURAL EFFECTS

Theoretical treatises on crisis stress the importance of structural contingencies in the detection of early warning signals and the ability to cope with crises (Richardson 1993 and 1995, Pearson and Mitroff 1993, Sheaffer et al. 1998). Organizational structures are seen as viable strategic choices rather than simple means conducive to organizational success (Wheelwright and Bowen 1996). Miles and Snow (1992: 69–70) associate crisis proneness as characterizing complex organizations, with slow response to changes in increasingly competitive environments, and with 'patchwork alterations' to existing forms without considering the ultimate systemic impact (Jelinik and Litterer 1995). Moreover, organizational structures are liable to harbour constraints that impede managerial skills in terms of their effectiveness in facilitating organizational processes (Baum and Rowley 2005). Various authors have indicated that crisis-prepared organizations can avoid failure owing to their flexible structures and effective work processes (D'Aveni 1990). According to Burns and Stalker (1961), less formalized organizations will improve their chances of coping with turbulent environments because formalization decreases organizational adaptability to environmental jolts, hence increasing the chances of failure (Wally and Baum 1994, Sine et al. 2006). Hence, we postulate that organizations typified by less formalized structures will be more crisis-prepared as they do not adhere to standardized functions and roles, thus will be less likely to respond rigidly to unanticipated events. While in general crisis-related mechanisms also include the use of organic (that is, malleable) structures, as against mechanistic and inflexible structures (Covin et al. 2001), fewer studies ask how well-designed and coherently synchronized structures withstand adverse circumstances in the NPO environment (Cumbey and Alexander 1998, Bryson et al. 2001). Pearson and Clair (1998: 65) consider unmanageable or uncontrollable disasters as resulting from inherent interactivity between structures and technologies (Orlikowski 2000, Perrow 1984, Radell 2006, Shoichet 1998). Weick (1979) noted that past structures shape present actions and Reilly (1993) then illustrates how structures induce or facilitate organizational outcomes and processes (Radell 2006), raising the levels of containment (Roberts 1994). We thus offer the following hypothesis:

H3: Perceived CC and CP will be higher among organizations typified by flexible structures – a higher number of volunteers and a lower level of salaried managers.

MANAGERIAL COMPETENCE

Managers in crisis-prone organizations often develop faulty presumptions and defence mechanisms regarding their perceived vulnerability. These flawed assumptions include such fallacies as 'Crises happen only to others', 'Size will protect us', or 'Well-managed firms don't encounter crises', all of which are suggestive of 'sloppy' management (Turner 1994, Pauchant and Mitroff 1990, Richardson 1993, 1995). As crises 'defy interpretations and impose severe demands on sensemaking' (Weick 1988: 305), managerial characteristics become paramount in organizational performance and outcomes. These characteristics include length of incumbency and level of education (Finkelstein and Hambrick 1990, Papadakis et al. 1998, Pfeffer and Veiga 1999) which lead some people to focus on self-control and self-esteem by not admitting that exogenous factors have affected them (Bandura 1990). Then, it is possible that managers' denial of the positive outcomes of a change diminishes and there is an increased focus on negative effects which are likely to affect their perception of crisis preparedness; in other words, containment and predictability (Radell 2006).

The literature on occupations and professionalism alludes to how differences in managerial competence – occupation, professionalism or experience – shape beliefs and organizational performance. Normally, NPOs allow a diverse managerial makeup (Papadakis et al. 1998, Watkins and Bazerman 2003). Some NPOs may be managed by social entrepreneurs lacking formal managerial expertise because in many cases NPOs are small and pursue highly specific goals. They represent the cause and credo upheld by the founders, who do not necessarily have professional skills (Finkelstein and Hambrick 1990). Such skills or their absence may affect perceptions and ideals of management (Mano-Negrin and Sheaffer 2004). Accordingly, it seems reasonable to assume that amateur managers will view past changes as threatening. For example, Greening and Johnson (1996) point to two critical characteristics for organizational performance: length of service in the company and skills (Finkelstein and

Hambrick 1990, Papadakis et al. 1998). As organizational performance has become increasingly important, reduced institutional funding and competition over resources induce stakeholders to stress higher managerial capabilities aimed at facilitating processes and accountability (Werther and Berman 2001). Consequently we hypothesize that:

H4a: Perceived CC and CP will be higher among NPO managers possessing higher professional qualifications.

H4b: Perceived CC and CP will be higher among NPO managers possessing higher managerial experience.

Methodology

SAMPLE

Questionnaires were sent to 225 organizations included in Shatil's list (an Israeli organization providing services to NPOs). One hundred and thirty-five managers (62 per cent) returned the questionnaires. Basic descriptive statistics show that mean organizational age was 14 years, and 30 per cent of the NPOs were located in metropolitan areas. Managers averaged six years of managerial experience and 50 per cent had salaried positions, suggesting that they mostly had professional managerial training.

MEASURES

Dependent variables   To explore the facets involved in crisis management evaluations, exploratory factor analysis (EFA) was chosen because the items are relatively unknown (Lievens and Anseel 2004). Two factors were extracted. Both factors – crisis containment (CC) and crisis predictability (CP) – loaded three pertinent items. The crisis items making up both CP and CC were derived from managerial rationalizations regarding the way crises are perceived or conceptualized (Richardson 1995), as validated by Sheaffer and Mano-Negrin (2003) and Mano-Negrin and Sheaffer (2004). CC was composed of answers to the following three questions, on a scale from 1 (lowest) to 10 (highest):

1.   'Is it possible to contain crises in general?'

2.   'Is it possible to control the duration of a crisis once it has occurred?'

3.   'Is it possible to be in control of the negative outcomes of a crisis once it has occurred?' ($\alpha = .79$).

Affirmative answers concerning the CC indicate that the respondents perceived themselves able to be in control when crises occur.

CP was composed of answers to the following three questions, on a scale from 1 (lowest) to 10 (highest):

1.   'Is it impossible to foresee crises?'

2.   'Is it impossible to foresee crises because they are affected by exogenous constraints, hence deemed unforeseeable?'

3.   'Is it impossible to foresee crisis because they occur mainly as a result of human error?' ($\alpha = .76$).

We postulated that because of the exposure to competition for ever-scarcer resources and the objective difficulties in measuring success, NPOs would differ from other types of organizations in the way they contain and prevent crises (Galaskiewicz and Bielefeld 2000, Alesch et al. 2001).

Independent variables   The variable 'Organizational change' measured whether or not the NPO experienced a significant organizational change. We did not elaborate the magnitude of the change, short of indicating that the change was significant, that is, not merely an incremental one. This was a dichotomous variable where 1 = 'Yes, we experienced change over the past year'; 0 = 'No, we did not'.

Moderating effects   The effects of 'Organizational context' included (a) organization age: years of organizational operations; (b) organization size: number of employees (Pugh et al. 1967); (c) organization location: 1 = metropolitan area, 0 = rural. 'Structure effects' included (a) number of volunteers; (b) number of managers; (c) number of administrative/clerical positions (Spillan and Crandall 2002). 'Managerial competence' included (a) experience: length of incumbency in position; (b) professional status: 1 = salaried position, 0 = volunteer.

Results

First, mean values for the model variables were examined (Appendix 1). Second, a step regression procedure was employed to test the additive effect of four sets of independent variables entered in the model predicting (a) CC and (b) CP. This common procedure permits gauging the relative predictive power of each set of independent variables.

Findings suggest that contextual variables (organizational age, size, and location) do not contribute significantly to the prediction of CC or CP in non-profit environments (see Table 6.1). Neither do managerial characteristics (education, professionalism, experience). But organizational structure plays a decisive role in predicting CC, contributing 35 per cent to the explained variance of the examined model (R^2 change = .35) and rises to 42 per cent of the model's total variance (R^2 = .42). Surprisingly, organizational structure does not significantly affect CP. This finding may be related to the assumed difference between CP and CC, suggesting that containment refers to an actual crisis whereas predictability refers to a hypothetical crisis occurrence. Finally, the model shows a significant effect of past experiences of change on both CC and CP. This variable contributes 21.6 per cent of the explained variance of CC (R^2 change = .22) and raises the model's total variance to 63 per cent (R^2 = .64). A lower, though significant effect is identified between past experiences of change and CP, producing 15.1 per cent explained variance (R^2 change = .15) of CP and raising the model's total variance to 47.6 per cent (R^2 = .48). These results suggest that some degree of learning from the past has a significant impact in determining managers' conception of the organizational potential to contain organizational crises in the future and to some extent prevent them. More specifically, the regression standardized estimates testing the direct effect of all independent variables entered in the model are presented in Table 6.2.

The results suggest a significant effect of the majority of independent variables on both CC and CP. Specifically context variables have a negative effect on both CC and CP. The negative effect of size on CC (B = -7.364; p = .000) and CP (B = -8.765; p = .000) suggests, as hypothesized by H2a and H2b, that as organizations become more bureaucratized they find it more difficult to handle crisis-related situations (Richardson 1993, 1995). Unexpectedly, however, age has no effect on CC and CP. Contrary to our hypothesis, location has a negative effect on CC (B = -.551; p = .000) and CP (B = -.457; p = .000) thus H2c is rejected. As to managerial competence, two opposing trends are apparent. Managerial experience has a significant effect on neither CC (B = -.267; p = .010) nor CP (B = -.180; p = .136). However, managerial professional status has a positive effect on both CC (B = .760; p = .000) and CP (B = -.678; p = .000). Hence, hypotheses H4a and H4b are corroborated by the data. A mixed relationship between inflexible structural components and higher awareness of CC and CP is also

Table 6.1 Model summary predicting CC and CP based on (1) organizational context, (2) managerial characteristics, (3) organizational structure, and (4) double-loop learning/past experience of change

	R	R²	Adjusted R²	Std error of the estimate	R² change	F change	Sig. F change
CRISIS CONTAINMENT							
Organizational context	.191(a)	.036	.007	6.0228	.036	1.245	.295
Managerial characteristics	.265(b)	.070	.012	6.0083	.034	1.159	.320
Organizational structure	.649(c)	.421	.242	5.2614	.351	2.622	.008
Past experience of change	.798(d)	.636	.515	4.2095	.216	30.238	.000
CRISIS PREDICTABILITY							
Organizational context	.235(a)	.055	.027	3.2168	.055	1.927	.154
Managerial characteristics	.331(b)	.109	.054	3.1715	.054	1.950	.151
Organizational structure	.570(c)	.325	.118	3.0624	.216	1.387	.202
Past experience of change	.690(d)	.476	.302	2.7241	.151	14.719	.000

Table 6.2 Unstandardized and standardized coefficients for model predicting crisis containment and crisis predictability based on (1) organizational context, (2) managerial characteristics, (3) organizational structure, and (4) past organizational changes

	CRISIS CONTAINMENT					CRISIS PREDICTABILITY				
	B	Std error	β	T	Sig.	B	Std error	β	T	Sig.
(Constant)	15.87	2.284		6.949	.000	15.467	1.478		10.47	.0.000
Organizational context										
Organizational size	-.745	.142	-7.364	-5.260	.000	-.479	.092	-8.765	5.218	.000
Organizational age	-.006	.038	-.152	-1.340	.186	-.0065	.025	-.360	2.641	.011
Metropolitan location	-7.26	1.281	-.551	-5.670	.000	-3.248	.829	-.457	3.917	.000
Managerial characteristics										
Managerial experience	-.200	.074	-.267	-2.690	.010	.0072	.048	.180	-1.513	.136
Managerial occupation	9.16	1.492	.760	6.137	.000	4.408	.966	.678	-4.565	.000
Organizational structure										
No. of volunteers	.001	.001	.109	1.240	.221	.0054	.000	.154	-1.455	.152
No. of managers	-4.78	.624	-1.703	-7.665	.000	-1.728	.404	-1.140	4.277	.000
No. of clerical positions	3.30	.516	1.201	6.390	.000	1.175	.334	-.793	-3.517	.001
Past organizational changes	8.23	1.496	.683	5.499	.000	-3.715	.968	-.572	-3.837	.000

apparent. Most structural-level variables (except for the non-significant effect of volunteers) have a positive effect on CC and CP.

More importantly, a larger number of managers, indicating a top-heavy (therefore inflexible) structure, has a negative effect on both CC (B = -4.787; p = .056) and CP (B = 1.728; p = .056). The results are partially consistent with hypothesis $H3$. Finally, and noteworthy, is that the first hypothesis is supported by the data. Past organizational change enhances CC significantly and positively (B = 8.229; p = .002), but surprisingly it affects CP negatively (B = -3.715; p = .000).

Discussion

Crisis preparedness as an inevitable ingredient of crisis management (CM) has become an increasingly important research theme in the wider domain of management as both practitioners and scholars acknowledge the magnitude and repercussions of multidimensional crises (Mellahi and Wilkinson 2004, Seeger et al. 2005) or disasters (Greenberg 2002). No less conspicuous is the relative scarcity of empirical as well as conceptual scholarly contributions to the research of organizational downturn trends, including failure, crisis and decline in the non-profit sector. This is probably owing to the long-held belief that crises occur or are primarily important in business settings (Spillan and Crandall 2002).

By all accounts crises are likely to occur more frequently and intensely. Radical changes thereof may have a spill-over effect on NPOs' crisis management because undergoing incessant changes raises the awareness of the inevitability of crises and the need to prepare NPOs for higher crisis preparedness in a context of greater crisis proneness.

In this study we heeded the implicit calls by both Estes and Alford (1990) and notably Mordaunt et al. (2004) for further research involving organizational failure and crisis in non-profits. In addition to existing studies addressing crises in non-profits, we add an important element that thus far has been only fleetingly addressed in studies about NPOs – how perceptions regarding CC and CP are affected by previously experienced organizational change. The question underlying this study focuses on the need to evaluate the possibility and inevitability of crises in NPOs. To tackle this issue we addressed crises in non-profits, and we add an important element regarding the perceptions of CC and CP and how they are affected by previously experienced organizational change.

Previous studies offer scant and unfocused information on how managerial psyche affects the perception and evaluation of crises. Even fewer studies have examined, albeit implicitly, what organizational-level phenomena shape these perceptions and evaluations. Moreover, research on organizational change focuses largely on how change affects performance and employees, and on how change is effectuated as well as on change processes. Experiences from past changes have been related to such organizational issues as threats emanating from change, change resistance, risk-taking or risk-aversion (Antonacopoulou and Gabriel 2001). However, the essential linkage between past changes and current perceptions of future crisis occurrence is only alluded to, not investigated.

We addressed this lacuna by employing this linkage to advance the notion that managers' previous experiences of past change may generate perceptions, attitudes and actions regarding crises. The model examined shows a significant effect of past experiences of change on managers' CC and CP alike. But we also asked whether or not managerial characteristics shape perceptions of CC and CP. In this vein we considered three aspects of organizational behaviour, the first of which was the individual level aspect or past managerial experiences of change and their impact on present perceptions of CC and CP. Second, we investigated how organizational structural and contextual variables moderate these effects. Third, we studied how managerial characteristics further affect this link. Results show expected and unexpected outcomes.

First, as expected, we identified a significant impact of the occurrence of past changes on perceived CP and also a negative effect of past changes on perceived CC. As indicated this shows that while managers who have experienced changes may have an improved understanding on the containment of crises, they do not necessarily perceive that crises can be prevented. This somewhat contradictory finding can be ascribed to the fact that the former reflects managers' view of a crisis as a foreseeable occurrence. Especially in the case of changes we indeed know that they are normally implemented to avert a crisis or following one.

Changes provide a proactive or 'buffering' effect. But this does not mean that crises are avoidable altogether. Once early warning signals loom near, managers are more likely to challenge them (Sheaffer et al. 1998) or they are forewarned by involving previous experiences with changes that integrate with or amplify awareness as to these early signals. Second, we found no significant impact of the contextual variables, that is, size, age and location. We believe the reason for this is that the normally hypothesized effects of these characteristics in business firms do not have similar effects in NPOs. Indeed, many of the organizations studied here are relatively small, and located in urban areas. In this respect the results do not support previous studies (Balser and McKlusky 2005, Dyck 1996). Third, corroborating classic essays on the impact of structural effects, it was possible to show that larger and mechanistic structures with a larger number of stable (that is, non-volunteer) positions induce or facilitate positive organizational outcomes and processes. CC and CP were both associated with these organizational structure properties. The results also revealed positive effects of managerial expertise in NPOs; the presence of top managers as well as a higher number of managers increase the probability that managers are better equipped to positively evaluate crisis containment and prevention. This explanation also indicates the existence of multiple tasks in the managerial positions in NPOs and the multiplicity of stakeholders in the boards of trustees. The board of directors is often composed of public opinion leaders whose value added is in the provision of a wider range of opinions and perspectives. This is despite the fact that often, these directors have no previous managerial experience.

Finally, of the two managerial characteristics examined, only managers' level of education affected containment and preventability of a perceived crisis. The role of managerial training (as opposed to managerial experience) proved to be the only relevant factor in evaluating crises, thus sustaining studies highlighting the importance of managerial skills. To summarize, much like their business counterparts, non-profits under intense pressures for performance can benefit from adopting flexible structures and by enhancing managerial CM competences. More importantly, managers can benefit from their own experience because the occurrence of past changes and insights drawn from them may potentially improve CM-related evaluations. Knowing how changes were handled in the past and restoring this in the organizational memory would be useful assets as these managers are more likely to have a higher awareness of future crises, thus are more likely to successfully prevent or contain them.

Limitations and Recommendations for Future Studies

The present study focuses on how organizational context and structure, and managers' characteristics linked to recollection of change, shape perceptions of CC and CP. The first limitation concerns the dataset, which did not allow a distinction to be made between managers' positive and negative experiences from past changes. We focused on how managerial perceptions reflect experiences from past changes on present perceptions. However, we could not control for the time lapse between the occurrence of the event and its present evaluations. This suggests that a history bias may be in effect. Consequently the subtle shift from past 'objective' situations to present 'subjective' or perceived attitudes may be a crucial link between successful and unsuccessful management of crises: it is indicated, but not fully tested. On the basis of these limitations future studies should involve longitudinal research methods and control for time-bias and use, where possible, observed variables rather than perceived constructs. Second, it is suggested that additional, rather than single (CEO) sources of information would be used to enhance content validity. Finally, comparative cross-cultural studies are called for where managers representing NPOs from various countries can be sampled.

A cross-cultural study involving NPOs would be particularly interesting, and could examine culture-based managerial evaluations towards change and crisis and global tendencies that make these differences salient in a world characterized by increasing international–regional cooperation.

References

Aldrich, H., and Ruef, M. 2006. *Organizations Evolving*. London: Sage.
Alesch, D.J., Holly, J.N., Mittler, E., and Nagy, R. 2001. Organizations at risk: what happens when small businesses and not-for-profits encounter natural disasters. *Small Organizations Natural Hazards Project First Year Technical Report*. University of Wisconsin-Green Bay, Center for Organizational Studies. Public Entity Risk Institute.
Amabile, T.M., and Conti, R. 1999. Changes in the work environment for creativity during downsizing. *Academy of Management Journal*, 42(6), 630–640.
Antonacopoulou, E.P., and Gabriel, Y. 2001. Emotion, learning and organisational change: towards an integration of psychoanalytic and other perspectives. *Journal of Organisational Change Management*, 14(5), 435–51.
Armenakis, A.A., and Bedeian, A.G. 1999. Organizational change: a review of theory and research in the 1990s. *Journal of Management*, 25(3), 293–315.
Balser, D., and McKlusky, J. 2005. Managing stakeholder relationships and nonprofit organization effectiveness. *Nonprofit Management and Leadership*, 15(3), 295–315.
Bandura, A. 1990. Perceived self-efficacy in the exercise of contain over AIDS infection, in *The Primary Prevention of AIDS: Psychological Approaches*, edited by K.L. Kaemingle and L. Sechrist. Newbury Park CA: Sage, 128–41.

Barnett, C.K., and Pratt, M.G., 2000. From threat-rigidity to flexibility – toward a learning model of autogenic crisis in organizations. *Journal of Organizational Change Management*, 13(1), 74–88.

Baum, J.A.C., and Rowley, T.J. 2005. Companion to organizations: an introduction, in *Companion to Organizations*, edited by J.A.C. Baum. Somerset UK: Blackwell, 1–34.

Baum, J.A.C., and Amburgey, T.L. 2005. Organizational ecology, in *Companion to Organizations*, edited by J.A.C. Baum. Somerset UK: Blackwell, 304–26.

Brockner, J. 1992. The escalation of commitment to a failing course of action: toward theoretical progress. *Academy of Management Review*, 17(1), 39–61.

Bryson, J.M., Gibbons, M.J., and Shaye, G. 2001. Enterprise schemes for nonprofit survival, growth, and effectiveness. *Nonprofit Management and Leadership*, 11(3), 271–88.

Burns, T., and Stalker, G.M. 1961. *The Management of Innovation*. London: Tavistock.

Caldart, A., and Ricart, J. 2003. *Corporate Strategy Revisited: A View from Complexity Theory*. Pamplona: IESE Business School/University of Navarra.

Cameron, K.S., Whetten, D.A., and Kim, M.U. 1987. Organizational dysfunctions of decline. *Academy of Management Journal*, 30, 126–38.

Casciaro, T., and Piskorski, M.J. 2005. Power imbalance, mutual dependence and constraint absorption: resource dependence theory revisited. *Administrative Science Quarterly*, 50(2), 167–99.

Covin, J.G., Slevin, D.P., and Heeley, M.B. 2001. Strategic decision making in an intuitive vs. technocratic mode: structural and environmental considerations. *Journal of Business Research*, 52(1), 51–67.

Cumbey, D.A., and Alexander, J.W. 1998. The relationship of job satisfaction with organizational variables in public health nursing. *Journal of Nursing Administration*, 28(5), 39–46.

Daft, R.L. 2004. *Organization Theory and Design*. Independence KY: Thomson South-Western.

D'Aveni, R.A. 1989. The aftermath of organizational decline: a longitudinal study of the strategic and managerial characteristics of declining firms. *Academy of Management Journal*, 32, 577–605.

D'Aveni, R.A. 1990. Top managerial prestige and organizational bankruptcy. *Organization Science*, 1(2), 121–42.

D'Aveni, R.A., and MacMillan, L.C. 1990. Crisis and the content of managerial communications: a study of the focus of attention of top managers in surviving and failing firms. *Administrative Science Quarterly*, 25, 634–57.

Davis, G.F., and Marquis, C. 2005. Prospects for organization theory in the early twenty-first century: institutional fields and mechanisms. *Organization Science*, 16(4), 332–43.

Drazin, R., and Sanderlands L. 1992. Autogenesis: a perspective on the process of organizing. *Organization Science*, 3(2), 32–45.

Durst, S.L., and Newell, C. 2001. The who, why, and how of reinvention in nonprofit organizations. *Nonprofit Management and Leadership*, 11(4), 443–57.

Dyck, B. 1996. The role of crises and opportunities in organizational change: a look at a nonprofit religious college. *Nonprofit and Voluntary Sector Quarterly*, 25(3), 321–46.

Eikenberry, A.M., and Kluver, J.D. 2004. The marketization of the nonprofit sector: civil society at risk? *Public Administration Review*, 64(2), 132–140.

Elliott, D. 2006. Crisis management into practice, in *Key Readings in Crisis Management: Systems and Structures from Prevention and Recovery*, edited by D. Smith and D. Elliott. London: Routledge, 393–412.

Elliott, D., and Smith, D. 2006. Football stadia disasters in the UK: learning from tragedy?, in *Key Readings in Crisis Management: Systems and Structures from Prevention and Recovery*, edited by D. Smith and D. Elliott. London: Routledge, 269–392.

Estes, C.L., and Alford, R.R. 1990. Systemic crisis and the nonprofit sector: toward a political economy of the nonprofit health and social services sector. *Theory and Society*, 19(2), 173–98.

Finkelstein, S., and Hambrick, D. 1990. Top management team tenure and organizational outcomes: the moderating role of managerial discretion. *Administrative Science Quarterly*, 35, 484–503.

Fiol, C.M., and Lyles, M.A. 1985. Organizational learning. *Academy of Management Review*, 10, 803–813.

Galaskiewicz, J., and Bielefeld, W. 1998. *Nonprofit Organizations in an Age of Uncertainty: A Study of Organizational Change*. New York: Aldine Transaction.

Galaskiewicz, J., and Bielefeld, W. 2000 The behavior of nonprofit organizations, in *Advances in Theories of the Nonprofit Sector*, edited by H.K. Anheier and A. Ben-Ner. New York: Kluwer/Plenum.

Greenberg, B.S. 2002. *Communication and Terrorism: Public and Media Responses to 9/11*. Cresskill NJ: Hampton Press.

Greening, D.W., and Johnson, R.A. 1996. Do managers and strategies matter? A study in crisis. *Journal of Management Studies*, 33 (1), 25–51.

Hambrick, D., Nadler, D., and Tushman, M. 1998. *Navigating Change: How CEOs, Top Teams and Boards steer Transformation*. Boston: Harvard Business School Press.

Hannan, M.T., and Freeman, J. 1984. Structural inertia and organizational change. *American Sociological Review*, 49(2), 149–64.

Hannan, M.T., and Freeman, J. 1989. *Organizational Ecology*. Cambridge MA: Harvard University Press.

Haveman, H.A. 1992. Between a rock and a hard place: organizational change and performance under conditions of fundamental environmental transformation. *Administrative Science Quarterly*, 37, 48–75.

Herman, R., and Renz, D. 2004, Doing things right: effectiveness in local nonprofit organizations, a panel study. *Public Administration Review*, 64(6), 694–722.

Hsu, G., and Hannan, M.T. 2005. Identities, genres, and organizational forms. *Organization Science*, 16(5), 474–490.

Jelinek, M., and Litterer, J.A. 1995. Toward entrepreneurial organizations: meeting ambiguity with engagement. *Entrepreneurship: Theory and Practice*, 19(3), 137–68.

Kettner, P.M., and Martin, L.L. 1996. The impact of declining resources and purchase of service contracting on private nonprofit agencies. *Administration in Social Work*, 20(3), 21–38.

Levinthal, D.A. 1997. Adaptation on rugged landscapes. *Management Science*, 43(7), 934–950.

Levitt, B., and March, J. 1988.Organizational learning. *Annual Review of Sociology*, 14, 319–340.

Lievens, F., and Anseel, F. 2004. Confirmatory factor analysis and invariance of an organizational citizenship behaviour measure across samples in a Dutch-speaking context. *Journal of Occupational and Organizational Psychology*, 77, 299–306.

Mano-Negrin, R., and Sheaffer, Z. 2004. Are women 'cooler' during crises? Exploring gender differences in perceiving organisational crisis preparedness/proneness. *Women in Management Review*, 19(2), 98–108.

McKinley, W., and Scherer, A.G. 2000. Some unanticipated consequences of organizational restructuring. *Academy of Management Review*, 25(4), 735–52.

Mellahi, K., and Wilkinson, A. 2004. Organizational failure: a critique of recent research and a proposed integrative framework. *International Journal of Management Reviews*, 5/6(1), 21–41.

Meyer, A.D. 1982. Adapting to environmental jolts. *Administrative Science Quarterly*, 27: 515–537.

Miles, R.E., and Snow, C.C. 1992. Causes of failure in network organizations. *California Management Review*, 34(4), 57–72.

Miller, D. 1990. Organizational configurations: cohesion, change, and prediction. *Human Relations*, 43(8), 771–89.

Mitroff, I.I., Pauchant, T.C., and Shrivastava, P. 2006. The structure of man-made organizational crises: conceptual and empirical issues in the development of a general theory of crisis management, in *Key Readings in Crisis Management: Systems and Structures from Prevention and Recovery*, edited by D. Smith and D. Elliott. London: Routledge, 47–74.

Mitroff, I.I, Pauchant, T., Finney, M., and Pearson, C. 1989. Do some organizations cause their own crises? The cultural profiles of crisis-prone vs crisis-prepared organizations. *Industrial Crisis Quarterly*, 3, 231–41.

Mitroff, I.I., Pearson, C.M., and Harrington, L.K. 1996, *The Essential Guide to Managing Corporate Crises*, Oxford: Oxford University Press.

Mone, M.A., McKinley, W., and Barker, V.C. 1998. Organization decline and innovation: a contingency framework. *Academy of Management Review*, 23, 113–115.

Mordaunt, J., Cornforth, C., and Otto, S. 2004. Crisis, failure and the governance of public and nonprofit organizations: the effects of participation. *Proceedings of the 6th International Society for Third Sector Research Conference, 11–14 July, Toronto, Canada*.

Nathan, M. 2000. The paradoxical nature of crisis. *Review of Business*, 21(3), 12–18.

Ocasio, W. 1993. *The Structuring of Organizational Attention and the Enactment of Economic Adversity: A Reconciliation of Theories of Failure-Induced Change and Threat-Rigidity*. Working Paper. Cambridge MA: MIT Sloan School of Management.

Orlikowski, W.J. 2000. Using technology and constituting structures: a practice lens for studying technology in organizations. *Organization Science*, 11(4), 404–28.

Papadakis, V.M., Lioukas, S., and Chambers, D. 1998. Strategic decision-making processes: the role of management and context. *Strategic Management Journal*, 19, 115–147.

Pauchant, T.C., and Mitroff, I.I. 1990. Crisis management: managing paradox in a chaotic world. The case of Bhopal. *Technological Forecasting and Social Change*, 38(2), 117–134.

Pauchant, T.C., and Mitroff, I.I. 1992. *Transforming the Crisis-Prone Organization: Preventing Individual, Organizational, and Environmental Tragedies*. San Francisco: Jossey-Bass.

Pearson, C.M., and Clair, J.A. 1998. Reframing crisis management. *Academy of Management Review*, 23(1), 59–76.

Pearson, C.M. and Mitroff, I.I. 1993. From crisis prone to crisis prepared: a framework for crisis management. *Academy of Management Executive*, 7(1), 48–59.

Perrow, C. 1984. *Normal Accidents: Living with High-Risk Technologies*. New York: Basic Books.

Pfeffer, J., and Veiga, F. 1999. Putting people first for organizational success. *Academy of Management Executive*, 13(2), 37–48.

Pugh, D.S, Hickson, D.J., Hinings, C.R., and Turner, C. 1969. The context of organization structures. *Administrative Science Quarterly*, 14(1), 91–114.

Radell, W.W. 2006. Storming and catastrophic system failures, in *Key Readings in Crisis Management: Systems and Structures from Prevention and Recovery*, edited by D. Smith and D. Elliott. London: Routledge, 284–300.

Reilly, A.H. 1993. Preparing for the worst: the process of effective crisis management. *Industrial and Environmental Crisis Quarterly*, 7, 144–55.

Richardson, B. 1993. Why we probably will not save mankind: a natural configuration of crisis-proneness. *Disaster Prevention and Management*, 2(4), 32–59.

Richardson, B. 1994. Crisis management and management strategy-time to 'loop the loop'? *Disaster Prevention and Management*, 3(3), 59–80.

Richardson, B. 1995. Paradox management for crisis avoidance. *Management Decision*, 33(1), 5–18.

Rijpma, J.A. 1997. Complexity, tight-coupling and reliability: connecting normal accidents theory and high reliability theory. *Journal of Contingencies and Crisis Management*, (5)1, 15–23.

Roberts, K. 1994. *Levers of Control: How Managers use Control Systems to Drive Strategic Renewal*. Cambridge MA: Harvard Business School.

Sastry, A. 1997. Problems and paradoxes in a model of punctuated organizational change. *Administrative Science Quarterly*, 42, 237–75.

Schmid, H., and Hasenfeld, Y. 1993. Organizational dilemmas in the provision of home care services. *Social Service Review*, 67, 40–54.

Schneiberg, M., and Clemens, E.S. 2006. The typical tools for the job: research strategies in institutional analysis. *Sociological Theory*, 24(3), 195–213.

Seeger, M.W., Ulmer, R.R., Novak, J.M., and Sellnow, T.L 2001. Virtuous responses to organizational crisis: Aaron Feuerstein and Milt Colt. *Journal of Business Ethics*, 31(4), 369–76.

Seeger, M.W., Ulmer, R.R., Novak, J.M., and Sellnow, T.L. 2005. Post-crisis discourse and organizational change, failure and renewal. *Journal of Organizational Change Management*, 18(1), 78–95.

Sheaffer, Z., and Mano-Negrin, R. 2003. Executives' orientations as indicators of crisis management policies and practices. *Journal of Management Studies*, 40(2), 573–606.

Sheaffer, Z., Richardson, B., and Rosenblatt, Z. 1998. Early warning signals management: a lesson from the Barings crisis. *Journal of Contingencies and Crisis Management*, 6(1), 1–23.

Shoichet, R. 1998. An organization design model for nonprofits. *Nonprofit Management and Leadership*, 9(1), 71–88.

Shrivastava, P. 1993. Crisis theory/practice: towards a sustainable future. *Industrial and Environmental Crisis Quarterly*, 7(1), 23–42.

Sine, W.D., Mitsuhashi, H., and Kirsch, D.A. 2006. Revisiting Burns and Stalker: formal structure and new venture performance in emerging economic sectors. *Academy of Management Journal*, 49, 121–32.

Singh, J.V., Tucker, D.J., and House, R.J. 1986. Organizational legitimacy and the liability of newness. *Administrative Science Quarterly*, 31(2), 171–93.

Slappendel, C. 1996. Perspective on innovation in organizations. *Organization Studies*, 17(1), 107–29.

Smart, C., and Vertinsky, I. 1984. Strategy and environment: a study of corporate responses to crisis. *Strategic Management Journal*, 5(3), 199–214.

Spillan, J.E., and Crandall, W. 2002. Crisis planning in the nonprofit sector: should we plan for something bad if it may not occur? *Southern Business Review*, 27(2), 18–29.

Staw, B.M., Sandelands, L.E., and Dutton, J.E. 1981. Threat-rigidity effects in organizational behavior: a multilevel analysis. *Administrative Science Quarterly*, 26, 501–24.

Stone, M.M., Bigelow, B., and Crittenden, W. 1999. Research on strategic management in nonprofit organizations: synthesis, analysis, and future. *Administration and Society*, 13(3), 378–423.

Thierry, C., Pauchant, C., and Mitroff, I.I. 2006. Crisis prone versus crisis avoiding organizations: is your company's culture its own worst enemy? in *Key Readings in Crisis Management: Systems and Structures from Prevention and Recovery*, edited by D. Smith and D. Elliott. London: Routledge, 136–47.

Tjosvold, D. 1984. Effects of crisis orientation on managers' approach to controversy in decision making. *Academy of Management Journal*, 27, 130–138.

Towler, J. 1990. Leave me alone, I'm having a crisis. *Canadian Banker*, 97(4), 46–9.

Turner, B.A. 1994. Causes of disaster: sloppy management. *British Journal of Management*, 5(3), 215–219.

Turner, B.A., and Toft, B. 2006. Organizational learning from disasters, in *Key Readings in Crisis Management: Systems and Structures from Prevention and Recovery*, edited by D. Smith and D. Elliott. London: Routledge, 191–204.

Tushman, M.L., Newman, W.H., and Romanelli, E. 1986. Convergence and upheaval: managing the unsteady pace of organizational evolution. *California Management Review*, 29(1), 29–44.

Tushman, M.L., and O'Reilly, C. 1996. Evolution and revolution: mastering the dynamics of innovation and change. *California Management Review*, 38(4), 8–30.

Ulmer, R.R. 2001. Effective crisis management through established stakeholder relationships: Malden Mills as a case study. *Management Communication Quarterly*, 14(4). 590–615.

Wally, S., and Baum, J.R. 1994. Personal and structural determinants of strategic decision making. *Academy of Management Journal*, 37, 932–56.

Walshe, K., Harvey, G., Hyde, P., and Pandit, N. 2004. Organizational failure and turnaround: lessons for public services from the non-profit sector. *Public Money and Management*, 24(4), 201–9.

Walter, I. 2003. Strategies in financial services, the shareholders, and the system: is bigger and broader better? *Brookings-Wharton Papers on Financial Services*. Washington DC: Brookings Institution, 1–36.

Watkins, M.D., and Bazerman, M.H., 2003. Predictable surprises: the disasters you should have seen coming. *Harvard Business Review*, March, 72–80.

Weick, K.E. 1979. *The Social Psychology of Organizing*. New York: Random House.

Weick, K.E. 1988. Enacted sensemaking in crisis situations. *Journal of Management Studies*, 25(4), 305–317.

Werther, W., and Berman, E. 2001. *Third Sector Management*. Washington DC: Georgetown University Press.

Wheelwright, S.C., and Bowen, H.K. 1996. The challenge of manufacturing advantage. *Production and Operation Management*, 5(1), 59–77.

Yasai-Ardekani, M., and Nystrom, P.C. 1996. Designs for environmental scanning systems: tests of a contingency theory. *Management Science*, 42(2), 187–204.

Zajak, E.J., and Westphel, J.D. 2005. Organizational economics, in *Companion to Organizations*, edited by J.A.C. Baum. Somerset UK: Blackwell, 233–55.

APPENDIX 1: DESCRIPTIVE STATISTICS

	Mean	SD	N
Crisis controllability	28.4	6.04	121
Crisis prevention	9.78	3.26	119
Organizational age	14.1	18.03	136
Metropolitan location	.29	.458	138
Managerial education	16.3	2.6	138
Managerial experience	6.4	8.06	132
Occupations status	.51	.502	138
No. of volunteers	138.4	924.5	118
No. of managers	1.48	2.15	87
Past organizational changes	.5000	.5018	138

SD = standard deviation
N = number

7

Anecdotal Performance Reporting: Can it Provide Sufficient Confidence for Third Sector Funding Bodies?

Richard Greatbanks and Graham Manville

Introduction

Our experience of the third sector leads us to the view that many voluntary organizations have a primary focus on the delivery of their vision and mission objectives to their specific community. As such, meeting the funding reporting requirements of the many funding bodies which support voluntary organizations is low down on the priority list, albeit still an important consideration if future funding is to be obtained. So, whilst obtaining future funding is important, it is often regarded as an unwelcome distraction from the primary objective, that of supporting the community needs.

On the other hand, the primary objective of a third sector funding organization is to be able to demonstrate that funding decisions are made in a transparent and objective manner, and that the beneficiaries of funding decisions use the monies to best effect, and in accordance with the original funding application. Most funding bodies, and particularly central or local government agencies, are generally open to public scrutiny, and often criticized if funding decisions are seen as biased, unwise or inappropriate for the prevailing economic or political climate. Being able to demonstrate that funding decisions are appropriate and that allocated funding is delivering some level of positive social impact is therefore the primary objective of the many third sector funding organizations.

Whilst both the funded and the funding organization want to achieve the same goals (that is, the delivery of programmes for positive social change), their innately different positions can lead to a potential dysfunctional yet essential reliance on each other. The dynamics of this funding relationship are the focus of this chapter.

The global financial crisis (GFC) has had, in hindsight at least, a profound effect on the role of community organizations. The effect of increasingly tight economic conditions has forced many governments to reconsider and re-evaluate the social and community services offered, and effectively changed the role and contribution of voluntary organizations to the communities they serve. Changing economic and political circumstances have therefore forced third sector organizations into a different space. This change of position is encapsulated with the 'Big Society' initiatives of the 2010 UK Conservative party's general election manifesto. The Big Society initiative placed significant emphasis on 'localism' and 'voluntarism', two important factors in the role of voluntary sector organizations. Along with this repositioning of voluntary and community organizations has come an increased focus and interest on the values of such organizations, and the cost of the services provided. Some initial research on the effect of the Big Society has revealed an issue of mistrust as the funding from the public sector is cut and commissioning bodies increasing demand competitive tendering (Milbourne and Cushman 2011).

As a consequence of this greater interest, many aspects of third sector organizations have now come under closer scrutiny, particularly regarding the value provided, and the ability to tangibly demonstrate the social impact of funded organizations. This chapter compares and contrasts the performance measurement expectations of third sector funding bodies, and the perceived appropriateness of these measures to the values and goals of the third sector organization itself.

Literature

We now briefly review the current literature around the themes of performance measurement within the third sector environment.

Over the last decade the not-for-profit sector has been the focus of considerable attention from several perspectives. Once considered low in terms of economic benefit and value, many authors (Hind 1995, Moxham and Boaden 2007, Poister 2003, Salamon and Anheier 1997, Sargeant and Lee 2004) have emphasized both the current contribution of third sector organizations to society, and their latent potential within the economy, albeit without profit generation as their primary goal. Sargeant and Lee (2004) comment on the size and contribution of the voluntary sector to the UK economy, and note that the voluntary sector plays a highly significant role in modern society (Sargeant and Lee 2004).

Many different terms exist for organizations which provide community and social development services. In the UK much of the literature uses the terms 'voluntary' or 'non-statutory' to describe this work. In the US such organizations are often referred to as 'not-for-profit' or 'third sector'. Other terms which describe this work, and are used in a broader context are 'non-government organizations' (NGOs), although NGOs are generally used to indicate larger national or international organizations (Martens 2002). Other terms include the 'social economy', the 'independent sector' and 'community organizations'. The term 'third sector' appears to derive from US academic literature which defined four sectors: public or state funded, private or commercial, independent or non-profit, and finally voluntary associations or households.

Whilst the literature considering performance measurement within the third sector context is beginning to develop, much of this is still focused on the appropriateness of other sector models such as those derived from the private sector. Very little research appears to have been focused on the dynamics of the relationship between the funded organization which receives the money, and the funding organization which offers or provides the funding.

From an operations and quality management perspective the associated performance measurement and management literature indicate three broad and dominant themes. The first of these dominant themes is the efficacy of adopting private sector models of performance for voluntary sector organizations. Private sector performance measurement frameworks and models, involving financial and non-financial measures, have evolved considerably during the last twenty five years to such a point where several prominent strategic frameworks, such as the Balanced Scorecard (Kaplan and Norton 1992), the Performance Pyramid (Cross and Lynch 1988), the Performance Prism (Neely et al. 2002), and others (Bititci et al. 1997, Fitzgerald et al. 1991, Keegan et al. 1989) have been developed. Many of these frameworks or approaches have subsequently been successfully implemented within public sector organizations (Brignall and Modell 2000, Hood 1991, Pollitt 2006). However, from an organizational performance measurement perspective, it is generally acknowledged that less research has been specifically undertaken on voluntary or third sector organizations (Darcy 2002, Dart 2004, Morton 2008, Moxham 2009, Moxham and Boaden 2007, Radnor and McGuire 2004), yet this sector has increasingly become the focus of increased attention from both central and local government and practitioners and academics of several disciplinary perspectives (Crampton et al. 2001, Darcy 2002).

Whilst many authors have contributed to this debate there appears to be little guidance, other than that private and public sector performance models 'can be used' (Moxham and Boaden 2007) or 'adapted' (Radnor and McGuire 2004) for third sector organizations. Several researchers report a lack of development and sophistication in voluntary organization performance measurement (Moxham and Boaden 2007, Speckbacher 2003). There is published literature on the implementation of a balanced scorecard within a charity organization; however, this case reports a lack of evidence of the performance dashboard metrics that were deployed and the subsequent impact post-implementation (Manville 2007).

The second theme of third sector performance literature is the general consensus that auditing approaches, largely based on financial audit procedures used in the private and public sectors, fail to capture the true value of the third sector organization's activities, outputs and achievements. There has been a gradual but tangible shift in the call for more appropriate and sympathetic approaches to measure and report performance in third sector organizations. The balanced scorecard, which is the most widely cited performance measurement framework (Marr and Schiuma 2003) has been adapted for non-profit organizations by Kaplan (2001) and Neely et al. (2002). Speckbacher (2003) argues that holistic frameworks such as the balanced scorecard can be applied in the charity and voluntary sectors, but reports observing a general lack of understanding of these frameworks. Other frequently observed problems include a mismatch between the funding body's requirements for performance information and reporting mechanisms (Moxham and Boaden 2007). In the instances of such mismatches, Greiling (2007) suggests trust can sometimes act a substitute for performance measurement. Paton and Foot (2000) propose alternatives to audit-based reporting, in the form of using standards such as the ISO 9000 accreditation, or the SA 8000 standard for corporate social responsibility, to recognize governance and management of voluntary sector organizations. Ferlie and Steane (2002) consider the use of audit culture-based measurement in non-profit environments, and comment on the rigidity and unforgiving nature of such systems which focus purely on the achievement of measurable outputs from not-for-profit organizations (Ferlie and Steane 2002).

Baxter and Chau (2003) cite the difficulties of measuring the intangible social aspects of non-profit activities, and argue that there should be greater flexibility in the application of private financial measurement models to non-profit organizations. Mook et al. (2003) advocate the development of integrated social accounting – the combination of economic and social impact reporting which, they claim, is more appropriate to the objectives and challenges of non-profit organizations. Shaw and Allen (2006) offer an alternative view of funding relationships which rely less on financial-based audit approaches, and more on establishing a trust between the funding parties.

A third theme prominent in the voluntary sector literature is the nature of the actual performance measures used. Over the last ten years there has been a swell of support for impact measurement, rather than input measurement. Osborne et al. (1995) were early advocates of impact reporting, and describe impact measures as 'outcomes achieved on a targeted client population or organisation' (Osborne et al. 1995). Shar (2003) takes a broader view of impact measurement and suggests this approach can be used to measure the effect of the organization on specific aspects of the environment within which it operates. There is also evidence which suggests that voluntary organizations are under mounting pressure to demonstrate their achievements (Wainwright 2003). This would seem to be particularly strong for voluntary sector organizations which receive government funding (Cairns et al. 2005, Speckbacher 2003).

Shaw and Allen (2006) discuss the role of trust in the dynamics of non-profit funding relationships, and report the predominant use of audit-based systems to measure outputs of non-profit organizations. Shaw and Allen (2006) observe the (inappropriate) usage of quantitative audit-based approaches, which can only value in financial terms the work and outputs of a non-profit organization. The use and imposition of generic 'tick-box' forms for collecting feedback regarding performance is also observed and criticized (Radnor and McGuire 2004).

So, to summarize the major issues within the general literature, there is limited agreement that performance approaches developed in the private sector environment can be transferred to voluntary organizations; however, the importance of measuring the achievements of voluntary sector organizations is increasing, and there is broad agreement that impact measures are considered more appropriate than measures of input. There appears to be agreement within the literature that non-profit organizations have a greater value to their community, their stakeholders and society in general, than can be defined by financial audit-based measurement alone.

Funding Models

Voluntary sector organizations which receive government funding appear to be under increasing pressure to demonstrate achievements, yet particularly within these funding relationships there is evidence to suggest a wide predominance for reporting of arbitrary numbers, in the form of tick-box measures, even though these do not readily convey or relate to the goals, values and achievements of the voluntary organization. As a consequence there is a growing call for some approach employing social measurement which aligns more closely with the activities and achievements of voluntary sector organizations.

Regarding the issue of funding dynamics two important questions emerge from the literature. First, which types of measure would be more empathetic to the values, goals and achievements of a voluntary sector organization? And second, would such measures which are empathetic to a voluntary organization satisfy the reciprocal requirements of funding bodies which provide or offer funding? Before these questions can be addressed it is worth considering the different dynamics between these two perspectives, those of the funded and the funding organization.

The funded organization is focused on the delivery of its specific services to its chosen community. However, whilst reporting on how its funding is being used is not its primary focus, it is still an important aspect of its continued operation, if only to ensure that subsequent funding can be obtained in the future. From the perspective of the funded organization typical expectations regarding performance reporting include:

- alignment with the values and objectives of the funded voluntary organization, and
- efficiency in terms of gathering and reporting of information.

The alignment with values means being asked to report in a way which supports or emphasizes what the voluntary organization is trying to achieve. The efficiency refers to the ease of data collection and reporting.

A highly simplified model of operation is offered in Figure 7.1. This identifies four sequential activities, those of:

- funding application against a call for projects
- receiving of the funding
- social or community application of project
- post-funding impact review.

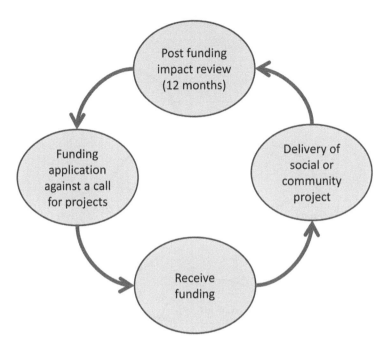

Figure 7.1   Typical annual cycle for funded organization

Though simplified, our experience suggests this is typical of the generic funding process and is reasonably representative.

The second perspective of the funding model is that of the funding body. The objectives here tend to be significantly different from those above. The funding organization is usually under pressure to demonstrate and appropriate funding process including:

- the transparency of the funding process
- to demonstrate an accountability and appropriate use of funding monies to its stakeholders
- to provide a robust process for finding allocation and decisions
- to obtain post-funding impact review data, and
- to ensure all process are appropriate to the economic and political climate.

When trying to ensure the above expectations are fulfilled, the funding body will almost certainly be at odds with the objectives and expectations of the voluntary organizations seeking funding. These conflicting expectations and requirements present a dilemma, where, in the majority of cases, the funding body holds the balance of power.

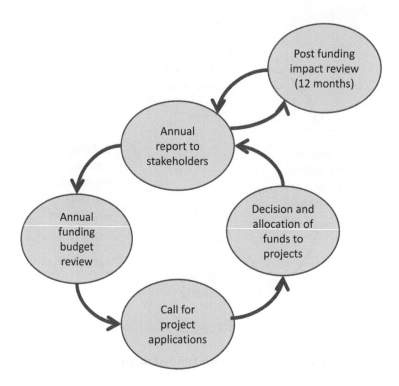

Figure 7.2   Typical annual cycle for funding organization

Figure 7.2 shows a simplified model of the typical funding cycle, which features a sequence of five activities:

- annual funding budget review
- call for project applications
- funding bid decision process
- report to stakeholders, and
- post-funding impact review.

Whilst both the above perspectives serve to deliver the same goal, that of positive social or community change, both processes are suited to their own specific needs and requirements. Ironically however, both perspectives are reliant on the other; they do not function without the involvement of each, so both must integrate to deliver the social or community change.

Figure 7.3 attempts to integrate both cycles, and indicates that the only activity in common to both is the post-funding impact review. This is where the funded organization is asked to report on the social impact of the funded project or programme, usually through the requirement of a formal reporting mechanism. It is this review activity, critical to both parties, which often lacks a relevance to the values and achievements of the funded organization.

We now consider the issues which emerge from both these models and contrast with themes found in the literature.

From the perspective of the funded organization a frequently observed theme is reporting of numeric data to provide information on the number of instances of an event. This form of performance reporting is often criticized because it does not align with the values and goals of the voluntary organization, and fails to convey their social and community achievements in a sympathetic way. This is a consistent theme within the third sector literature where mandatory performance reporting based on imposed or numeric targets is often criticized. Within the literature 'outcomes' are considered a measure of impact (Osborne et al. 1995) and are widely accepted as more appropriate, and of greater benefit to a voluntary organization than input measures alone (Shar 2003). Baxter and Chau (2003) and Shaw and Allen (2006), amongst others, discuss the observance of a 'tick-box' mentality in many funding agencies. Shaw and Allen (2006)

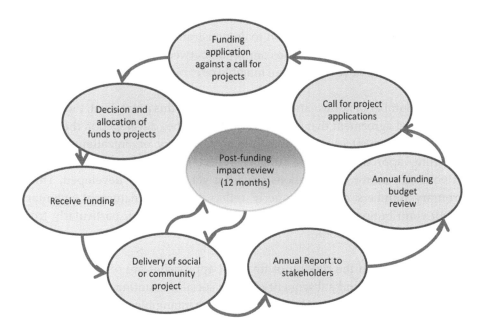

Figure 7.3   Combined funding model showing post-funding impact review common to both cycles

identify the intangibility of community services outcomes, which do not lend themselves to audit-based reporting. When assessing the mechanisms by which performance is reported a clear distinction can be seen between the requirements of government funding bodies and funding providers of a more philanthropic nature. For instance several examples were found where philanthropic funding organizations were more open to accept more social positioned performance evidence, such as visits to funded community schemes, and to meet and greet those that have benefited from, and contributed to, voluntary sector services.

From the funding body's perspective an important theme to emerge was the growing need to demonstrate achievements. In discussions with a local government funding body the requirement to ensure accountability for transparent and robust funding decisions appears to be paramount. The use of a post-funding impact review process to understand and quantify the outcomes of funding is also becoming more popular within third sector funding. Whereas ten years ago a voluntary organization might have been funded through rates relief or the provision of a property, with little expectation of performance reporting, today there is an expectation not only to justify their funding requirements (property and operating expenses), but also to clearly demonstrate what has been achieved or delivered through such funding; that is, the impact of funding on the community. In today's post-GFC economic climate, the social appropriateness of funding decisions is even more important, so as to be in a position to demonstrate how funding is being used for positive social outcomes. The connection between funding and delivery of social change has never been more tangible or explicit.

So, a number of issues can be in summarized at this point. First, there is still only limited agreement that performance approaches developed in the private sector environment can be transferred to voluntary organizations. Second, reporting approaches which suitably reflect the values and achievement of voluntary sector organizations have not yet been fully developed. Third, arbitrary numbers do not properly reflect the social nature of voluntary sector contributions, yet are still required to be reported, particularly from government funding bodies.

Problems with the rigidity of financial approaches are often cited (Ferlie and Steane 2002), and subsequent calls for social accounting appear to be on the rise (Mook et al. 2003). Difficulties with the intangible nature of voluntary sector work are also frequently noted (Baxter and Chau 2003, Shaw and Allen 2006). Whilst many authors are critical of these approaches, little appears to be offered as a way of an alternative.

When required to report organizational performance through measures which do not align well with the organizational values and achievements, many voluntary organization managers often become frustrated and dissatisfied with the reporting process. The objective of performance reporting is often to provide factual data regarding the progress of the funded project or initiative. Whilst reporting numbers, referred to as 'ticking boxes', provides this factual information to the funding provider, such an approach fails to recognize the detailed and often socially complex context of such programmes. It appears to be this reductionist approach to this complexity which often irritates and frustrates community organization managers; we recognize, however, that ultimately, if reporting of numbers is actually required by the funding body, then this situation is unlikely to change. So what alternatives are there to audit-based or financial reporting?

Anecdotal Performance Reporting

There is little, if any, reported research on the role and use of anecdotal performance reporting, and as yet it does not appear to have been defined or considered from a research perspective. Clearly, anecdotal performance reporting is not quantitative in the sense of providing hard numbers; it is qualitative in that it describes in greater detail the changes and effect on one's individual circumstances, much the same as a case study is deep and rich, and a survey is broad and shallow. It could be argued, however, that anecdotal evidence does provide an example of the outcome or impact of the community programme, albeit from one individual's perspective. As such, we consider anecdotal performance to be generally more sympathetic to, and reflecting of, a voluntary organization's values, goals and achievements.

Since by its very nature anecdotal evidence is generated from outside the voluntary organization it does not require any internal resources to produce it. It does, however, require management and coordination to be useful, but these tasks are considered minimal within the context of managing an organization. The potential for voluntary organizations to collect and produce a portfolio of anecdotal evidence, which can be provided alongside other reported performance metrics, may be worthy of further consideration. Perhaps the best feature of anecdotal performance reporting is that voluntary organization managers feel good about it, and that it reflects accurately and appropriately their activities and achievements. This in itself must have some value.

Despite the appeal of anecdotal performance reporting, we see several barriers to the greater use of this approach. First and foremost it remains contrary to accounting and audit-based approaches, and in spite of increasing criticisms of such approaches in the third sector, these are unlikely to change radically. Second, and related to the first point, is the fact that anecdotal performance reporting is by its nature intangible. It therefore remains to be seen if, and which type of, funding bodies will be more open to 'deeper and richer' outcome statements in this form. Finally, there is as yet no definition of what form and nature anecdotal performance reporting could be provided in. Nonetheless, we feel there is some validity in considering further the use of anecdotal performance as a potential parallel, if not alternative, means of reporting performance within a third sector organization.

Conclusion

In conclusion this chapter calls for further research to consider what forms of parallel performance reporting support and are compatible with audit-based approaches. There is clear circumstantial evidence that philanthropic funding bodies appear to be more flexible in the nature of performance reporting, to the extent of receiving anecdotal evidence in the form of newspaper clippings and visits to see programmes in action. Yet there is also evidence that many government funding bodies are yet to move from their intractable requirement for the reporting of arbitrary numbers, which in most cases fail to relate to the values or achievement of the voluntary organizations they support.

References

Baxter, J., and Chau, W.F. 2003. Alternative management and accounting research – whence and whither. *Accounting, Organizations, and Society*, 28, 97–126.

Bititci, U.S., Carrie, A.S., and McDevitt, L. 1997. Integrated performance measurement systems: a development guide. *International Journal of Operations and Production Management*, 17(5), 522–34.

Brignall, S., and Modell, S. 2000. An institutional perspective on performance measurement and management in the 'new public sector'. *Management Accounting Research*, 11, 281–306.

Cairns, B., Harris, M., Hutchinson, R., and Tricker, M. 2005. Improving performance? The adoption and implementation of quality systems in UK nonprofits. *Non-profit Management and Leadership*, 16(2), 135–51.

Crampton, P., Woodward, A., and Dowell, A. 2001. The role of the third sector in providing primary care services – theoretical and policy issues. *Social Policy Journal of New Zealand*, 17, 1–21.

Cross, K.F., and Lynch, R.L. 1988. The 'SMART' way to define and sustain success. *National Productivity Review*, 8(1), 23–33.

Darcy, M. 2002. Community management. How discourse killed participation. *Critical Quarterly*, 44, 32–9.

Dart, R. 2004. Being 'business-like' in a non-profit organisation: a grounded and inductive typology. *Non-Profit and Voluntary Sector Quarterly*, 33(2), 290–310.

Ferlie, E., and Steane, P. 2002. Changing development in NPM. *International Journal of Public Administration*, 25(12), 1459–69.

Fitzgerald, L., Johnston, R., Brignall, T.J., Silvestro, R., and Voss, C. 1991. *Performance Measurement in Service Businesses*. London: CIMA.

Greiling, D. 2007. Trust and performance management in non-profit organizations. *The Innovation Journal: Public Sector Innovation Journal*, 12(3), article 9.

Hind, A. 1995. *The Governance and Management of Charities*. Cambridge: Voluntary Sector Press.

Hood, C.C. 1991. A public management for all seasons? *Public Administration*, 69(1), 3–19.

Kaplan, R.S. 2001. Strategic performance measurement and management in non-profit organisations. *Nonprofit Management and Leadership*, 11(3), 353–370.

Kaplan, R.S., and Norton, D.P. 1992. The balanced scorecard – measures that drive performance. *Harvard Business Review*, January/February, 71–9.

Keegan, D.P., Eiler, R.G., and Jones, C.R. 1989. Are your performance measures obsolete? *Management Accounting*, June, 45–50.

Manville, G. 2007. Implementing a balanced scorecard framework in a not-for-profit SME. *International Journal of Productivity and Performance Management*, 56(2), 162–9.

Marr, B., and Schiuma, G. 2003. Business performance measurement – past, present and future. *Management Decision*, 41(8), 680–687.

Martens, K. 2002. Mission impossible? Defining nongovernmental organizations. *Voluntas: International Journal of Voluntary and Non-Profit Organisations*, 13(3), 271–85.

Milbourne, L., and Cushman, M. 2011. *From the Third Sector to the Big Society: how changing UK government policies have eroded third sector trust*. The 7th International Critical Management Studies Conference, Naples, Italy.

Ministry of Social Development website, at: www.msd.govt.nz [accessed: November 2009].

Ministry of Youth Development website, at: www.msd.govt.nz [accessed: November 2009].

Mook, L., Richmond, B., and Quarter, J. 2003. Integrated social accounting for nonprofits: a case from Canada. *Voluntas: International Journal of Voluntary and Non-Profit Organizations*, 14(3), 283–97.

Morton, S.A. 2008. Performance management in the voluntary sector, in *Performance Management: Multidisciplinary Perspectives*, edited by R. Thorpe and J. Holloway. Basingstoke: Palgrave Macmillan.

Moxham, C. 2009. Performance measurement: examining the applicability of the existing body of knowledge to non-profit organisations. *International Journal of Operations and Production Management*, 29(7), 740–763.

Moxham, C., and Boaden, R. 2007. The impact of performance measurement in the voluntary sector: identification of contextual and processual factors. *International Journal of Operations and Production Management*, 27(8), 826–45.

Neely, A., Adams, C., and Kennerley, M. 2002. *The Performance Prism*. Englewood Cliffs NJ: Prentice-Hall.

Osborne, S.P., Bovaird, T., Martin, S., Tricker, M., and Waterson, P. 1995. Performance management and accountability in complex public programmes. *Financial Accountability and Management*, 11(1), 19–37.

Paton, R., and Foot, J. 2000. Non-profit's use of awards to improve and demonstrate performance: valuable discipline or burdensome formalities? *Voluntas: International Journal of Voluntary and Non-Profit Organizations*, 11(4), 329–53.

Poister, T.H. 2003. *Measuring Performance in Non-Profit Organisations*. New York: Wiley.

Pollitt, C. 2006. Performance management in practice: a comparative study of executive, agencies. *Journal of Public Administration Research and Theory*, 16(1), 25–44.

Radnor, Z., and McGuire, M. 2004. Performance management in public sector: fact or fiction? *International Journal of Productivity and Performance Management*, 53(3), 245–260.

Salamon, L.M., and Anheier, H.K. (eds). 1997. *Defining the Nonprofit Sector: A Cross-National Analysis*. Manchester: Manchester University Press.

Sargeant, A., and Lee, S. 2004. Trust and relationships in the United Kingdom voluntary sector: determinants of donor behaviour. *Psychology and Marketing*, 21(8), 613–635.

Shar, R. 2003. *Ideas Underpinning Impact Assessment*. London: National Council for Voluntary Organisations.

Shaw, S., and Allen, J. 2006. 'We actually trust the community': examining the dynamics of a non-profit funding relationship in New Zealand. *Voluntas*, 17, 211–220, published online 27 September.

Speckbacher, G. 2003. The economics of performance management in nonprofit organisations. *Nonprofit Management and Leadership*, 13(3), 267–81.

Wainwright, S. 2003. *Measuring Impact: A Guide to Resources*. London: National Council for Voluntary Organisations.

8

Public Value and Performance Management in Third Sector Organizations

Pratima Dattani

Introduction

Over the past twenty years, the political economy of the UK's third sector has meant that third sector organizations (TSOs) have become increasingly involved in public service delivery: this involvement has threatened the sector's purpose, identity and independence and brought increased pressures for it to become more accountable and manage its performance. The majority of TSOs are small and have limited resources to assess how to measure and demonstrate effectiveness and performance and there has also been a huge growth in the quality systems industry, much of which uses models more applicable to the private sector which TSOs have often adopted these in order to win contracts or funding.

This chapter presents research which assessed whether 'public value', the new paradigm for public sector reform proposed by Moore (1995) and Benington and Moore (2011a), and the development of a performance management system (PMS), based on the 'public value scorecard' (Moore 2003), offer an 'alternative' to support TSOs so they can assume greater control over their purpose, demonstrate effectiveness and maintain independence. The research also considered whether the development of a public value scorecard through action research with TSOs provides an effective means of collaboration to achieve what Moore (2003) calls 'wider social results' and the 'strengthening of the (third sector) industry'.

The questions the research proposed were as follows:

1.   What is the understanding of performance management within the third sector organizations (TSOs) and how do they currently manage performance?

2.   Drawing on the concept of public value and the public value scorecard and using action research, can third sector organizations develop an 'alternative' performance management system (PMS) that could support them to demonstrate their effectiveness and independence?

Literature Review

CHANGING RELATIONS – A HISTORICAL CONTEXT

In a review of the changing nature of state and voluntary sector relationships, Lewis (1999: 258–9) identified three major shifts. Firstly, the balance within what was a 'mixed economy of welfare' shifted towards the state, with greater welfare effort and central government control. Then, there was the move towards the 'extension ladders approach'[1] associated with Beveridge (1948), a strong supporter of voluntary action who saw it providing a necessary complement to state services. The third 'sea change' came at the end of the twentieth century, under the influence of Thatcherite consumerism, with its challenge to the monopoly of public services.

THE THATCHER GOVERNMENT

The dominant philosophy of the Thatcher government was based on neo-liberalism,[2] which sought to expand the scale of the private sector and introduced quasi-markets in the public sector. The relationship was characterized by the third sector fulfilling a service agent role and it was

---

1   Throughout the rest of the twentieth century, the relationship between the two sectors focused on whether voluntary sector provision should operate between *parallel bars* (that is, competition) or *extension ladders* (that is, complementariness) (Sidney and Beatrice Webb 1912, cited in Alcock et al. 2004).

2   Neo-liberalism has been defined by Harvey as a theory of political economic practices that proposes that human well-being can best be advanced by liberating individual entrepreneurial freedoms and skills within an institutional framework characterized by strong private property rights, free markets and free trade. The role of the state is to ensure proper functioning of markets but otherwise the state should keep intervention to the minimum.

the impact of the community care legislation (1990) which had the greatest direct impact on changing the relationships between government and voluntary organizations. In the earlier part of the twentieth century, most public funding for voluntary organizations was provided in the form of grants. Contract funding changed this to fund the provision of particular services and was conditional upon performance and legal agreements. This new 'contract culture' involved significant changes in the operation of many TSOs including social care providers who were involved in this research.

The ideologically rooted cluster of techniques adopted in UK public service reforms in 1980s and 1990s were articulated by Hood (1991: 4–5, cited in Lewis 2005) as 'new public management' (NPM) encompassing public choice theory[3] and the principal agent theory where contracts provided the connection between 'principal' and the 'agent' and influenced the structural separation of purchasers and providers. NPM was based on the principle that economic markets should be models for relationships in the public sector. It suggested that policy and delivery functions should be separated and constructed as a series of contracts, and that a range of new administration technology should be introduced, including performance-based contracting, competition, market incentives and deregulation (Kaboolian 1998, cited in O'Flynn 2007).

NEW LABOUR AND THE THIRD WAY

NPM application became embedded within the UK's public sector and was pursued by New Labour from 1997. New Labour's 'Third Way' in a globalized marketplace portrayed the welfare state as inhibiting economic performance. It came with a new pragmatism to replace an era of the 'nanny state' of the left with market-led preferences of the right and an era of partnership between the state, market and civil society (Quinn 2008). The Third Way drew indirectly upon the communitarian writings of US commentators like Etzioni (1995)[4] and Putnam (1995) on the role of 'social capital'.

---

3   Public choice theory is that governments were unresponsive, inefficient, monopolistic and reflected inherent failures of government because politicians act on their own self-interest and there are self-interested bureaucrats who are not interested in efficiency (Hood 1991, in Hartley et al. 2008).

4   Etzioni's main idea is that individual rights and aspirations should be protected but that they should be inserted into a sense of the community (hence the name of the movement he created, 'Communitarianism'). Within the movement, the communitarian thinking developed in reaction to the 'me-first' attitude of the 1980s. Also the movement has sought to establish a common ground between liberals and conservatives, thus bridging

Under New Labour, while a mixed economy approach to welfare provision continued, the new relations between the state and the third sector were marked by significant investments that massively increased the scale and profile of the third sector in policy, planning and delivery.[5] The number of charities grew from 98,000 in 1991 to 169,000 in 2004. Total public funding to the voluntary and community sector doubled from less than £5 billion in 1996/97 to more than £10 billion in 2004/05. Public service delivery has become central to the third sector, with government funding now accounting for 38 per cent of total income for general charities, making it their largest contributor (Chater 2008). Within social care, the third sector earns 62 per cent of its income from statutory sources (IFF 2007, cited in Chater 2008).

CRITIQUE OF THE THIRD WAY – LOSS OF INDEPENDENCE AND 'DEVOLUNTARIZATION'?

The criticism about the Third Way's focus on the third sector supported this research's findings, particularly that of loss of independence and identity. Quinn (2008), for example, found that while there had been significant new investment, the funding agreements focused on government contracts and the sector was in danger of being co-opted as a tool of government compromising its independence and advocacy role. Lord Dahrendorf (cited in Brindle 2001) claimed that many TSOs had become nationalized: 'Larger charities have become … "quasi-government organizations"' and asked 'Is there not a an issue of independence which is the oxygen of charity …?' For Dahrendorf, the true spirit of civil society is found in thousands of initiatives that have nothing to do with government.

The NHS and Community Care Act 1990 removed a TSO's ability to even set the type of work undertaken (Kramer 1981, cited in Quinn 2008). For Quinn (2008) the 'contract culture' is associated with 'devoluntarization' (loss of identity) of service providers with upward accountability to the local authority

---

the continual division. The movement works to strengthen the ability of all aspects of the community, including families and schools, in order to introduce more positive values.

5   The Cross-Cutting Review (HM Treasury 2002) made the role of the third sector explicit in the reform of public services and delivery of statutory services. It identified barriers to effective involvement that lay in inadequate infrastructure and established Futurebuilders (2003), a £125 million capital investment fund to build capacity, and the ChangeUp (2004), involving £80 million to strengthen infrastructure including performance management. The Social Enterprise Unit was created in the Department of Trade and Industry and launched the Social Enterprise strategy. In 2006 the Office of the Third Sector was established in the Cabinet Office with a Minister for the Third Sector. There was a growing acceptance that overhead costs should be covered within contracts for public services – the full cost recovery principle.

and standards of professionalism associated with state provision. Seldon (2007, cited in Quinn 2008) argues that charities receiving more than 70 per cent of their income from statutory sources are already de facto state agencies and this can apply to one third of charities which deliver public services; Manser's (1974, cited in Quinn 2008) law states that an 'agency's freedom and effectiveness in social action or advocacy are in inverse proportion to the amount of public money it receives'.

Najam (2000, cited in Quinn 2008) claimed 'devoluntarization' is self-reinforcing, which introduces a risk of institutional isomorphism which Blake et al. (2006, cited in Quinn 2008) identifies as an '*Animal Farm* syndrome' where TSOs grow and change and look more like statutory departments whose functions they hope to inherit.

For McLaughlin (2004) the agenda of voluntary sector modernization involves the third sector embracing core tenets of the NPM and 'the sector is propelled from a role as an *agent* of modernisation able to exert pressure for change to a *subject* of modernisation with challenges for its own governance and performance' (my italics).

2009 – COALITION GOVERNMENT

In 2008, the Conservative Party published its Green Paper[6] that has formed the basis of its policy towards the third sector. David Cameron emphasized the centrality of voluntary action in his vision of 'social responsibility' where citizens take responsibility in their own communities. NCVO,[7] however, remained concerned that it only mentioned the service delivery role of TSOs with no explicit recognition of TSOs' campaigning and advocacy role.[8] The third sector's independence to speak out on issues and campaign for change continued to remain in serious doubt.

Following the Comprehensive Spending Review 2010, the current scale and pace of public spending reductions has significantly affected levels of funding for the third sector and local authorities are working towards providing only the statutory minimum level of services. Stephen Cook (2011) of *Third Sector* claimed there had been a 'sea change' in the coalition's approach to the

---

6 Conservative Party Green Paper titled 'Voluntary Action in the 21st Century'.
7 National Council for Voluntary Organisations, a representative body of over 8,000 voluntary and community sector organizations.
8 NCVO response (2009) to the 2008 Green Paper.

voluntary sector; for example, recent decisions about the strategic partners programme where, under Labour, 40 strategic partners (including NCVOs) received £62.9 million as core funding from central government grants. Now only 17 partners will receive £8.2 million until 2014 when this programme will end. These strategic partners have been told they must develop the 'Big Society' agenda. Cook claims: 'It doesn't look like core funding any more and one suspects there won't be much speaking out against the government. This approach is altogether more hard-nosed and businesslike.' The independence of the third sector and its core investment base is once again being called into serious doubt.

PERFORMANCE MANAGEMENT

Hood (2007) argued that the UK stands out amongst other countries in relation to the importance attributed to performance management. New Labour tried to improve the effectiveness of public services through the use of private sector principles, resulting in more than 300 headline performance targets applied to all government departments in 1998 (Radnor 2008). This centralized target approach to public service management has made notable improvements (such as patient waiting times for operations); however, Radnor's research (2008) describes major types of gaming and strategic behaviour surrounding targets.[9] Radnor and McGuire's (2004) research found that parallel systems were operated and concluded that performance management in the public sector is closer to fiction than to fact.

Performance Management Systems (PMS)

For Paton (2000, cited in CVAR 2003), 'performance' is a contested notion and a social construct that helps explains how it can be so multifaceted, problematic and ambiguous. Therefore, Radnor and McGuire (2004) contend that PMSs should constitute four building blocks which organizations need to understand: if performance management is about continuous service improvements there needs to be a relationship between strategy, people, organizational form/design and performance systems (see Figure 8.1).

---

9   The ratchet effect is where performance is restricted to well below productive possibility by target setters; the threshold effect is where a uniform output applying to all units gives no incentive for excellence; and lastly, where behaviour consists of manipulation of reported results – that is, 'hitting the target and missing the point' – a term coined by a senior civil servant in relation to health targets (Radnor 2008).

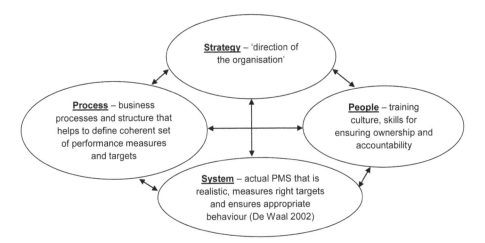

Figure 8.1   Radnor and McGuire's basis for performance management systems

Source: Adapted from Radnor and McGuire 2004.

Radnor (2004) claims that currently within the public sector performance is about measurement not management; the system is diagnostic not interactive; it does not allow for improvement; and overall there is a lack of ownership at all levels.

THIRD SECTOR AND PERFORMANCE MANAGEMENT

There is a range of drivers and trends including NPM strategies that means the third sector today operates in an environment permeated by 'expectations of measurement' (Paton 2003). Alcock et al. (2004) say there are, however, some particular features that need to be taken into account when considering implementation of performance improvement in the third sector; for example:

- *The stakeholder* mix is multiple and there is a pluralistic power structure where each stakeholder is likely to have different expectations of accountability and what constitutes performance improvement.
- *The environment* is ambiguous and complex. It comprises the specific *task* environment (such as other agencies operating in the field) and the *general* external environment which may be made turbulent because of changes in public policy.

- *The power of a TSO governing body* – TSOs are rarely free to define themselves without regard to external influences. While the governing body remains the point of final accountability, external influences need to be held in balance with internally established goals, mission and values (Harris 1998, cited in Alcock at al. 2004).

Manville (2007) and Somers (2005) found that although the knowledge base of performance management for social enterprise has increased, the literature covering TSOs is inadequate. Aston University (CVAR 2003) research found little research literature on the subject of performance improvement in the third sector and that the concept of 'performance improvement' appears to encompass such diverse issues as demonstrating accountability to stakeholders, setting objectives and meeting them efficiently and effectively, and developing organizational capacity.

PUBLIC VALUE

Mark Moore (1995) first developed the concept of public value as he was concerned that all too often public services were 'hitting the target but missing the point'. He proposed that public bodies re-orient to 'ends' such as health or well-being rather than value for money.

Moore's book *Creating Public Value* (1995) was written at the height of the dominance of the neo-liberal ideology around NPM and public value forms the basis for a paradigmatic change. Moore claims a *'post-competitive'* paradigm could signal a shift away from the primary focus on results and efficiency toward achievement of the broader goal of public value creation. In essence, Moore presents public value thinking as a means of focusing public services on delivering ends endorsed and supported by service users and their communities, where the role of the public service leader was to maximize the amount of public value created. This would then necessitate consideration of:

- *whether the proposed outcome is publicly valuable* – ensuring strategic goals and action are in line with the values, mission and purpose of the organization
- *whether it will be politically and legally supported* – ensuring that customers, citizens, stakeholders, sponsors and funders support the proposed action.

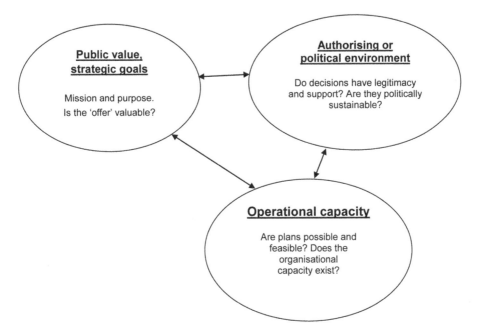

Figure 8.2   Creating public value – Moore's strategic triangle

Source: Moore 1995.

- *whether it is administratively and operationally feasible* – ensuring that the organization has the operational capacity, skills and competences to carry out the proposed action.
- Moore's strategic triangle represents this diagrammatically (Figure 8.2).

CREATING PUBLIC VALUE

The *scope* of the authorizing environment and the *process* of seeking authorization are key to Moore's proposition. Moore makes an important distinction between 'clients' – direct customers – and citizens. He argues that support is needed not just from those who will benefit directly but also from the wider community within which services are delivered. For example, taxpayers may implicitly support the provision of sheltered housing because they recognize the value to the wider society, even if they do not personally benefit. Co-production is also a vital component of a public value framework, which sees the dissolution of the boundaries between client and provider where the centrality of the user is a distinction between the user as consumer who seeks what is good for her/himself and the user as citizen who seeks what is good for society. The legitimacy of public bodies grows as their accountability to the public is strengthened and users behave as 'citizens acting through politics rather than consumers acting through markets' (Moore 1995: 44). Moore suggests that this public acceptance needs to be sought explicitly and deliberately to establish robust authority for action. If this authorization is not achieved, then the enterprise is vulnerable to criticism or to being abandoned. To achieve this authorization, there needs to be a process of engagement and deliberation. For Moore, the legitimacy of such public bodies is earned not just by their achievement of government targets, but by their relationship with publics – customers, citizens and stakeholders.

Benington (2011) defines public value as:

1. *'What the public values'* – the current focus is on public satisfaction but to establish robust measures the public is asked to 'make trade-offs' between competing sources of satisfaction; for example, in cases where public services may be of a regulatory kind.

2. *What adds value to the public sphere* – the 'public sphere' is about focusing on the wider public interest, not just current users but also on the long-term public good and needs of generations to come.

While neo-liberal economic approaches to value have concentrated on the measurement of exchange value (price in open markets), public value encompasses wider political (democratic dialogue and citizen engagement), social, economic and cultural and environmental aspects. Benington (2011) has argued that public value offers a potential development to NPM theory, which sought to bring in private sector doctrines and practices to public sector performance management and promoted the importance of consumers rather than citizens and the numerical quantification of quality through targets. Public value theory brings back accountability downwards towards the customer and citizen and emphasizes the importance of informed and knowledgeable citizens to give legitimacy to public services.

Integral to Moore's theory is a challenge to the prevalent performance management approaches that encourage compliance and managerial approaches rather than the entrepreneurial and innovative approaches needed to maximize the impact of public services.

HOW CAN PUBLIC VALUE BE MEASURED?

Collins (n.d.) says that public value challenges NPM's emphasis on reducing what is valuable to what can be quantified. NPM has a clear focus on results and achievement of performance targets, and critical performance objectives are centred on efficiency and economy and reconstruction of citizens as customers. In the public value paradigm, public managers have multiple goals in addition to achieving performance targets; for example, steering networks of providers to create public value, creating and maintaining trust and responding to collective preferences of the citizenry. In public value multiple objectives are pursued by public managers including service objectives, broader outcomes, creation of trust and legitimacy which requires a focus for managers from *results* to *relationships*.

Performance Management Systems

MEASUREMENT AND DEMOCRACY

Horner and Hutton (2011) say that public value involves advocacy for the greater role of public in decision-making and therefore performance management frameworks need to reflect key principles of public value measurement; in other words, the very process of measurement should create value, the system of performance management should blend with the strategic goals of an organization and it should allow for public debate and scrutiny and not be a top-down process.

PUBLIC VALUE CHAIN

For Benington (2011) the concept of public value highlights the importance of focusing on processes and outcomes not just inputs and outputs; it goes beyond public satisfaction towards economic, social, political and ecological value added to the public sphere. Moore's 'Value Chain' is an open systems model that envisions a complex production process (Figure 8.3).

The theory of public value urges creation of PMSs that tilt in the direction of the measurements down the value chain (satisfaction and outcomes) but continue to play close attention to organizational process measures as they support learning and reassure all that the organization is operating fairly, efficiently and effectively.

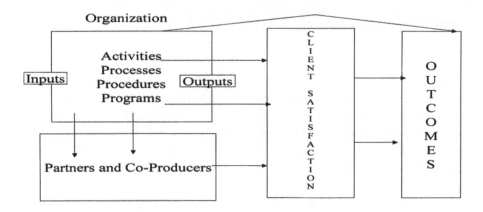

Figure 8.3   Production processes and value chains

Source: Moore 1995.

THE IMPORTANCE OF THE STRATEGIC TRIANGLE AS A MEANS OF MEASUREMENT

For Benington and Moore (2011) to be practically useful, a concept of public value has to not only stand alone and a philosophical concept made concrete with the technical construction of a measurement system but should also link closely to existing political aspirations (authorizing environment) and to organizational production and implementation (operations capacity). They claim that developing performance measures that recognize public value has to be dynamic and as contested as the political world and as uncertain and challenging as the operations world.

FOCUS ON OUTCOMES

Benington (2011) claims that public value is a focus on outcomes measured over the medium to long term. Public value outcomes are complex and contested, frequently involving trade-offs between competing priorities (Mulgan 2011). However, the concept of public value helps focus attention on the processes by which it is created or co-created and can therefore be used not only as a conceptual tool for strategic planning but also as a heuristic device to stimulate debate and dialogue on how to improve services, benefits and trust (Benington and Moore 2011).

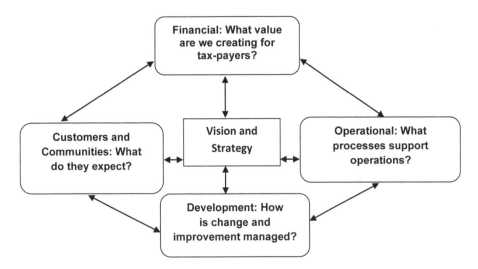

Figure 8.4   Financial and operational questions which assess an organization's system

Source: Adapted from Kaplan and Norton 1992.

The Balanced Scorecard

By the early 1980s there was a growing realization in the private sector that it was no longer appropriate to use financial measures as the sole criteria for assessing organizational success (Kennerley and Neely 2002). Kaplan and Norton (1996: 25) developed the Balanced Scorecard (BSC) to translate mission and strategy into objectives and measures, and organized this into four different perspectives: financial, customer, internal business process, and learning and growth. In Kaplan and Norton's view (1996: 30, 2001), strategies developed a cause-and-effect nature; for example, investments in learning lead to a better internal business process, which is likely to improve customer satisfaction, resulting in a higher return on investments to satisfy shareholders. They found that the organization's measurement system affects the behaviour of employees, and managers want to see a balanced presentation of both financial and operational measures that provide answers to four basic questions, as posed in Figure 8.4.

Radnor and McGuire (2004) say the BSC methodology is centred on a holistic vision of a PMS, a multi-dimensional framework that utilizes measurement as a means of describing an organization's strategy. Manville (2007) and others have shown how the BSC has evolved over the last decade (Table 8.1).

Table 8.1   Three generations of the Balanced Scorecard

First Generation Balanced Scorecard Johnson and Kaplan (1987) and Kaplan and Norton's seminal work (1992) which developed the BSC	Broke new ground by combining financial and non-financial performance measures grouped into 4 perspectives
Second Generation Balanced Scorecard Kaplan and Norton (1996)	Provided the basis for implementation and defined strategic objectives, linked together with a causal 'strategy map' to help identify activities and results to be measured
Third Generation Balanced Scorecard Neely et al. (2003) and Lawrie and Cobbold (2004)	Used 'Destination Statements' as the starting point for choosing strategic objectives, selecting measures and targets as a statement of where the organization seeks to be at a pre-determined time in the future

Source: Manville 2007.

Manville (2007) says there is a current gap in the literature regarding implementation of BSC in the third sector.

Public Value Scorecard

Moore (2003) in '"A rejoinder and an alternative to strategic performance measurement and management in non-profit organizations" by Kaplan and Norton', argues says there are some difficulties in adapting the BSC for the non-profit world. For example, financial measures are only a means to an end for TSOs and it is not clear who the 'customers' are. The BSC is also based on a competitive strategy and yet the key issue for the TSOs is not about developing a competitive advantage in the market but to 'strengthen the industry' and cooperate to deal with social problems, pooling combined resources that can make a greater contribution to the achievement of 'wider social results'.

AN ALTERNATIVE PUBLIC VALUE SCORECARD

Moore (2003) takes 'important wisdom offered by BSC' that non-financial process and outcome measures are important, that a measurement system can support execution of a strategy and that working through a strategic concept is more appropriate to TSOs than a competitive strategy. However, he challenges the reliance on a few outcomes because efforts to measure outcomes are expensive, slow to provide feedback and there is a need for information to hold organizations to account in real-time basis. Therefore he says TSOs will need a mix of outcomes, outputs, process and input measures to recognize value and ways of improving performance. Moore captures the 'public value scorecard' through the strategic triangle directing TSOs to three calculations (see Figure 8.5).

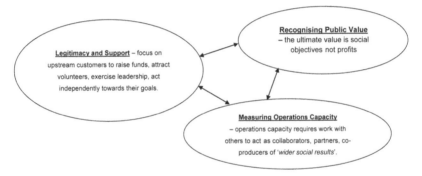

Figure 8.5   Public value scorecard

Source: Moore 2003.

For Moore there are crucial difference between the two concepts; in the public value scorecard the ultimate value is measured in non-financial terms and in desired aggregate social outcomes; it focuses attention on not just clients who benefit but also on other legitimators and authorizers. It focuses attention on productive capabilities for addressing large social results outside the organizational boundary and sees others in industry not as competitive but partners and co-producers. TSOs use measures of performance to strengthen the industry, not assume market share.

Research Strategy and Purpose

The purpose of this action research was to test if the development of Moore's public value scorecard could support third sector organizations to demonstrate collaboration, effectiveness and independence. Seven Chief Executive Officers (CEOs) were involved in the action research, of whom five headed social care providers. One organization, supporting people with learning disabilities, was supported to develop an organization strategy, and focus groups of service users, carers and staff provided the means of developing public value performance outcome measures. The outcomes of each stage were debated at the CEOs' sessions and the public value scorecard developed from this.

Research Analysis

UNDERSTANDING OF PERFORMANCE MANAGEMENT

This study confirms that TSOs need time and resources to understand performance management systems (PMSs) and that TSOs are using different quality systems or running parallel systems to serve the needs of multiple stakeholders and to attract funding.

The public value scorecard developed in this study demonstrated the potential to be the single PMS supporting Alcock et al.'s (2004) findings about particular features of performance improvement required in TSOs; that is, the potential to respond to TSOs' multiple stakeholders through a single and transparent reporting system, to be responsive to the TSO's general external environment and to enable the governing body to hold in balance external influences with the internally established mission, goals and values.

THE NEED OF TSOs FOR AN ORGANIZATIONAL STRATEGY TO DRIVE PERFORMANCE

The research confirmed that TSOs need to invest time and resources in developing organizational strategies with their stakeholders. The CEOs in the study recognized the importance of having an organizational strategy to drive performance improvements. The strategic triangle provides important guidance about how work could be done (Benington and Moore 2011b). For example, the participants in the study recognized that their authorizing environment was much wider than just funders and that managing these relationships could also create public value and would enable them to diversify their funding base.

THE CHALLENGE OF MEASURING PUBLIC VALUE

However, the process of developing a public value scorecard can challenge concepts of 'outcomes' and 'performance management' and can develop a better understanding of public value so that TSOs can overcome constraints presented by NPM. The study confirmed that TSOs are unclear how to demonstrate or measure 'outcomes'. The process of involving service users, carers and staff in selecting public value performance measures and the development of the scorecard with CEOs began to broaden the debate about what is meant by 'outcomes' and' performance management'. These discussions supported Benington's (2011) notion that public value is a focus on outcomes and confirmed Mulgan's (2011) view that the lessons for social value are that measures of value are only useful to the extent that they support negotiations and arguments about what needs to be done, about choices and trade-offs. The conversations undertaken with focus groups became value-creating and increased dialogue at different levels, increased involvement and increased trust amongst stakeholders.

For Moore (2003), public value has wider application to strengthen the third sector industry, and the collaborative efforts demonstrated by CEOs confirmed this. For Moore the public value scorecard works better for TSOs because their ultimate goal is not to capture and seize value for themselves but to give away their capabilities to achieve the largest impact on social conditions and find ways to leverage their capabilities with those of others.

The potential of TSOs adopting the public value paradigm and using the public value scorecard could enable them, as Benington and Moore (2011a) say, to strive for the 'ideal' of public value and become stronger and more effective at managing the 'real' which is politics and operations. For TSOs this research suggests that the 'real' is the political economy of the third sector presenting constraints such radical changes in social policy, new commissioning strategies that do not sufficiently involve the third sector in planning, competitive tendering processes and contracting that constrain third sector operations.

USING THE SECOND AND THIRD GENERATION BALANCED SCORECARD METHODOLOGIES

Using these methodologies to produce strategy maps and destinations statements respectively can support the development of a public value scorecard with stakeholders and this could support third sector organizations to develop 'alternative' performance management systems that can demonstrate their effectiveness and independence.

Using Different Methodologies   The research found that using the second and third generation balanced scorecard methodologies of strategy maps and destinations statements[10] respectively to develop the public value scorecard can have benefits. The strategy maps enabled stakeholders to understand the organizational strategy and develop public value measures against these using a simple 'Activities' and 'Outcomes' methodology. Developing strategy maps through facilitated dialogue enabled stakeholders to contribute actively to developing public value measures and it appeared to provide greater transparency and trust amongst the participants. Mapping the destination statements against the strategic triangle can offer both a clear view of the organization's strategy and demonstrate the organization's vision, values and ambition. As a tool, it can provide a balanced overview of the organization that could prove useful for reporting performance and developing greater legitimacy with the authorizing environment, including the wider public.

Demonstrating Effectiveness and Independence   For Benington and Moore (2011a) successive efforts to define public value can be key instruments of organizational leadership. This study demonstrates that when organizational leaders agreed to apply the concept of public value to develop specific performance measures with their authorizing environment (users, carers and staff) they gave their authorizers a chance to say whether they agreed or not. While the study did not test implementation, Benington and Moore say that when they create measurements that can record the degree to which an organization achieves these results, it challenges the organization to produce more. This dialogue and contestation helps the organization to explore possible ideas of public value and it affords the opportunity to gain control over the organization's purpose, create opportunities for co-production and allows TSOs to work in collaboration with others in the industry to achieve Moore calls 'wider social results'.

ACTION RESEARCH

Developing the public value scorecard through action research can be value-creating and can facilitate greater levels of collaboration, empowerment,

---

10 Kaplan and Norton (1996), Neeley et al. (2003) and Lawrie and Cobbold (2004) developed strategy maps and destinations statements to enhance the work of the BSC.

involvement and improvement amongst third sector organizations. The process of developing the public value scorecard through action research demonstrated that action research can be value-creating. The level of participation achieved and the levels of confidence, collaboration and empowerment (or Stringer's (1999: 9–10) 'liberating' and 'life-enhancing' aspects) that were demonstrated in such a short time was an unanticipated outcome of the research. The process itself appeared to create greater levels of trust and confidence within the focus groups and between CEOs. The CEO of Organization G's presentation to the staff workshop demonstrated the empowerment that he had experienced and that the process had helped him to reinforce the values of the organization and given him greater confidence to negotiate with commissioners, 'on the terms of the organization rather than that of the commissioners'. The CEO group felt encouraged by the contributions made by service users, carers and staff and about what they saw as '*real*' engagement. They felt this involvement would empower them in their negotiations with commissioners and other funders and would provide them with the evidence to demonstrate stakeholder engagement and strategy implementation to their Board members.

The research design shows that *improvement* and *involvement* are central to action research and this research demonstrated improvement of:

- *A practice of some kind* – the involvement of stakeholders, in understanding the organizational strategy and working towards defining public value measures, was a key improvement in practice.
- *The understanding of a practice by its practitioners* – the development of a public value PMS improved understanding amongst CEOs about the need for an organization strategy and that PMSs can enable them to both demonstrate effectiveness and exercise greater control and independence.
- *The situation in which the practice takes place* – the key improvement in the situation appeared to be the potential created within the CEO group for greater practical and ideological collaboration that could lead 'to strengthen(ing) the third sector industry' (Moore 2003).

Conclusion

All the literature points to the fact that there has been little research on the application of performance management systems (PMSs) for the UK's third sector. This research suggests that public value could offer an alternative to current PMSs and be a corrective to the pressures presented by NPM. It also points to the fact that public value could have wider application for UK's TSOs at a time when they have an important role in addressing inequality, social exclusion and disenfranchisement exacerbated by the current economic crisis.

There are other changes affecting the third sector: the coalition government is offering public sector employees the chance to create mutuals, cooperatives and social enterprises and is planning to 'outsource' the delivery of public services to ex-employees.[11] While this may present opportunities for the third sector, it could also mean that new players are entering the third sector and civil society with an agenda not necessarily that of social change and public value but as an extension of government and its claim of 'Big Society'.

Walker (2011) claims that there is a backlash to the top-down ideology of the Big Society, fuelled by people's anger at the cuts and the state of the economy. There are new movements forming; for example, national community movements such as 'Our Society' and 'UK Uncut' which mobilized people at the anti-cuts march in London on 26 March 2011. Besides them, Walker claims there are countless grass-roots activists and groups, many of them new, such as the campaign that defeated the government's recent forestry policy. For Walker, 'These movements are pushing back the ideology of big society and creating, um, big society ... [Has the government created] a bigger and better big society as a backlash to the policy of big society – is this the biggest nudge of all?'

The UK's third sector and civil society face unprecedented and significant new challenges in this new economic order. The findings of this action research hint at the potential for public value application for the UK's third sector. The current economic crisis and reduction of the role of the state means that members of the UK's third sector now have a greater responsibility to match their organizational effectiveness with real impact to affect social change.

References

Alcock, P., Brannelly, T., and Ross, L. 2004. *Formality or Flexibility: Voluntary Sector Contracting in Social Care and Health.* University of Birmingham website, at: www.bham.ac.uk.

---

11 Frances Maude, Minister for the Cabinet Office, Cabinet Office, 17 November 2010, Mutual Speech – Final Version, www.cabinetoffice.gov.uk.

Atweh, B., Kemmis, S., and Weeks, P. (eds). 1998. *Action Research in Practice: Partnership for Social Justice in Education.* London: Routledge.

Benington, J. 2011. From private choice to public value?, in *Public Value: Theory and Practice.* Basingstoke: Palgrave Macmillan, 31–49.

Benington, J., and Moore, M. 2011a. *Public Value: Theory and Practice.* Basingstoke: Palgrave Macmillan.

Benington, J., and Moore, M. 2011b. Conclusions and looking ahead, in *Public Value: Theory and Practice,* edited by J. Benington and M. Moore. Basingstoke: Palgrave Macmillan, 256–74.

Beveridge, W. (Lord). 1948. *Voluntary Action: A Report on the Method of Social Advance.* London: Allen & Unwin.

Blaug, R., Horner, L., and Lekhi, R. 2006. *Deliberative Democracy and the Role of Public Managers.* The Work Foundation [Online]. Available at: www. theworkfoundation.com.

Boyne, G., Farrell, C., Law, J., Powell, M., and Walker, R. 2003. *Evaluating Public Management Reforms.* Buckingham: Open University Press.

Brindle, D. 2001. The weaker partner, charities warned on sacrificing independence to the state. *The Guardian* [Online]. Wednesday 18 July.

Cairns, B., Harris, M., and Young, P. 2005. Building the capacity of the voluntary nonprofit sector: challenges of theory and practice. *International Journal of Public Administration*, 28, 869–85.

Cairns, B., Harris, M., Hutchison, R., and Tricker, M. 2005. Improving performance – the adoption and implementation of quality systems in the UK nonprofits. *Nonprofit Management and Leadership*, 16(2), 135–51.

Chater, D. 2008. *Coming in from the Cold? The Impact of the Contract Culture on Voluntary Sector Homelessness Agencies in England.* Voluntary Sector Working Papers no. 10. London: London School of Economics and Centre for Civil Society.

Collins, R. n.d. *Public Value and the BBC: A Report Prepared for The Work Foundation's Public Value Consortium* [Online]. Available at: www.theworkfoundation.com.

Cook, S. 2011. Editorial: Hard-nosed approach to strategic partnerships. *Third Sector*, 4 April [Online]. Available at: www.thirdsector.co.uk.

CVAR (Centre for Voluntary Action Research, Aston University Business School). 2003. *A Strategy for Performance Improvement for the Voluntary and Community Sector: A Scoping Paper for the Performance Improvement Strategy Steering Group* [Online]. Available at: www.cvar.org.uk.

Ellis, J., and Gregory, T. 2008. *Developing Monitoring and Evaluation in the Third Sector.* Charities Evaluation Services [Online]. Available at: www.ces-vol. org.uk.

Etzioni, A. 1995. *The Spirit of Community: Rights, Responsibilities and the Communitarian Agenda.* London: Fontana.

Gomes, R.C., and Liddle, R. 2009. The Balanced Scorecard as a performance management tool for third sector organizations: the case of the Arthur Bernardes Foundation, Curitiba, Brazil. *BAR*, 6(4), art. 5, 354–66, October/December [Online]. Available at: http://www.anpad.org.br/bar.

Hartley, J., Donaldson, C., Skelcher, C., and Wallace, M. (eds). 2008. *Managing to Improve Public Services*. Cambridge: Cambridge University Press.

Harvey, D. 2009. *A Brief History of Neoliberalism*. Oxford: Oxford University Press.

Haugh, H., and Kitson, M. 2007. The Third Way and the third sector: New Labour's economic policy and the Social Economy. *Cambridge Journal of Economics*, 31, 973–94.

Hill, D., and Sullivan, F. n.d. *Measuring Public Value 2: Practical Approaches*. The Work Foundation [Online]. Available at: workfoundation.net/assets/.../publications.

HM Treasury. 2002. *The Role of the Voluntary and Community Sector in Service Delivery: A Cross Cutting Review*. London: HM Treasury.

Hood, C. 2004. Gaming in Targetworld: the targets approach to managing British public services. *Public Administration Review*, 66(4), 515–521.

Hood, C. 2007. Public services management by numbers. Why does it vary? Where has it come from? What are the gaps and puzzles? *Public Money and Management*, 27(2), 95–102.

Horner, L., and Hutton, W. 2011. Public value, deliberative democracy and the role of public managers, in *Public Value: Theory and Practice*, edited by J. Benington and M. Moore. Basingstoke: Palgrave Macmillan, 112–125.

Horner, L., Lekhi, R., and Blaug, R. 2006. *Deliberative Democracy and the Role of Public Managers, The Work Foundation's Public Value Consortium* [Online]. Available at: www.the workfoundation.com.

Johnson, H.T., and Kaplan, R.S. 1987. *Relevance Lost*. Boston: Harvard Business School Press.

Kaplan R.S. 2002. The Balanced Scorecard and nonprofit organizations, *Balanced Scorecard Report*, November–December, 1–4.

Kaplan, R.S., and Norton, D.P. 1992. The balanced scorecard – measures that drive performance. *Harvard Business Review*, 70(1), 71–9.

Kaplan, R.S., and Norton, D.P. 1996. *The Balanced Scorecard: Translating Strategy into Action*. Boston: Harvard Business School Press.

Kaplan, R.S., and Norton, D.P. 2001. Transforming the balanced scorecard from performance measurement to strategic management: Part I. *Accounting Horizons*, 15(1), 87–104.

Kaplan R.S., and Norton, D.P. 2004. *Strategy Maps: Converting Intangible Assets into Tangible Outcomes*. Boston: Harvard Business School Press, Chs 1 and 2.

Kelly, G., and Muers, S. 2002. *Creating Public Value: An Analytical Framework for Public Service Reform*. London: London Strategy Unit, Cabinet Office [Online]. Available at: www.strategy.gov.uk.

Kennerly, M., and Neely, K. 2002. A framework of the factors affecting the evolution of performance measurement systems. *International Journal of Operations and Production Management*, 22(11), 1222–45.

Lawrie, G., and Cobbold, I. 2004. Third-generation balanced scorecard: evolution of an effective strategic control tool. *International Journal of Productivity and Performance Management*, 53(7), 611–623.

Lewis, J. 1999. Reviewing the relationship between the voluntary sector and the state in Britain in the 1990s. *International Journal of Voluntary and Nonprofit Organisations*, 10(3), 255–270.

Lewis, J. 2005. New Labour's approach to the voluntary sector: independence and the meaning of partnership. *Social Policy and Society*, 4(2), 121–31.

Manchester Business School. 2008. *Managing within Performance Regimes and Delivering Public Value*. Development and Research Consortium, Centre for Public Policy and Management, University of Manchester [Online]. Available at: www.mbs.ac.uk/research/performanceregimes.

Manville, G. 2007. Implementing a balanced scorecard framework in a not-for-profit SME: Bournemouth University, Poole, UK. *International Journal of Productivity and Performance Management*, 56(2), 162–9.

McLaughlin, K. 2004. Towards a 'modernised voluntary and community sector? Emerging lessons from government – voluntary and community sector relationships in the UK. *Public Management Review*, 6(4), 555–62.

Moore, M. 1995. *Creating Public Value*. Cambridge MA: Harvard University Press.

Moore, M. 2003. *The Public Value Scorecard: A Rejoinder and an Alternative to 'Strategic Performance Measurement and Management in Non-Profit Organizations' by Robert Kaplan*. The Hauser Center for Nonprofit Organizations, The Kennedy School of Government, Harvard University, May, Working Paper no. 18.

Moore, M. 2011. Public value in complex and changing times, in *Public Value: Theory and Practice*, edited by J. Benington and M. Moore. Basingstoke: Palgrave Macmillan, 3–7.

Moxham, C., and Boaden, R. 2007. The impact of performance measurement in the voluntary sector: identification of contextual and processual factors. *International Journal of Operations and Production Management*, 27(8), 826–45.

Mulgan, G. 2011. Effective supply and demand and measurement of public and social value, in *Public Value: Theory and Practice*, edited by J. Benington and M. Moore. Basingstoke: Palgrave Macmillan, 212–223.

Neely, A. 1999. The performance management revolution: why now and what next? *International Journal of Operations and Production Management*, 19(2), 205–28.

Neely, A., Bourne, M., Mills, J., Platts, K., and Richards, H. 2002. *Strategy and Performance, Getting the Measure of your Business.* Cambridge: Cambridge University Press.

Neely, A., Marr, B., Roos, G., Pike, S., and Gupta, O. 2003. Towards the third generation of performance measurement. *Controlling,* March/April, 129–35.

New Economics Foundation and the Performance Hub. 2007. *Banking on Outcomes for the Third Sector: Useful? Possible? Feasible?* [Online]. Available at: www.performancehub.gov.uk.

O'Flynn, J. 2007. Research and evaluation: from new public management to public value: paradigmatic change and managerial implications, *The Australian Journal of Public Administration,* 66(3), 353–66.

Osborne, S.P., and McLaughlin, K. 2004. The cross-cutting review of the voluntary sector: where next for local government–voluntary sector relationships? *Regional Studies,* 38(5), 573–82.

Paton, R. 2003. *Managing and Measuring Social Enterprises.* London: Sage.

Punniyamoorthy, M., and Murali, R. 2008. Balanced score for the balanced scorecard: a benchmarking tool. *Benchmarking: An International Journal,* 15(4), 420–443.

Putnam, R. 1995. Bowling alone: America's declining social capital. *Journal of Democracy,* 6 (January), 65–78.

Quality Standards Task Group. 2004. *Improving our Performance: A Strategy for the Voluntary and Community Sector.* London: NCVO.

Quinn, A.G. 2008. *Social Capital: An Assessment of its Relevance as a Conceptual and Policy Tool.* Voluntary Sector Working Paper no. 9. London: London School of Economics and Centre for Civil Society.

Radnor, Z. 2008. Introduction to process and performance management for public services and strategic performance management systems. Presentation slides at the Performance Management Module, December, University of Warwick.

Radnor, Z., and De Waal, A.A. 2007. Performance management analysis for public sector and non-profit companies: how is performance driven in your organisaton? Handout at Performance Management Module, December.

Radnor, Z., and Lovell, B. 2003. Success factors for implementation of the balanced scorecard in a NHS multi-agency setting. *International Journal of Health Care Quality Assurance,* 16, 99–108.

Radnor, Z., and McGuire, M. 2004. Performance management in the public sector: fact or fiction? *International Journal of Productivity and Performance Management,* 53(3), 245–260.

Somers, A. 2005. *Shaping the Balanced Scorecard for Use in UK Social Enterprises.* London: Social Enterprise London.

Stringer, E.T. 1999. *Action Research*, 2nd edn. Thousand Oaks CA: Sage.

Walker, C. 2011. Big society is dead – long live big society. *Third Sector*, 4 April [Online]. Available at: www.thirdsector.co.uk.

PART III:

REFLECTIVE PRACTICE FROM THE

THIRD SECTOR

Overview of Part III: Reflective Practice from the Third Sector

As previously discussed in Parts I and II of this text, the third sector has traditionally comprised community-based organizations which rely on voluntary support to deliver public services. This environment is vastly different from the large corporate, private for-profit sector from which many of the performance measurement and management models and frameworks are developed and first emerge. Whilst third sector practitioners have long been aware of this important differentiation, several chapters presented in this text argue that a shift to a more surplus-centred business model would be appropriate for many third sector organizations. Our experience of third sector organizations does indeed suggest that whilst profit is not a primary objective, there is usually a desire in make a small surplus on funded projects, which can be used for discretionary projects and to underpin other non-funded but necessary work.

This section offers practitioners the opportunity to contribute their experience in the form of case studies and the application of practical experience from working with and within the third sector. All the chapters are therefore contributed by practitioners with experience of consulting for or managing third sector enterprises. The first chapter in this section, by Aonghus Sammin, John O'Byrne, Cáthál Wilson and Patrizia Garengo, provides a case study of performance measurement design and implementation in a not-for-profit organization in Galway, Ireland. COPE Galway is a charity that provides services to the most isolated in their community, including a refuge for women and children affected by domestic violence, accommodation for those experiencing homelessness, and sustenance and social supports for older people at home.

The second contribution, by John Merritt from Coastal Credit Union, UK, considers the role and position of credit unions from a democratic sociopolitical perspective. This is an exploration of the changing 'space' within which credit unions are operating now and potentially will have to operate within in the foreseeable future.

The third chapter, by Brett Knowles (Founder of PM2 Consultancy, Canada), Richard Greatbanks and Graham Manville looks at the application of two popular strategy performance models, scorecards and strategy maps, and their application to third sector organizations. This short contribution identifies ways in which third sector organizations can improve their approach to service provision, and bring their organizational processes to a more business-like model.

The fourth contribution in this section, by Gareth Rees and Richard Greatbanks, outlines the structure and nature of the Peruvian third sector and then provides a brief case study of a Peruvian non-government organization (NGO), SOS Faim. This analysis serves to highlight some of the similarities and differences across the third sector globally.

The final contribution to the practitioner section, by Iain Lucas from RISE Computers Ltd and David Newton of West Itchen Community Trust, offers an informal review of a six-year collaborative effort to develop effective performance management tools for small and medium-sized social enterprises (SMSEs). This chapter examines the requirements for measuring and managing performance, and the challenges of ensuring such measurement is appropriate and valuable to the social enterprise.

This section draws together the experience of several third sector practitioners and provides a real-world international view of the changes, challenges and potential in third sector organizations around the world.

9

A Cooperative Development Approach to Performance Measurement in a Not-for-Profit Organization: The COPE Galway Case Study

Aonghus Sammin, John O'Byrne, Cáthál Wilson and Patrizia Garengo

Introduction

Performance measurement can often be overlooked in charitable or not-for-profit (NFP) organizations as it can be seen as something that belongs in the private sector and commercial organizations. However, NFP organizations have similar challenges to commercial organizations, albeit with a different focus. On one hand, they should have a purpose and therefore strategic objectives that need to be tracked. They have income, expenses and a balance sheet that need to be managed, and whereas the focus may not be on making a profit, it is essential to fund services and operations. Finally, they have many stakeholders and therefore have a much broader accountability to society as a whole than the average private company. This means that performance measurement and being accountable for what is done is essential for NFP organizations. On the other hand, NFP organizations are differentiated in comparison with their commercial counterparts and, as a consequence, there is a need for a different approach in performance measurement. As Boland and Fowler (2000) highlight, NFP organizations have no profit-maximizing focus, little potential for income generation and no bottom line against which performance can ultimately be measured. Most of the NFP sector organizations still generate most of their income from the government and non-government funders, and have to account to several stakeholders, including funders, donors, volunteers, employees, clients and beneficiaries.

This study outlines a cooperative development approach to performance measurement in an NFP organization called COPE Galway, to highlight both the relevance of performance measurement in NFP organizations and the need for a different approach. What follows is, firstly, a description of the organization, in which a suitable performance measurement system is defined, outlined and put in place using predefined methods and software tools. The system was designed and implemented using an action research approach by simply examining the practicalities of what was required, defining an approach and focusing a software tool to make the system as efficient as possible. Secondly, looking back to the available studies on performance measurement in NFP organizations, we identify the main determinants that a NFP organization should consider in implementing an effective performance measurement system.

A Cooperative Development Approach based on Action Research

Given the poor literature on the investigated topic, and the difficulty in gathering information on managerial practices in NFP organizations, the action research approach was considered as the most appropriate methodology to use: it supports practical problem-solving and expands scientific knowledge by involving researchers and practitioners, acting together on a cycle of activities with underlying generative mechanisms, to contribute to the development of a theory (Eden and Huxham 1996). That is because the approach is performed collaboratively in a real situation, using data feedback in a cyclical process, and it increases the understanding of a given organizational situation. The convergence of managers' and researchers' interests makes it easier to access a large amount of information, which is usually not available to researchers when carrying out case studies or surveys (Schein 1987). As a matter of fact, when researchers support managers' decisions, they gain access to detailed quantitative data from documents and databases and gain qualitative knowledge about the actual organizational context which are otherwise difficult to obtain.

Even Kaplan (1998), the designer of the Balanced Scorecard, described the importance of action research in developing research on the implementation of a Balanced Scorecard. He defined action research as the methodology able to promote the linkage of theory and practice, and the creation of new knowledge and new practices to study the performance measurement field.

This methodological consideration drove our decision to illustrate the COPE Galway case. In the following, we briefly describe the organizational profile of COPE Galway and its experience in implementing a performance measurement system.

COPE Galway Profile

COPE Galway is a charity based in Galway city in the west of Ireland. It was founded in the 1970s. Currently, the organization employs approximately 100 people, headed by a CEO and management team, with the majority of employees working directly in service provision. The company also has a strong network of volunteers.

The organization has a budget of almost €4 million of which 80 per cent is funded by state agencies, the balance being made up of fundraising and service income. Over 80 per cent of expenditure is on staff costs, as the service provided requires a high level of staff contact.

It has a Board of Directors, which provides governance and oversight through meetings and through the effective operation of four sub-committees; namely, finance, operations, property and marketing. The Board is primarily made up of local people who bring a broad range of skills, experience and contacts to the organization.

COPE Galway has three primary service areas – homelessness, domestic violence and older people. It also has an administration function, which provides shared services like human resources, finance, communications and fundraising. The organization has a head office and several centres throughout Galway, from which it provides emergency and follow-on accommodation, drop-in centres and catering services as well as running outreach services for the wider county.

The Performance Measurement System Implementation

In 2004, COPE Galway created an integrated strategic plan, with mixed success. The strategic planning process was productive and motivating for service staff, who were very much involved in the execution of the strategy. However, tracking and measuring the achievement of strategic objectives was difficult. Some of the reasons for this difficulty were the lack of an effective performance measurement system along with the integrated nature of the plan across different service areas and the lack of useful tools to track progress and report back.

When the company restarted the strategic planning process in 2007, it was decided that each service area would create its own plan, consistent with the overall company vision and values. In tandem with this, the Board of Directors initiated its own development plan for the company, to clarify its 'brand', its place in the community and its funding strategy as a whole.

With these different initiatives taking place, the Board required a performance measurement system to simply answer the question 'Are we doing what we said we would do?' Although the measurement of performance was difficult in the first strategy review which took place, some key needs for implementing a performance measurement system became clearer. For instance, an underlying goal or vision for each service area, especially ones that dealt with disadvantaged or vulnerable people, was about the prevention or elimination of the conditions that caused these problems in the first place. This was a recurrent theme which staff were passionate about and was reflected in the vision and values of the organization. However, as time elapsed, it was difficult to show any progress in the achievement of these goals as the activities which could drive change, for example, advocacy or resettlement work, were not funded and therefore impossible to implement fully, notwithstanding the efforts by staff across the services. The Board of Directors, in its development plan, took a view that if the organization was serious about these goals then it needed to put resources behind the drive to reach them and measures to track their achievement.

Another problem with the initial strategic planning process was the number of initiatives that were included. A wish list of goals was published, without implementation being thought through, creating an undeliverable expectation. In an ever-present situation of scarce resources, performance measurement forces participants to prioritize and focus on the really important things and keep wish lists for another day.

The last major reason for implementation was to give the Board line of sight of the organization. There was a need for a scorecard or a dashboard of some kind to maintain a balanced view and to coordinate the various reporting tools and processes that were in place, such as financials, risk register, quality assurance and service reports. In this way, the Board felt it could measure its own stewardship of the organization.

The First Design of the Performance Measurement System

In order to implement a performance measurement system, the Balanced Scorecard proposed by Kaplan and Norton (1996) with its four perspectives (financial, customer, internal and growth) was considered, but its application was not possible as the organization needed to maintain the focus on the four departments before applying the perspectives of the Balanced Scorecard. As a lot of the strategic objectives had been developed and clarified for all service areas, COPE would be faithful to this process and use these objectives as the basis for identifying performance measures.

This simpler approach meant that the four key departments – of homeless services, domestic violence, senior support services and head office – were used as the top level perspectives, with strategic themes and objectives below this. As the organization set out on this type of performance measurement, it was appropriate (as it is in every organization) to change 'as much as necessary but as little as possible'. This involved using the terminology and data that were already familiar rather than introducing unnecessary changes.

Once the sub-plans, themes and objectives were laid out there were over 400 objectives within 76 strategic themes across 7 departments (or sub-departments), as illustrated in Table 9.1. This presented a challenge in terms of the number of initiatives to be tracked and was similar in that regard to the previous strategic planning process of some years earlier. Furthermore, the 400+ objectives stated at the detail level were not a homogenous set of 'SMART'

Table 9.1   Objectives within COPE Galway

Department	Themes	Objectives
Homeless Services	11	50
Senior Support Services		
Community Catering	13	87
Sonas	13	64
Domestic Violence	14	48
Head Quarters		
Human Resources	7	34
Finance	3	20
Development Plan	15	103
Totals	**76**	**406**

Table 9.2   Implementation process in COPE Galway

Department	Themes	Objectives
Homeless Services	Range of Accommodation	
		To identify the accommodation needs of homeless people
		The provision of one bedroom units for single person households
		The provision of appropriate long term housing for people
		A housing access service to assist people who are homeless
		Develop working relationships with the Probation and Welfare Service
	Campaigning	To have a clear mechanism within Cope to progress campaigning issues in relation to homelessness
		To campaign for an increase in the rent allowance rent cap levels
		To campaign for a full and comprehensive count of the number of homeless people
		To campaign for all year round low threshold accommodation for rough sleepers
		To campaign for an increased provision of one bed social housing units
		To campaign for the provision of residential and community based detox and rehab services
	Partnerships	That Copes input at Homeless Forum Level is focused, specific and effective
		To seek to review the membership and operation of the membership of the VHS Galway
		To put in place arrangements for quarterly liaison meetings at organisational level
		Develop closer working relationships between Cope homeless services
		Develop working partnerships with organisations
		To seek to meet with voluntary housing providers operating in Galway
	Quality/Evaluation/ Review/Research measurement	
		The full roll out of the Cope quality standards system
		Introduce the national standards for emergency accommodation
		To plan for and implement changes arising from the quality standards introduction and roll out
		Quarterly seminars and workshops on best practice and developments
		That annual service plans for each individual Cope service/project is in place
	Supports	To identify and document the gaps in current service provision within Cope emergency accommodation projects
		Devise a plan to address these gaps by reviewing and updating this plan
	Staff Development	An audit of the current skills base and deficits/gaps for individual homeless services staff be carried out
		The current training planning process to be reviewed and changes implemented
		Develop a specification and role brief for a training and development representative
		A system to be devised to ensure that adequate staffing cover is available
		That regular supervision and annual appraisal are taking place for all staff.
		That a compulsory system for feedback and reflection following individual and team training within one month of the training taking place is put in place
		That staff team away days are scheduled to take place twice yearly - to be introduced in 2008
		An ethos of consultation with front line staff be developed
	Resources	Secure ongoing funding for Ruislip Manor
		Secure the necessary office space required for the operation of resettlement services
		Carry out a costing of this strategic plan

objectives but rather a mixture of objectives, tasks, projects and so on, as would be expected when different plans with different authors are combined. To illustrate this, Table 9.2 sets out 6 of the 11 themes for homeless services and their relevant objectives.

In order to measure whether the objectives were being achieved or not we took a pragmatic, if quite simplistic, approach to this and gave each objective a simple 0–100 per cent score (this was mainly due to the limitations of the software used – see below). A zero score meant no progress at all and a 100 per cent score meant the objective was achieved. Although simplistic and subjective, it was a starting point and did not require a lot of set-up time.

The Implementation Process

Although the design process was at the first phase, and numerous further improvements would be necessary, the researchers, along with the Board of Directors, decided to start the implementation phase. It was clear that the change process would be long and difficult, and the people involved needed to see some positive impact to be involved. An incremental approach would have delayed the entire project, so the team decided to use simple software to support the first collection and analysis of data.

Improving an organization's performance should start with measuring it and gaining an understanding of the factors that influence it. In order to do this effectively, successful companies have expanded the exercise from just top management to involve the entire organization and provide insight as to where the organization has been, where it is now and where management envisions it is headed. Doing this requires more than an in-house solution based on Microsoft Excel. An integrated environment is required that combines forward- and backward-looking metrics, business rules, performance maps and dashboards that speak to an individual's specific requirements, predictive analytics and flexibility. This all needs to integrate easily with existing information systems and offer an easy-to-use 'adopt and roll-out' package. Finally, a strong, experienced implementation team is needed that provides education, training and change management in order to secure organizational buy-in. A number of solutions were considered and a simple piece of software that represented the Balanced Scorecard was used. This was inexpensive and intuitive to use and, although limited in its application (for instance the 0–100 scoring as outlined above), it allowed for rapid implementation, even if it could not satisfy all the organizational needs.

Once the hierarchy (see Table 9.1) was clear, the administration assistant entered the data into the system. This was followed by a simple meeting with each relevant centre manager and they were asked to give a subjective view of 0–100 for each objective that they owned. This first set of interviews gave an approximate view of overall progress but also raised some issues around the consistency of data entry, subjective judgements and a perceptible level of resistance among users. To deal with the resistance among staff the Board prepared a communication which simply stated the objective of finding out how the individual plans were going and what, if any, issues were preventing progress. It was not going to be used as a punitive tool, for poor performance against objectives. It was agreed to update progress at two-monthly intervals to coincide with sub-committee and board meetings. Staff have now got used to the bi-monthly process and it allows them to reflect on the bigger picture of service development.

During this time other software solutions were also researched to overcome the limitations of the existing one. Eventually a vendor called QPR was selected, as their scorecard software had a number of improvements such as:

- more flexibility on defining performance measures
- multi-user functionality to allow researchers to roll out directly to staff enabling a more collaborative real-time process
- ability to also combine some of other controls such as risk management and quality framework processes.

QPR's software and support options were the preferred solution and it was agreed that COPE Galway would act as a reference site. It looked a flexible and quick-to-implement performance management software supporting a multitude of areas; from managing strategy to monitoring risk, controls, quality and operational performance. It offered powerful online collaboration features, accountability and target-setting that engaged employees across the organization to continuously improve performance, quality and compliance. The QPR performance management solution provided a complete suite to manage and communicate company strategy, to measure and improve performance, performing powerful ad hoc analysis on business data, and for making performance improvement an organization-wide exercise. It helped the organization gain insight into its strategy and operations, its execution, weaknesses and strengths, and into the ongoing prioritization and management of initiatives towards improving performance and managing transformation.

It should be noted that there is a cost–benefit consideration with the introduction of the new software as QPR had already been through this process once and wanted to augment what they already had. It was determined, however, after much consideration that the benefits which are outlined below outweighed the two primary costs which included the investment in additional training requirements and the time required to work out new performance measures and key performance indicators (KPIs).

It was determined, however, that the impact from the introduction of the QPR system should be minimized as much as possible. This was done primarily through training.

- The software vendor provided training while at the same time its staff were able to migrate their current scorecards onto the new platform. In addition to the capabilities of the software, it would enable them to manage and communicate in a more efficient way.
- A one-day training course/workshop was designed specifically for COPE Galway and delivered on site by Katalis and the staff of the software vendor in an intensive session. In that session, key COPE Galway staff members were introduced to the features of the products and a sample of COPE Galway's existing scorecard was entered into the products.

Subsequent to this workshop COPE Galway and QPR have had a remote working session where a QPR expert was able to access the developed scorecard and make changes in collaboration with the COPE Galway staff.

During the implementation of the new software, the existing scorecard measures were migrated to the new system in order to facilitate the process. The existing method of meeting with centre managers and recording their subjective comments continued. In this way the transition was made to seem less serious, albeit without the improvements in the system being implemented. Throughout 2009 and 2010, good incremental progress was noted across a range of objectives, and experimentation with the system was encouraged. The QPR report was also supplemented with a short narrative from each plan-holder, including some detail, about areas progressing well, and those requiring further focus. By combining QPR ScoreCard, QPR FactView and QPR Portal, the identified software offered an end-to-end performance management solution that spans planning, communication, measuring and consolidation, operational analytics, business intelligence, reporting, alerting, initiatives management and data integration: its target is to help organizations improve their performance effectively and achieve defined targets.

In the fourth quarter of 2010, the organization began another round of strategic planning to cover the 2011 to 2013 period. This process was quicker and easier due to the inputs from the existing scorecard and key information about how objectives had been achieved. Currently, the new agreed objectives are being updated into the system for the next three years. There is also a plan to include the organizational risk register and to extend the system out to the centre managers to update their own information. Further experimentation on how performance is measured (such as actual real scores rather than 0–100 scoring) is continuing.

Discussion

In the last ten years, academic and practitioners have underlined the growing need for NFP organizations to demonstrate their achievement (Moxham and Boaden 2007, Speckbacher 2003, Wainwright 2003) and recent studies have investigated performance measurement in NFP organizations (Paton 2003, Poister 2003). Reviewing literature, we found some studies focused on the difficulty in measuring performance in SMEs (Little 2005, Stone and Ostrower 2007); other describe empirical experience (Cairns et al. 2005, Collins et al. 2003, Kaplan 2001) and also some guides to measuring performance in NFP organizations (Connexions 2001, Cupitt 2005). Despite this growing attention, the literature on performance measurement still mainly focuses on the private and public sectors and the available studies are fragmented and not able to guide the performance measurement system implementation in NFP organizations (Dart 2004, Moxham 2009). Moving from this literature background, we look at the COPE Galway case study and we identify some key factors characterizing performance measurement in NFP organizations. In the following we synthesize them.

LACK AND RELEVANCE OF STRATEGIC PERFORMANCE MEASUREMENT

In the last decade, scholars and practitioners have been increasingly concerned about measuring and managing organizational results (Kaplan 2001, Forbes 1998). Some authors (Sheehan 1996, Sawhill and Williamson 2001) highlight that, although most of the NFP organizations have clear statements of mission, very few develop a performance measurement system that reveals whether the organization has an impact on its mission. As a consequence, most of the NFP organizations have no way to distinguish whether their strategic objectives are achieved or not.

That is exactly what happened in the case investigated. In order to fill the gap between mission and measures COPE Galway identify a much more balanced set of measures, better linked to its organizational mission, but the difficulties in defining a common strategy obstruct the immediate adoption of the BSC model. It is not a difficulty specific to COPE Galway but it demonstrates the need to adopt an incremental approach that is able to comply with the specific characteristics of these kinds of organizations.

In COPE Galway, as in the NFP organization investigated by Kaplan (2001), most of the strategy documents represent a combined wish list from all the participants invited to engage in the strategy-setting process. Once the mission and vision are articulated, most of the documents consist of lists of programmes and initiatives rather than the outcomes the organization is trying to achieve. Such organizations, when implementing a performance measurement system, typically measure progress in achieving milestones on their initiatives

CULTURAL BARRIERS TO IMPLEMENTATION OF STRATEGIC PERFORMANCE MEASUREMENT

The implementation of integrated performance measurement systems may be particularly difficult for NFP organizations, as there are relevant obstructions in achieving internal focus and alignment. In these organizations employees voluntarily accept below-market compensation because they believe in the mission of the institution. Their personal values motivate them to work as they desire to contribute to society through the organization's programmes. This is an extraordinary source of strength that profit-based organizations cannot benefit from.

APPLICABILITY OF BALANCED SCORECARD MODEL

Non-profit performance measurement is receiving increasing attention from both scholars and practitioners, but the design of non-profit performance measurement systems is still insufficient investigated; as a consequence, it is currently not clear if performance measurement system models developed for the private and public sectors are suitable for the non-profit organization.

In the 1980s, the Balanced Scorecard was developed for supporting private organizations in overcoming the limits of the traditional performance measurement systems. Such organizations collected many critics as they focused on financial performance, neglecting the intangible assets, such as the skills, motivation, and capabilities of its employees, customer acquisition and retention, innovative products and services, and information technology.

In the same period, some scholars advocated that multi-dimensional approaches should be used not just for measuring private organization effectiveness but also to manage the organizations belonging to the third sector (see for instance Cameron 1981, 1982, Connolly et al. 1980).

As matter of fact, the opportunity for the Balanced Scorecard to improve the management of non-profits should be even greater than in private companies. However, there are important differences that cannot be neglected. In for-profit organizations, the financial perspective provides key objectives, while the achievement of financial success is not the primary objective for NFP organizations. Certainly, they have to monitor their spending and comply with financial budgets, but their success cannot be measured by profit results or considering if their actual expenses are kept well below budgeted amounts.

Literature underlines that most non-profit organizations had difficulty with the architecture of the Balanced Scorecard suggested by Kaplan and Norton (1996), as the financial perspective is on the top of the hierarchy and many NFP organizations have rearranged the structure of their Balanced Scorecard, placing the customer perspective at the top (Kaplan 2001). However, this modification determines also the need to redefine the definition of 'customer', an operation that is not always easy in NFP organizations. In for-profit corporations, customers both pay for the service and receive the service. In NFP organizations the two roles are separate but complementary and often it is not easy to define if the customer is the donor or the person who receives the service or both.

DIFFICULTIES IN IDENTIFYING PERFORMANCE CATALOGUE

In all the organizations, financial measures supplemented with a collection of ad hoc non-financial measures are not enough to motivate and evaluate mission accomplishments, so it is necessary to carefully select the group of the strategic indicators suitable for measuring the achievement of strategic objectives.

This issue is even more difficult in NFP organizations as they lack the simple financial measures, such as profitability or shareholder returns, used by for-profit organizations to assess their performance (Forbes 1998), and they should disclose non-financial quantitative measures of the quantity and quality of the intangible services provided. On one hand, non-profits organizations have difficulty in developing quantitative measures of organizational performance because they frequently offer intangible services and have to manage specific internal cultural barriers (Forbes 1998). Performance measurement in the NFP sector has to consider a wide range of stakeholders, including government and non-government funders, donors, volunteers, employees, clients and beneficiaries, not comparable with private or public organizations (Van Iwaarden et al. 2009). The role of government is becoming more significant as non-profits progressively engage in the provision of state-funded services and it has to be carefully balanced with strategic objectives. On the other hand, literature does not offer enough support on how these organizations should select effective measures (Herzlinger 1996).

Conclusions

The main contribution of PMS implementation in COPE has been a renewed focus by managers and staff on the strategic objectives. The tendency is to get absorbed in operations to the detriment of the bigger picture. The system helps them to keep the objectives operational and to prioritize resources in focusing on the more important ones. It also gives them more ownership of the strategy.

Over the course of the year, the performance measurement has been moving in a generally positive upward direction with issues clearly visible. For the Board it has given line of sight of how the organization as a whole is progressing and, crucially, has identified the major issues and areas of concern with the strategy. It has also allowed more integration between the different reporting processes that are in place and will make possible linking risk management with objectives.

Strategic planning and monitoring is a journey, rather than a destination, and as it begins again for 2011, there will be a much better starting point and a more focused approach which will speed up the process.

COPE Galway are essentially looking for a more structured and manageable system. As well as the improvements mentioned in the previous section the company is hoping to maintain what it already has in a more manageable, user-friendly and scalable format. The key benefits COPE Galway are hoping to retain and obtain from the introduction of its performance measurement system include:

- ongoing focus toward goal alignment and achievement
- business agility via improved decision-making
- comprehensive regulatory compliance

- improved information consolidation process
- streamlined reporting
- collaborative management.

In term of cost savings, it is difficult to give an objective assessment at this point. In any organization with a large staffing and volunteer complements the most valuable resource is people's time. If the performance measurement system makes the company more effective, and if it assists in achieving objectives, then this is where any savings are likely to be made.

From an organizational viewpoint there are three main conclusions about the use of the scorecard and performance measures in NFP organizations. Firstly, getting key personnel involved in measuring their own performance against strategic objectives can make people more mindful of the bigger picture and how they can contribute. Strategy becomes operational. Secondly, for the Board and CEO there is a comprehensive view of what is going on, enabling issues and opportunities to be identified in a timely manner. Finally, the strategy-setting process can become more continuous and fluid for all participants, which makes it easier for everyone to engage and be enthusiastic about the process.

References

Baskerville, R., Wood-Harper, A., and Trevor. A. 1996. Critical perspective on action research as a method for information systems research. *Journal of Information Technology*, 11, 235–46.

Boland, T., and Fowler, A. 2000. A systems perspective of performance management in public sector organisations. *International Journal of Public Sector Management*, 13(5), 417–446.

Cairns, B., Harris, M., Hutchison, R., and Tricker, M. 2005. Improving performance? The adoption and implementation of quality systems in UK nonprofits. *Nonprofit Management and Leadership*, 16(2), 135–51.

Cameron, K.S. 1981. Domains of organizational effectiveness in institutions of higher education. *Academy of Management Journal*, 24, 25–47.

Cameron, K.S. 1982. The relationship between faculty unionism and organizational effectiveness. *Academy of Management Journal*, 25, 6–24.

Coghlan D., and Brannick. T. 2001. *Doing Action Research in Your Own Organization*. London: Sage.

Collins, B., Lacey, M., O'Hagan, S., Shah, R., Wainwright, S., and Wilding, K. 2003. *Measuring Impact: Case-Studies of Impact Assessment in Small and Medium-Sized Voluntary Organisations*. London: NCVO.

Connexions. 2001. *A Little Book of Evaluation*. Sheffield: CSNU.

Connolly, T., Conlon, E., and Deutsch, S. 1980. Organizational effectiveness: a multiple-constituency approach. *Academy of Management Review*, 5, 211–217.

Cupitt, S. 2005. *Measuring Up: Assessing Outcomes in the Voluntary Sector*. London: Charities Evaluation Services.

Dart, R. 2004. Being 'business-like' in a nonprofit organization: a grounded inductive typology. *Nonprofit and Voluntary Sector Quarterly*, 33(2), 290–310.

Eden, C., and Huxham, C. 1996. Action research for management research. *British Journal of Management*, 7(1), 75–86.

Forbes, D.P. 1998. Measuring the unmeasurable: empirical studies of nonprofit organization effectiveness from 1977 to 1997. *Nonprofit and Voluntary Sector Quarterly*, 27(2), 183–202.

Kaplan, R.S. 1998. *Innovation action research: creating new management theory and practice. Journal of Management Accounting Research*, 10, 89–118.

Kaplan, R.S. 2001. Strategic performance measurement and management in non-profit organisations. *Nonprofit Management and Leadership*, 11(3), 353–370.

Kaplan, R.S., and Norton, D.P. 1996. *The Balanced Scorecard: Translating Strategy into Action*. Cambridge MA: Harvard Business School Press.

Herzlinger, R.E. 1996. Can public trust in nonprofits and governments be restored? *Harvard Business Review*, Mar–Apr, 97–107.

Lipsky, M., and Smith, S.R. 1989/90), Nonprofit organizations, government, and the welfare state. *Political Science Quarterly*, 104(4), 625–48.

Little, W. 2005. Charities ready to play with the big boys but say 'let's be fair'. *Health Service Journal*, 27, 14–15.

Moxham, C. 2009. Performance measurement: examining the applicability of the existing body of knowledge to nonprofit organisations. *International Journal of Operations and Production Management*, 29(7), 740–763.

Moxham, C., and Boaden, R. 2007. The impact of performance measurement in the voluntary sector: identification of contextual and processual factors. *International Journal of Operations and Production Management*, 27(8), 826–45.

Paton, R. 2003. *Managing and Measuring Social Enterprises*. London: Sage.

Poister, T.H. 2003. *Measuring Performance in Public and Nonprofit Organisations*. New York: Wiley.

Sawhill, J.C., Williamson, D. 2001. Mission impossible? Measuring success in nonprofit organizations. *Nonprofit Management and Leadership*, 11(3), 371–87.

Schein, E.H. 1987. *The Clinical Perspective in Fieldwork*. Newbury Park CA: Sage.

Sheehan, R. 1996. Mission accomplishment as philanthropic organization effectiveness: key findings from the Excellence in Philanthropy Project. *Nonprofit and Voluntary Sector Quarterly*, 25, 110–123.

Speckbacher, G. 2003. The economics of performance management in nonprofit organisations. *Nonprofit Management and Leadership*, 13(3), 267–81.

Stone, M., and Ostrower, F. 2007. Acting in the public interest? Another look at research on nonprofit governance. *Nonprofit and Voluntary Sector Quarterly*, 36(3), 416–438.

Van Eynde, D., and Bledsoe, J. 1990. The changing practice of organization development. *Leadership and Organization Development Journal*, 11(2), 25–30.

Van Iwaarden, J., Der Wiele, T., Williams, R., and Moxham, C. 2009. Charities: how important is performance to donors? *International Journal of Quality and Reliability Management*, 26(1), 5–22.

Wainwright, S. 2003. *Measuring Impact: A Guide to Resources*. London: NVCO.

10

Social Enterprises and Democracy: Credit Unions, Social Enterprises and Engagement with a Democratic Political Economy

John Merritt

Introduction

Alongside my academic work for a BSc in politics and sociology and an MPhil in social sciences (with democracy and art at its core), my experience in political parties, trade unions, the cooperative and credit union movement, community projects and emerging social enterprises has given me many insights into the theory and practice of democracy. And it is the vein of praxis that I offer in this contribution. Being a work of both theory and practice the arguments and concepts sometimes stray as I try to pull the two together. However, by the end of the chapter I hope you will find the arguments and issues compelling, coherent and of sufficient importance to motivate you to become more centrally involved in their many manifestations, if you are not already.

To begin, we need a framework for our thinking in order to give action meaning. We have our key concepts democracy, social enterprise and political economy, but these are hardly clear in themselves. Like the mystifying Third Sector, these also remain 'essentially contested' concepts. Democracy embraces a range of practices and structures. Certainly in 'the West' we are hardly ever able to get our views, knowledge or belief presented directly except in small forums. We are forced to consider tactical voting or keeping and only having partial representation. In 'constituency'-based democracies, it is not uncommon that the majority of voters' choices are not represented, as often the elected representatives were chosen by less than 30 per cent of the population. We are given choices between options we do not want and we have representatives who display traits we do not approve of, and even when we can get our views heard many lack the confidence or the articulation to present them. Again, we only have limited knowledge of the terms of a debate or are consumed by conflicting ideological frameworks which only distort the debate. For credit unions in the UK democratic participation takes on two forms. Firstly, the directors and some officers are elected by the membership at annual general meetings. If contested, the candidate with the highest number of votes wins. Secondly, decision-making by the board is largely a one-person one-vote structure, with decisions being those supported by the majority on the board. I take these two requirements as fundamental to democracy, but also I would argue that employees need a structured democratic involvement; I will discuss that further, later.

Of course, these type of organizations (which sometimes include charities, social enterprises, cooperatives, mutual organizations and even environmental private sector companies) may

> adopt a constitution and rule book which commits them to democratic governance and even for those that do, there is plenty of disenchantment (and evidence) amongst both democratic theorists and writers on the social economy, that organizations which institute formal political equality (for example one member one vote) often fail to live up to democratic expectation in practice. (Smith and Teasdale 2010, cited in Smith 2010: 15)

Social enterprises similarly have many terms of reference and discretionary definitions, so much so that we can often be surprised by the differences of meaning deployed by people using the same terms. Smith and Teasdale explore this at some length and suggest government incentives and good legislation could help the social economy act as a 'vehicle for renewal' (ibid.: 27). However, I still find myself dissatisfied with the frame of reference. Credit unions as cooperatives are by almost any definition a social enterprise, but the boundaries around what is 'not for profit', voluntary or third sector, charitable or social purpose and so forth prevent an easy link between social enterprise, third sector, voluntary sector and the social economy.

Perhaps the growing number of 'benchmarks' for social enterprises will help and, as I argue later, I think democracy should be one. However, at this stage, I would like to offer the concept of a 'fourth sector', which can distinguish itself as the sector of social enterprises (including cooperatives and mutual organizations). This title draws itself from the work in the US on this issue during the 1990s evident in, for example various fourth sector websites (see www.fourthsector.net, for example). This is as distinct from the 'third sector' but, like the third sector, sometimes retains a voluntary component. Simply, I would like to suggest that social enterprises, cooperatives and mutual organizations (the fourth sector), are organizations, companies and/or businesses which:

1. aim to create a socially beneficial and economically self-sustaining enterprise through trading;

2. return any surplus or profit to the business, its members and/or the 'community' and also maintain a common ownership of assets

3. have 'volunteer' representation on its board (although this is volunteered skills, not necessarily 'unpaid time', and may enable volunteers to take part in its practice) and commits itself to some form of democratic control.

Finally, I will be recurrently using the term 'political economy'. This is an unfashionable term and the separation of 'politics' and 'economy' has been in vogue for well over a century. But, as Hahnel states, 'unlike mainstream economists, political economists have always tried to situate the study of economics within the broader project of understanding how society functions ... and give a realistic value to ... the importance of human agency compared to social forces' (Hahnel 2002: 1).

The intrinsic link of politics and economics to the way we live is so strong, it is surprising that the concepts of unemployment, alienation, health and other work/life issues were not sustained in mainstream political and economic discourse. At a time when bankers' bonuses, financial bailouts and economic possibilities (and life chances) obscure a lot of positive and progressive discourse, the fourth sector is able to offer a refreshing alternative and a real opportunity for mutual, cooperative and more democratically controlled finances to help regenerate the economies of the world. It is worth noting that credit unions and mutual organizations were not bailed out by governments in the recent banking crisis and have a far more financially secure business model than banks. Importantly, credit unions operate with people, economy, democracy, financial well-being and the risk of exclusion as part of their very being. Therefore, they are ideal for consideration in regard to issues of social enterprises and a democratic political economy. With an environmental investment potential, perhaps credit unions could be at the centre of a future of more equitable, socially driven and accountable future.

I will now present a few models of democracy and arguments around their value and development as well as reasons why we should do all we can to support democratic practice, especially in credit unions and the wider fourth sector.

Democracy and its Relationship to Political Economy

Democracy became popularized in political language with the French and American Revolutions and has been refined, played with, reviled and revered widely since. At that time, voters were male, home-owners and people of business, and the study of political economy was the study of what they did and how best they could practise it in societies. Specialization in work and study was relentless in the nineteenth and early twentieth centuries, especially in the West, and one manifestation of this was the separation of politics, economics, social studies (sociology). etc. Politics and its study became an issue of electing 'governments' while the practice of democracy at work was largely left to maverick cooperatives and businesses.

In the twentieth century state enterprises, notably throughout the communist bloc and nationalized industries made some gesture towards enabling people to engage in the political economy, however poorly practised, and 'democracy' was always given a principled position in the claims made by 'socialist' figureheads. In politics though, democracy is almost universally the watchword of progress, regardless of people's political and ideological commitments and beliefs. By the 1950s and more evidently the 1960s 'democratic management', as a style of management, widely entered the mainstream academic literature. For example, Pateman notes: 'It is frequently claimed that democracy already exists in Western Countries. Perhaps the best known example of this view is Clegg, one of the foremost British experts on industrial matters, in his book *A New Approach to Industrial Democracy* (1960)' (Pateman 1970: 71–2). What this means regarding a 'social' enterprise and the whys and wherefores of engagement in political economy is not so clear, as Pateman shows in the full text of *Participation and Political Theory* (Pateman

1970). Management studies, economics, politics and sociology (even social studies) provided a home for some part of the study and recommendations of how to engage and the consequences of intervention in a 'political economy'; however, none was as comprehensive as historical materialism had been as a core term in political economy. Hahnel notes, that 'During the second half of the twentieth century dissatisfaction with traditional political economy theory of social change, known as historical materialism, increased to the point where many political economists and social activists no longer espouse it' (Hahnel 2002: 1).

A 'big picture' notion of political economy re-emerged with the idea of a 'shareholder democracy', notably cited by Margaret Thatcher. Largely harping back to the values of the eighteenth and nineteenth centuries (and the political economists of the time, such as Adam Smith, etc.), it did help to re-associate politics and economics. However, Thatcher's famous denial of the existence of 'society' gave further question as to the value of this type of notion in a 'virtuous' political economy. During the twentieth century, democracy had an almost unassailable claim to moral and meritocratic superiority, even if not accepted prima facie as a perfect system. Figures central to Conservative, Liberal and Socialist traditions espoused it. Winston Churchill described democracy as 'the worst form of government except for all those others that have been tried before' (Churchill 1947). Marx approvingly regarded the ancient Greeks as living through the childhood of democracy and by implication hoped for a democratic future. J.S. Mill was an avid advocate of democratic processes. The specific forms of democracy still maintained some inequalities, inefficiencies and perhaps even immorality in British democratic decisions of the nineteenth and twentieth centuries, but it was the form of democracy, not democracy itself, that needed change. While there are many inefficiencies, wastages and bureaucratic frustrations that may be associated with its practice, democracy shows itself overall to be more efficient, more effective, and more open to change and more fair than any other structural and organizational style. Keane presents the argument that

> Democratic procedures are superior to all other types of decision making, not because they guarantee both a consensus and 'good' decisions, but because they provide citizens who are affected by certain decisions with the possibility of reconsidering their judgements about the quality and unintended consequences of these decisions. Democratic procedures sometimes allow the majority to decide things about which they are blissfully ignorant, but they also enable minorities to challenge ... to

> *think twice or say no … and … encourage incremental learning and trial and error modification or muddling through' (Keene in Held 1992: 127–8).*

These procedures, I would argue, apply equally to any reasonable size social institution from the United Nations to the state, from the 'mindscape' of a class (see reference list), social movement or other geo-political entity to the small business or local community group. I employ the term 'mindscape', in preference to communicative community or conceptual entity as it carries with it an ontological and ethical presence. The notion is explored further in my unpublished essay 'Mindscapes: creating the future by doing what you believe in'.

Whether using a democratic system of 'first past the post', constituency-based, proportional, alternative vote or a hybrid system, and whether being 'direct', 'delegatory' or 'representative', there is a possibility that wider and some consensual views of a 'population' will be heard.

But to give the greatest voice, I believe a mixture of association, geography and proportionality needs to embodied in a democratic process. The fourth sector could lead this, as the social purpose of the sector lends itself to cooperation, democracy and concern for political and economic outcomes. All of these are aspects of social interaction, especially as the fair trade concept aims to prove. Without meaning to be glib, the fourth sector could be the fair trade sector – counterposed to the free trade sector?

There is still a lot of room for research into the practices of 'a democratic political economy' and I will only be able to provide some small recent examples, which will highlight opportunities, but also show that there are still dilemmas I still find unresolved.

Ethical Benchmarking

Benchmarking offers tools for the measurement, management and goal-setting of organizations. However, this could be enhanced by measuring democratic and fair governance, social purpose activity and surplus distribution, percentage of trading or subsidized income, social ambitions and positive environmental engagement. The fourth sector has been the subject of a lot of benchmarking and performance management tools but none I have encountered include democracy as a benchmark. I would argue this is an essential criterion and while the models of democracy need some work, I have no doubt that it should be a central component of a social enterprise. Further, while I do not have room to explore this in more depth, some of the unresolved issues in this chapter can be framed within the benchmarking process, so I want to make reference to them here.

Triple bottom line management (*people, profit* and *planet*) is now widely well received, but I believe there is room for a further bottom line and the costs of this are not necessarily prohibitive. Referring back to Smith and Teasdale's suggestion of incentives and with a reassessment of tax income and distribution these bottom lines could promote a far more effective future, with massive health benefits, reduced ecological catastrophe clear-up costs and far greater efficiency, as many studies of social enterprises have indicated. I am working on creating acceptance of a quadruple bottom line as a benchmark. These are:

1.   Social purpose and social impact targets: here the distinction and overlap with charitable purpose needs configuring.

2.   Economic integrity: solvency and stability and the target of 100 per cent core income from trading (here the definition and use of surplus and capital will be crucial).

3.   Governance and efficiency: democratic governance, external audit and external regulation should be required (though cost may be an issue – but the cost of minimal regulation can be evidenced by the cost to the public purse in subsidizing the private sector, bailing out banks, putting right Enron's wrongs, remedying Bhopal's nightmare, etc., etc.).

4.   Progressive environmental practices need to be in evidence.

I am aware of some of the work of McLoughlin, based at Brighton University, who has used the quadruple bottom line idea in the past year where he identifies the *social, financial, environmental* and *economic* parts of the business and I hope to work in cooperation to align our definitions. Hopefully these ideas will largely speak for themselves and for those who may have read the '1,000,000 climate jobs' proposals or who are sympathetic to the UNCUT ambitions to ensure taxation due is paid, so there is plenty of scope for supporting these proposals. While I cannot explore these further here, as a central subject of this chapter, I would like to say a little more about a hierarchy of democratic models for these enterprises. While is not easy to create a perfect model, I offer a few ideas for ways of keeping up a higher level of democratic engagement in social enterprises and credit unions. Depending on the size of the organization any fourth sector organization should have:

1. An annual general meeting with elections for boards and most senior committees. The minimum on a board should be five people (with regular meetings, fairly fixed agendas, reports ready a few days before the meeting, minutes taken and good management information). The widest membership possible needs to be involved in these elections and there should be places for employees and service users/consumers on the board. If employees are members as well as partners and consumers there should be a widespread representation of interests. The board should have paid employees/ directors and directors paid for from social responsibility funds, including giving employees time from one firm to volunteer as directors of another. Some examples of this exist apart from worker cooperatives: for example trade union representation on boards in some German companies are constitutionally established; there are tenant participation representatives on housing association boards and, indeed, as with my own credit union and some local social enterprises, other organizations have allowed people to stand as directors for the Credit Union and Social Enterprise Link and they undertake their duties during normal working hours. A conflict of interest in both cases may arise and, as in any cooperative, this needs serious consideration; however, the basis of this practice is that people want the best for the company and its social purpose – cooperation not competition. There are a number of difficulties and potential changes in UK credit unions in this regard. Questions of payment for board work and employee representation need to be refigured. Furthermore, the relationship between credit unions, their trade associations and the credit union support organizations which are beginning to emerge needs to be looked at. Of course, it is impossible to regulate and govern all actions that undermine or damage a cooperative, but the governance needs on the whole to be enabling rather than punitive.

2. Annually elected departmental committees (for any organization or business with 'departments' or with 'areas of operation' which have 50 or more employees as well as volunteers contributing to their successes – which suggests well in excess of £5 million business turnover including wages). These committees need regular meetings, fairly fixed agendas, reports ready a few days

before the meetings, minutes taken and good management information. They should be constituted by at least three people and should give feedback to their constituents. For credit unions, when active volunteers are included, the numbers needed to run an organization with a Live or Work Common Bond can easily reach 50, but for many reasons elections have been constrained to being about directors and officers. These committees need fairly strict terms of reference and time-limited activities but this should include consultation time and resources. Consideration of this structure creates interesting thoughts about trade union roles and employer representative bodies, as everyone is potentially both an employer (director) and an employee. It also provides a model partially transferable to the public sector: however, in that instance the 'board' has traditionally been the ministerial team of the elected party and the employees have a say largely only as citizens, whereas with the fourth sector people have much more direct engagement.

3. A strong commitment to consultations, participation, openness and a democratic process in its regulatory constitution.

The Fourth Sector, Credit Unions and the Development of a Democratic Political Economy

Liberating theory as Hahnel describes it, is the theory used to understand and plan actions in political economy if we want 'to plan our joint endeavours democratically, equitably and efficiently' (Hahnel 2002: 291). My own social concept of mindscapes is intended to link the theory and practice of joint endeavours with the mindful qualities of passion, purpose, reason and action, and the mindscape of people working for a progressive, democratic political economy can find commonalities in the fourth sector. Indeed, it is the contention of this chapter that social enterprises, comprising the 'fourth sector' and credit unions centrally, could play a central role in helping bring about the realization of that desire. Nationalized and publicly owned industries and shareholder-owned industries may aspire to practise a democratic political economy, but they have shown enormous shortfalls. This fact has disillusioned many and with the collapse of the eastern bloc a 'dictatorship of the proletariat' seems as unlikely as it does undesirable. Andrew Mawson reflected recently that while there have been attempts at providing cash injections to 'community businesses', for example, the 'Local Enterprise Growth Initiative', it failed miserably, because it was '100 per cent process. Five hundred million pounds of public money wasted, most of it going on the salaries of civil servants, university academics and government bureaucracy' (Mawson 2009: 152). This vast input of money to help the third and/or fourth sector was poorly directed and did not create the sustainable jobs that social purpose social enterprises, cooperatives and mutuals would have done had the money been given to social entrepreneurs. However, £130 million put into third sector lenders, largely credit unions, over the past few years has had a significant impact on personal saving and borrowing habits, financial and healthy well-being and general improvement in social conditions in a number of areas of multiple deprivation. Further, Andrew Mawson, whose exemplar project has been Bromley-by-Bow centre, gives numerous accounts of successful social enterprises providing jobs, products and services that people want and need.

Lost public and indeed 'private' money, which has been sucked into the pockets of senior business people in tax havens, bankers and civil servants or offered to people as sweeteners, etc., is truly shocking. Similarly, the hundreds of millions of pounds paid in compensation to firms for major contract foreclosures or for delays, lost by withheld tax payments and the hundred-and-one accountants' ways to make a million, are often hardly noticed. There is money around and more democratic control is likely to help its fairer distribution. Money which travels through organizations which have a social purpose, a democratic structure and which operate with others of a similar ethos (the fourth sector), could well help break into a virtuous political economy. With new legislation proposed in 2009 (as a Legislative Reform Order) and awaiting its final 25 days of parliamentary time in September 2011, credit unions will be able to take deposits from and lend to businesses, and here I foresee a huge opportunity for a major banker for the fourth sector which is democratically controlled and regulated in a way which prevents it creating high-risk products, dealing on the Stock Exchange and playing the currency markets.

Extend this to the whole fourth sector and we are offered the opportunity to extend the virtues of a democratically controlled political economy. In many ways, forth sector organizations offer more direct democratic engagement than most of the public sector and as the booklet *Transitions* identifies (Jarrett 2011), the UK government's desire to allow government services to be run by social enterprises could produce a new political and economic landscape. It will fail, if this is just a cost-cutting procedure and an attempt to replace paid jobs with voluntary posts. But it will have interesting and important consequences if it is invested in as a means of political and economic progress, without the necessity of growth.

Conclusion

Democratic control of economic resources beyond the secondary control of 'state enterprises' and the highly unrepresentative 'share' listed companies offers an engagement of an individual with his or her future for ordinary people. There is an intrinsic interest in the outcome of an organization whose performance affects one's working conditions, terms and conditions and pay, etc., and while business leaders appeal to the goodwill of the workers, if the latter are not involved in the decision-making, they will be alienated, disenchanted and be beholden to decision-makers.

The fourth sector is already a dynamic and growing part of the economy and with legislative developments in the UK, it could help both credit unions and social enterprises develop a more consistent identity and give tenable social and environmental targets as central parts of that identity. Some of these are emerging through Private Members Bills and Legislative Reform Orders and there is even recent money available for developing these laws through European grant finance, but there is as yet little coherence. What is needed is a more unified, identifiable and legislatively enabled sector. As part of a wider democratic rejuvenation this engagement with making history feeds into Hirst's notion of 'associative democracy' which promotes the union of knowledge and position in democratic input. It makes being a citizen more than just being a voter but rather a full contributor to the development of an economy. By giving democracy a benchmark value for the fourth sector we would add one further effective and strengthening attribute, which I am sure would only add value to the title and experience of a business with a social purpose.

References

Benn, T., and Hood, A. 1993. *Common Sense: New Constitution for Britain*. London: Hutchinson.

Churchill, W. 1947. Speech in the House of Commons. *The Official Report, House of Commons (5th Series)*, 11 November 1947, vol. 444, cc. 206–7.

Hahnel, R. 2002. *The ABCs of Political Economy*. Chippenham: Pluto.

Held, D. (ed.). 1992. *Political Studies*, vol. XL, special issue, *Prospects for Democracy*. Oxford: Blackwell.

Hirst, P. 1993. *Associative Democracy*. Cambridge: Polity.

Jarrett, M. 2011. *Transitions* [Online]. Available at: http://www.sel.org.uk/uploads/TransitionsUpdated.pdf.

Mawson, A. 2009. *The Social Entrepreneur*. London: Atlantic.

Merritt, J. 2010. *Mindscapes: Creating the Future by Doing What You Believe In*. Unpublished essay, 'personal papers'.

Pateman, C. 1970. *Participation and Democratic Theory*. Cambridge: Cambridge University Press.

Schecter, D. 1994. *Radical Theories*. Manchester: Manchester University Press.

Smith, G. 2010. *Associative Democracy and Social Economy*, unpublished, University of Southampton.

11

Scorecards and Strategy Maps: The Top Ten Factors of Performance Measurement in Non-Profit Organizations

Brett Knowles, Richard Greatbanks and Graham Manville

Introduction

Almost all the learning and best practices established around performance measurement and management (PMM) originate in the private and public sectors. Yet much of this knowledge is applicable to non-profit organizations and their community focus. From our experience in working with voluntary sector organizations there are several areas which can make an important difference to how a third sector organization is managed and therefore performs. Balanced scorecards and strategy maps are used as the primary approach for reviewing these performance measurement issues within non-profit organizations. Performance management is becoming ever more important as organizations are required to benchmark against their peers and compete for renewable contracts. Moreover, the balanced scorecard also provides transparency and evidence of continuous improvement, which is becoming increasingly important for funders and commissioning agents. This chapter identifies and explores ten areas where, with careful consideration, management can address and improve organizational performance.

Multiple Stakeholders with Diverse Expectations

One of the most frequently cited problems associated with non-profit organizations is the need to satisfy their many and varied customers and stakeholders. Not only do non-profit organizations need to meet the needs of their customers and stakeholders, but they are increasingly held to account and subjected to the scrutiny of elected officials, legislative bodies, interest groups, employees, the media and related businesses, not to mention service users. Such groups rarely coordinate with each other, and often have their own agendas which, from the perspective of the non-profit, might appear to be in conflict. Customer groups are often in a position of power, providing funding for key projects and community services. As such they cannot easily be ignored; they expect and deserve their own hearing and response, and, most importantly, they may expect completely different things in terms of performance reporting from the non-profit organization. So how can the non-profit organization optimize against those constraints? Communication is the key: by using the balanced scorecard and strategy map the organization can clearly communicate to all stakeholders what it is trying to do relative to the needs and expectations of specific customers and stakeholders.

Whilst gathering all stakeholders together in a single meeting is often impractical, a strategy map, developed by the non-profit organization, is an excellent means of creating a visual with which to communicate with key customers and stakeholders, and it can indicate the prioritization and potential conflicts which arise from the non-profit organization attempting to meet their needs and requirements. Rather than building different strategy maps for each of the different stakeholders, thus adding to the complexity of the management team's task of coordinating across all stakeholders, it is necessary to focus on only the most critical few stakeholders with a single strategy map, helping the others to see that their needs will be met through the key stakeholders' needs. A stakeholder power interest matrix may be employed for identifying the key players and determining a communicative strategy to all of the constituency members (Mendelow 1981) (see Figure 11.1).

Transparency

Transparency is about sharing detailed performance information with many stakeholders. The performance goals and subsequent achievements of non-profit organizations inevitably become a matter of public record, and if performance drops significantly below target there is a risk of this being reported in the

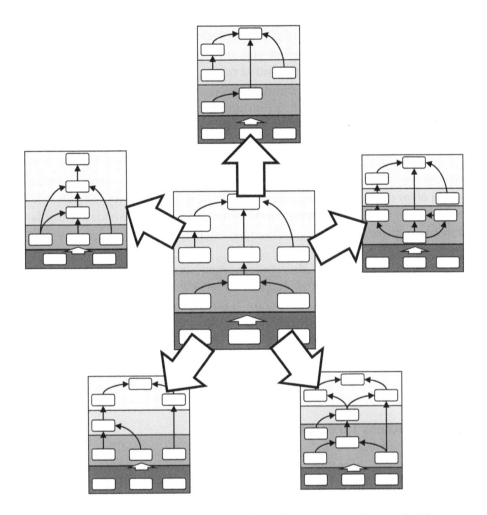

Figure 11.1   A single strategy map reflects the needs of all stakeholders

Source: © BalancedScorecard.net.

press and political environments. Such risks result in non-profit organizations being less committal about performance objectives, goals or actual performance levels than those in the private sector. Increasing transparency has the inherent risk of appearing to invite external stakeholders into the internal management process and exposing the organization to additional time and complexity in making decisions. However, if the decision to adopt a formalized performance measurement framework such as the balanced scorecard is internally motivated, transparency will be viewed more positively. There is a maxim that what gets measured gets managed and this is often quoted as a truism. If simply measuring leads to effective management, then serious questions need to be asked as to why 70 per cent of scorecard implementations fail (Neely and Bourne 2000). Perhaps what gets measured simply gets measured, as measuring can also lead to unintended consequences of behaviour which can distort performance such as gaming, sub-optimization and myopia (Milgrom and Roberts 1992, Smith 1995, Smith and Goddard 2002, de Waal 2007). In many balanced scorecard implementations, managers and executives pay lip service to the learning and growth perspective yet this is invariably the last perspective developed (Niven 2008). Another unintended consequence is the explosion of performance indicators, which has led to a measurement culture which often detracts from the core processes of service delivery. Therefore it is important to have an appropriate level of measures which provide appropriate transparency and yet do not constrain the organization.

As already discussed, the strategy map can be used as the primary communication tool to all stakeholders, providing a clear and simple message of what the organization does and how it is performing, at a very low cost and with a rapid update capability. Strategy maps provide detailed performance attainment reporting and therefore allow different stakeholders to look at a single common view of the organization, but see just the elements that are important to them.

Proven Success Takes a Long Time

The measurable outcomes from non-profit sector programmes, such as community healthcare improvement or poverty relief, can take years if not decades to achieve. In many cases it is therefore not clear to non-profit managers how daily, weekly or monthly activities help the organization progress closer to its goals in these areas. A strategy map describes the three to five year strategic direction, and the consequent strategic and operational goals of the organization. Using a weighting allows the focus of key strategic objectives to be changed from year to year, thus reflecting the need to develop a dynamic approach to achieving the organization's long-term goals. One approach is to provide the stakeholders with two weightings: a five-year weighting and a one-year weighting. This approach allows non-profit staff and external stakeholders a view of how the focus of the organization will change over these timescales. It then also allows staff to focus on how operational objectives will change over the time period to support the overall strategy.

The non-profit organization's board establishes the need to do things now, in order to be in a position to accomplish things later. The strategy map (with

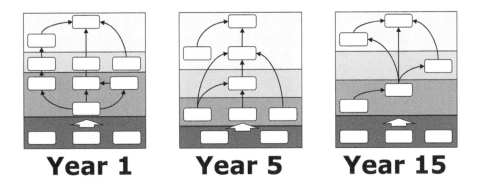

Figure 11.2   Scorecard offers an approach to managing the timeliness of results

Source: © BalancedScorecard.net.

annual weighting) then becomes a service-level agreement between the board and management. This future-oriented expectation setting provides the time/ space needed by management in order to change the organization's trajectory over time. In some cases the best solution is to develop several strategy maps – each describing major milestones in the evolution of the organization – say at five-year intervals (Figure 11.2). This allows the senior team to describe the future state while ensuring the necessary things are done today to maintain the business. It must be borne in mind that senior management commitment over several years is vital to the success of a scorecard. Performance management should be viewed as a long hike rather than a quick march (Neely et al. 1995)

Many Organizations Must Work Together

For most, if not all, non-profit organizations a number of departments and organizations must work together. Not only does this require alignment across an even broader stakeholder population, but it also requires activity alignment (such as on budget and outcome) across organizational boundaries. To achieve this a non-profit organization must create an performance architecture that enables agreement and seamless alignment across organizational (and departmental) boundaries through articulated and shared goals. Scorecards should be designed to reflect the value stream across multiple organizations of key customers and stakeholders. Focusing on the value stream across stakeholder organizations identifies the shared objectives – those which are either mandatory or contributory for each organization across the value stream. By building 'cascade' strategy maps and scorecards for all stakeholders a clear

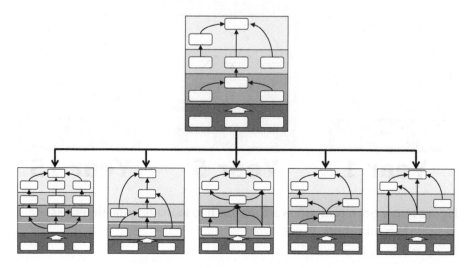

Figure 11.3   Each stakeholder has a Scorecard which corresponds to their value stream contribution

Source: © BalancedScorecard.net.

value stream emerges which links non-profit performance to stakeholder deliverables and, ultimately, to their strategic objectives (Figure 11.3). Non-profit scorecards can have as many as a third of all key performance indicators (KPIs) being externally driven by regulators, funders and other stakeholders. This is viewed as vital for achieving the linkages across the different agencies. Nevertheless, the scorecard should not be compromised by misalignment to the organizational strategy.

Budget Uncertainty

Most non-profit organizations are at the mercy of the external budget forces of funding bodies. The non-profit's destiny is therefore not guaranteed by good performance or the actual financial requirements in order to achieve its expected results. Its budgets may ultimately be determined by politicians, local government bodies, social groups or even the media. The strategy goals and expectations of non-profit organizations also shift over time, through activities such as shared-services initiatives. The service/deliverable for the end customer must continue across these changes in ownership, and therefore budgets must get adjusted in real time. The private and public sectors are rapidly evolving the flexible budgeting concepts that were introduced in the mid-1980s into corporate performance management (CPM) systems. CPM integrates strategy (scorecards), detailed performance information (business intelligence) and planning and budgeting (enterprise planning).

The prioritized strategy map becomes the agreement between leadership and management. The map transcends time and therefore provides a stability that unchanging financial budgets provided years ago. It is therefore the role of the non-profit management to deliver the strategic objectives with the shifting resources available (people, money and assets). Management therefore needs an ability to align rapidly shifting resources as it sees fit, while remaining accountable to the agreed strategic objectives of the organization. Strategy is a top-down, bottom-up system. The effects of budget changes need to be rippled up and used to refine the strategy map/scorecard based on the new realities. From a post-2008 perspective, the world now looks considerably different, consisting of budgetary cuts brought about by the steering media (money, power and law) of the age of austerity, itself born out of the banking crisis which has become a sovereign debt crisis. Looking to the future, non-profit organizations will need to be more entrepreneurial and more agile and light-footed. What this means in practice is that the opportunities and threats may present themselves in the wake of the financial crisis.

'Fuzziness' of Outcomes

Even when non-profit organizations have a clear mandate, their actual outcomes may still be 'fuzzy'. For instance, improving literacy appears to be a clear mandate, but what is literacy? What level is satisfactory? How do you know when it is achieved? With any strategic objective, fuzzy or not, when using a scorecard, the focus is more likely to be concerned with the general trend, rather than the specific value at any point in time. Scorecards require management to reflect on the components of the strategic objective and not just the top line deliverable. Therefore, if we have a lack of definition in our strategic objectives, then scorecards should promote questions such as 'Are we moving toward defining that fuzzy outcome or are we ignoring it?', and 'What are the implications of ignoring it?'

For example, research proves that training is an important component to job satisfaction, retaining the right people and doing a better job – three fuzzy outcomes. Although you cannot measure the impact of training on these issues, we do know that if we do no training, these outcomes will suffer. We also know that people vote with their feet: if a training session is bad, word travels and people stop going. If training is enjoyable and helps employees, more will go. The indicator of training hours allows us to see if we are working on this objective and, by implication, moving toward the fuzzy outcome. Over time, progress against fuzzy outcomes becomes clearer and can be measured directly.

Stakeholder/Political Interference

Experience tells us that many non-profit organizations are not only at the mercy of external stakeholders for their funding and budgets, but even their mandate, objectives and accountabilities can shift throughout the year. Politicians, local councils and other public bodies have the power to change an organization's accountabilities with very little forethought or restraining forces.

Where political or stakeholder interference is a major concern the need for strategic adjustment can be minimized in advance by making the prioritized strategy map the agreement between the organization and stakeholders for an agreed time period, such as two years. Forming and using this agreement in all communications helps ensure all parties that the organization is fulfilling its charter. Where strategic repositioning is required it should be done through a formal process of changing the strategy map and weighting, not through ad hoc demands. In this manner all stakeholders have a voice (which will tend to offset each other) and the organization has some degree of strategic stability.

Unclear Personal Accountabilities

Inside most organizations, including non-profits, the accountabilities of individuals are often unclear or poorly defined. We hire and manage as if qualifications and activities are enough – not the actual delivery of outcomes. A classic example is that we hire through CVs and resumés, and manage through job descriptions (listing what we do, not what we are to deliver). In over 80 per cent of our clients, it is unclear who is accountable for what outcomes.

Early in its evolution, the scorecard should be integrated with individual accountabilities and deliverables. Individuals or teams should be linked to specific outcomes and weightings from the strategy map or associated processes and projects. If the strategy or its operational execution changes, so should the associated processes and projects and, consequently, the accountabilities of the teams/individuals. A simple visual for achieving transparent roles and responsibilities which can supplement job descriptions and performance appraisals is an 'organogram' or organizational chart.

Culture of Consensus

It seems that most non-profit organizations have business practices and cultures that encourage team-based decision-making or cultures of consensus. This may be due to the innate altruism associated with working for a community or voluntary sector organization, but whilst this may lead to consensus-based decisions, to be effective consensus requires alignment of goals, priorities and access to necessary information. We find these elements to be weaker in most non-profit organizations than in private or more commercially oriented organizations.

Where consensus-based decision-making is appropriate, the organization must lay the foundation of alignment upon goals, priorities and available information. The strategy map and weighting informs the organization of the goals and priorities; the scorecard and business intelligence layer ensure that the appropriate information is available around the specific issues at hand.

Where grants of authority are required to ensure the correct people are making appropriate decisions for their skill and knowledge level, the accountability framework should be linked to each objective and/or process/project on the strategy map. For example, each objective may have an owner, who must approve changes; others may review authority and still others must inform performance issues.

Unclear Relationship between Performance and Consequences

Many non-profit organizations argue that because they cannot offer incentive-based compensation to employees and staff they are at a performance disadvantage. In fact, the problem is deeper than just salary: organizations in the non-profit sector could offer non-monetary rewards, such as the opportunity to take on more challenging or higher-profile assignments, permission to become apprentices in other processes, or even honorary mention at the next team meeting as incentives. In our experience it seems that the root cause might be more associated with a culture that does not support performance-related acknowledgement. Likewise, it is often unclear how poor performance leads to unfavourable consequences.

Most of our non-profit clients are concerned with the complexity of creating a performance-based reward structure. We have discovered that, with the scorecard, these can be established through simple one-week workshops across the organization. A recent study showed that over 80 per cent of senior managers do not understand their organization's strategy. Without such understanding, it is impossible to even begin linking performance to consequences. This may be due to the fact that many business strategy documents end up in a filing cabinet or on a shelf gathering dust. The balanced scorecard brings the strategy to life and can motivate the commitment of the entire workforce. Once again, the weighted strategy map clearly communicates what matters – and how much it matters. This becomes the foundation of a performance-based culture. Ensuring that the strategy map describes objectives – not tasks – allows departments and individuals to quickly understand their contribution and describe it to management. Linking those contributions to specific roles creates accountabilities that underpin the performance-based feedback system of the scorecard.

References

De Waal, A. 2007. *Strategic Performance Management: A Managerial and Behavioural Approach*. Basingstoke: Palgrave Macmillan.

Mendelow, A. 1981. *Environmental Scanning: The Impact of Stakeholder Concept,* Proceedings of the Second International Conference on Information Systems, December 1981, Cambridge MA, 1981.

Milgrom, P.. and Roberts, J. 1992. *Economics, Organization and Management*. Englewood Cliffs NJ: Prentice Hall.

Neely, A., and Bourne, M. 2000. Why measurement initiatives fail. *Measuring Business Excellence*, 4(4), 3–7.

Neely, A.D., Gregory, M., and Platts, K. 1995. Performance measurement system design: a literature review and research agenda. *International Journal of Operations and Production Management*, 15(4), 80–116.

Niven, P.R. 2008. *Balanced Scorecard: Step-by-Step for Government and Non-Profit Agencies*, 2nd edn. New York: Wiley.

Smith, P. 1995. On the unintended consequences of publishing performance data in the public sector. *International Journal of Public Administration*, 18, 277–310.

Smith, P.C., and Goddard, M. 2002. Performance management and operational research: a marriage made in heaven? *Journal of Operational Research Society*, 53(3), 247–55.

12

Measuring or Managing?
NGO Performance in Peru

Gareth Rees and Richard Greatbanks

Introduction

Peru has a vibrant and diverse third sector reflecting the needs of the country. Its history and development echoes the country's history of indigenous imperialism, imported religion and republican statehood, and is reflected in the place and the activities of today's third sector throughout the lives of its citizens.

This chapter draws on global studies of the third sector, country studies, economic statistics, practitioner and academic literature on NGO management, and interviews with NGO sector personnel to develop a view of performance management in the Peruvian third sector. Peru has social and economic challenges to overcome, particularly in terms of its third sector. Whilst it is impossible to fully represent the sector in one brief analysis, this chapter is divided into five short discussions: an introduction to the country, an introduction to its third sector, the influence of bilateral aid, Peruvian NGO performance management and, finally, a short case study. The case study examines performance management in the context of how one international donor agency representative is managing a micro credit programme with its client producer cooperatives. The case considers how performance is managed, and what innovations have been introduced to overcome structural barriers. The chapter then closes with a short conclusion.

Peru's Recent Economic and Social History

Peru has a population of 29 million, with Lima, the capital city, accounting for close to 8.5 million. A former colony of Spain through the conquest of the Incas by Pizzaro, it gained its independence in 1824. Peru's geography and its social history are the source of internal conflicts, some of which have lead to social exclusion for some citizens and continue to impact the country today (Alasino 2008).

Peru is classified as an upper middle income country with a GNI per capita of $4,200 (World Bank 2009). (The US dollar is used throughout this analysis.) This status demonstrates Peru's significant economic growth throughout the first decade of this century, where at mid-decade GNI per capita stood at $2,360 and when Peru was rated as a lower middle income country (Alasino 2008). Extractive and energy industries are key drivers of the present economy, with Peru's significant metal ore resources and natural gas being exploited in its southern and Amazonian provinces. This commodity-led growth has driven Peru's GDP growth for the last 10 years, stimulated by the growing worldwide mineral and energy demand.

The growth observed over the last decade has been assisted by low inflation and a stable currency. However, this period of relative prosperity was preceded by crises featuring rampant inflation and civil insurrection. During this time there was significant population growth in cities, with people from rural areas who sought safety migrating to urban areas, especially to Lima.

Economic stability and growth has seen a steady decrease in poverty rates from 54.3 per cent in 2001 (World Bank 2009) to 39.3 per cent in 2007 (INEI, reported in *Peruvian Times* 2008). Even though the average GNI figure makes Peru a middle income country on the development ascendancy, this status belies inequities that remain within the country, where 'the income received by the poorest part of the population receives less than the average GDP per capita in Sierra Leone' (Alasino 2008: 3). There is also an unevenness present within the 2007 poverty statistics; for example the highland province of Huancavelica experiences poverty rates of 85.7 per cent, while the Lima urban area, at 19.4 per cent, experiences a substantially lower rate (INEI 2009). This phenomenon is highlighted by Alasino (2008: 13), where it is stated that 'failure of growth distribution is clearly shown in the fact that GDP per capita in Lima is five times that of the regions. Rural and indigenous people have thus been largely excluded from the benefits of economic growth' (Alasino 2008), typified by unequal access to education, water and electricity (UNDP, 2010).

Peru's Third Sector

Peru's Third Sector has been influenced by three factors. The first has been termed 'Andean reciprocity' – the traditions of solidarity and mutual self-help that were part of the pre-Spanish Peruvian society. The second is the presence of Catholic Church affiliated organizations – a legacy of Spanish rule. Finally, and more recently, is the increase in issues-based NGOs advocating for improved environment, human rights and gender conditions (Sanborn et al. 1999). The roots of Peru's community welfare sector can therefore be seen in terms of its social history, where Andean kinship ties, the advent of religious brotherhoods and the emergence of post-independence mutual aid societies and beneficial charities were defining features of consecutive periods. The post-1950 urbanization unveiled new social and cultural concerns which were met with modern interpretations of Andean reciprocity through the formation of support networks, which later became 'neighbourhood defence organizations, *comedores populares* (community soup kitchens), and *comités de vaso de leche* ("Glass of Milk" committees)' (Sanborn et al. 1999: 451) that relied on significant inputs from volunteers.

Since the 1980s more modern, independent and critical civil society entities have developed, addressing not only poverty and welfare issues but those of women's rights, human rights in general and the environment (Alasino 2008, Sanborn et al. 1999). This has resulted in some Peruvian third sector activities, such as social research, drifting to academic institutions and consultancies, and the development of representative bodies to interact with the state (Alasino 2008, Guerra et al. 2011).

For instance, Sanborn et al. (1999) reported 'approximately 110,621 private non-profit [*sic*] organizations in existence as of 1995, without including places of religious worship, cooperatives, unions, or political parties. Of this number, 64,905 are community-based organizations, 29,491 are sports and cultural organizations, and 14,346 are education institutions' (ibid.: 446). Data was gathered from existing databases and because of the informal nature of many of the organizations identified, the dataset for more detailed analysis on employment and financial affairs was limited to 49,400 non-profit organizations.

In 1995 the Peruvian non-profit sector produced $1.2 billion in expenditures (2.0 per cent of GDP) and paid 126,988 employees. These employees accounted for 2.4 per cent of total non-agricultural employment, 3.2 per cent of total service employment, and 16.5 per cent of public sector employment. When volunteers are added, non-profit employment represents 2.9 per cent of the total employment in Peru (Sanborn et al. 1999: 447–8). The Peruvian non-profit sector is therefore a significant economic force, a major employer, and one which utilizes significant volunteer inputs.

Sanborn et al. (1999) further report that Peru's third sector is dominated by the education sector, which employs a sizeable number of people – over 60, 000 (48 per cent of non-profit employees). This feature is a likely remnant of the Catholic Church's history of providing primary and secondary education throughout the country. Funds for non-profits are largely from self-generated sources (67.8 per cent), with other funds received being public sector sources (19.3 per cent) and philanthropy (12.9 per cent). The reliance on self-generated income is therefore significant, and is made up of fees for services (such as school tuition), memberships and contributions for access. When contributions in kind are added the only significant difference is found in comparative inputs from the public sector, 26.7 per cent as compared to 19.3 per cent, represented by inputs such as food to the *comedores populares* and *comités de vaso de leche*.

The pattern of Peruvian non-profit income is typical of other Latin American countries, but varies against global averages. Globally non-profit incomes tend to have more public sector receipts comprising 'a considerably larger share of non-profit income in these other countries (40.1 per cent vs. 19.3 per cent in Peru)' (Sanborn et al. 1999: 457).

The informality and number of individual groups is not surprising, as Peruvian third sector organizations operate under civil law and can be easily constituted (Guerra et al. 2011, Luna 2005). Those organizations that receive non-reimbursable overseas aid should be registered, according to government law implemented during the last decade to meet the global drive for aid transparency and its effective use and management of funds (Luna 2005). In Peru, the third sector registration requirement is for 'only those organizations that both (1) carry out programs or projects for development, and (2) channel technical international cooperation' (Luna 2005: 12). Agencies which receive informal or privately arranged donations are therefore exempt from registration. However, these changes were introduced in a climate where little trust existed between civil society and the government. In light of this, representative or coordination bodies have emerged, responding to constituent needs by lobbying government or entering dialogue regarding regulatory measures and compliance issues (Alasino 2008, Guerra et al. 2011, Luna 2005).

Peru and International Aid

As a country climbs the ranks of the development ladder it becomes less attractive to aid donors. Peru has been relatively fortunate that its accounts do not rely on foreign aid, with Official Development Assistance[1] (ODA) flows being less than 1 per cent for at least the last five years (Alasino 2008, World Bank 2009). Nevertheless, ODA funds are still a significant numerical figure, being $584.6 million in 2005 (Alasino 2008) and $444 million in 2009 (World Bank 2009). However, the decentralized pattern of poverty presents three major challenges: first, to ensure funds flow to communities in need – some distance from policy-makers in Lima; second, to meet with accords that govern aid harmonization; and, third, to manage the performance of those funds and organizations which apply them.

The Paris Declaration on Aid Effectiveness, signed in 2005 and latterly further endorsed in Accra in 2007, is an agreement to seek to reform the ways in which aid is delivered and managed in light of the Millennium Development Goals. It was signed by donors, agencies and recipient countries, and committed them to monitorable actions through strategies and plans, alignment, accountability and simplification and to reducing duplication across and within these countries (OECD 2005). Peru is a signatory to the Paris Declaration but since signing, only limited progress has been achieved towards Peru's obligations to the declaration (Alasino 2008).

To develop an improved capacity for coordination or to instigate the development planning required to meet the declaration's expectations, Peru created a new government agency, the Peruvian Agency for International Cooperation (APCI) (Luna 2005). APCI's role is one of '... conducting, programming, organizing and supervising international non-reimbursable aid as part of the National Development Policy, within the framework of the legal directives regulating international technical aid (Law no. 27692, Art. 3)' (Alasino 2008). The mechanisms created are to provide for a central registry for not-for-profit organizations, receive returns on funds used by agents and donors and to enable access taxation relief by qualifying organizations (Luna 2005). The APCI has interpreted a raft of national and international documents and strategies to develop a strategic development framework; a structure that can enable performance to be at least monitored, if not proactively managed in terms of a development direction (Alasino 2008).

---

1   http://stats.oecd.org/glossary/detail.asp?ID=6043.

However, not all eligible organizations have registered with the APCI or SUNAT, the Peruvian taxation agency. As such, there appear to be few functional opportunities for these government agencies to engage with the third sector organizations directly, exacerbating the distance between the state and the country's NGOs, and resulting in a fragmented and diverse third sector (Alasino 2008). Furthermore, the APCI civil accountability framework makes a coordinated approach to aid the delivery that is relatively difficult to achieve (Alasino 2008).

Part of the accountability drive that initiated the Paris Declaration donors refined their planning requirements and some introduced a more quantifiable approaches, by either modifying the use of logical framework planning or introducing their own performance management tool – results-based management (Binnendijk 2001) – for local NGOs to comply with.

These tools, through their methodology, 'involve several phases: e.g., articulating and agreeing on objectives, selecting indicators and setting targets, monitoring performance (collecting data on results), and analyzing those results vis-à-vis targets' (Binnendijk 2001: 2). However, a weakness of the above process is the clarity of the objectives. In early plan iterations these objectives may not be the most appropriate and later the objective-setting decisions may be clouded by the attraction of framing in terms of what is easily measured rather than measuring what is important (Binnendijk 2001). For Peruvian ODA-funded groups these performance tools have become the main accountability method and significant resources are directed to them (Guerra et al. 2011).

Performance Management in Peruvian Third Sector Organizations

Defining performance management in terms of Peruvian third sector organizations is difficult. The size, variety and dispersal of third sector groups throughout the country means there is little homogeneity, nor is there an equal access to physical and knowledge resources.

Peruvian civilly constituted bodies require some form of financial record keeping or accountability as outlined in each organization's constitution. Further, those groups who avail themselves of taxation relief will need to meet the administrative requirements for the registration and returns as part of ACPI/SUNAT regulations (Luna 2005). The range of methods employed for data-gathering are through objective-setting, stakeholder consultations, planning, budgets and financial targets, with each of these having a measurement criterion (Guerra et al. 2011, Necochea 2011).

Recent research suggests Peruvian managers act instinctively and use intuitive practices (Matzkin 2008, Necochea 2011) which are appropriate for a complex environment such as Latin America. Intuitive management is different from the data-based problem-solving approaches for structured situations that is a hallmark of rational management science (Dávila and Samper 1994). This difference is probably more apparent in rural areas where, for example, agricultural cooperative managers work in informal and traditional ways, making decisions largely by past experience, but therefore being slow to respond to market signals (Necochea 2011). In this situation, any performance data collected may be used to manage the organization in its pauperized state, rather than being used to improve performance or develop growth strategies (Matzkin 2008). Peruvian NGOs are also at the mercy of structural issues, including project-based funding cycles, temporary staffing, governance turnover and poor matching of training access and needs (Guerra et al. 2011, Matzkin 2008, Necochea 2011). So even if they are able to apply collected data to management decisions, structurally the above impediments may impair any benefits being realized. Organizations that may be better placed to act on performance data are those that have relationships or are partners of overseas organizations, as they will tend to use prescribed performance management tools, for which they may have improved data collection and analysis hardware and trained staff, producing further improvement in organizational systems (Guerra et al. 2011).

Peruvian NGOs which receive overseas funds tend to be driven by the requirements of those donor programmes (Alasino 2008, Guerra et al. 2011, Necochea 2011). Their performance measurement requires reports on budgets and activities as well as the use of planning and project design tools such as logical frameworks and results-based management, thus providing, at a minimum, an accountability for results (Austin et al. 2006, Binnendijk 2001). For some organizations, this data is also used for management decision-making. Such results-based management has been imperilled in Peru by 'the huge geographical and sector-based dispersion of resources, the lack of trustworthy information mechanisms, and the limited monetary value of non-reimbursable aid' (Alasino 2008: 4). Moreover, 'donor agencies rarely have the capacity to carry out proper control over the management and execution of their projects. Control is narrowed down to account checking, and is rarely extended to management and project impact' (Alasino 2008: 26).

The multi-funded NGO finds the myriad of templates and reporting idiosyncrasies frustrating. Guerra et al. (2011) reported that there is no standard template for Peruvian organizations, with different formats required for the ACPI and for other funding bodies, making performance reporting complex and time-consuming. 'Staff could better use this time building social impact assessment capacity, or maximizing their human and organizational capital' (Matzkin 2008: 156). As a consequence, aid harmonization has been slow to develop in Peru (Alasino 2008), thus tending to maintain the effect of results-based management that was introduced for the donor government's benefit in the first instance (Binnendijk 2001).

Those NGOs who operate in data-driven industries such as micro finance use the existing industry metrics that quantify mainly lending performance parameters (Guerra et al. 2011), with some software and templates being provided by the donors, which assist with data-gathering, accuracy and homogeneity (Necochea 2011). However, both Necochea (2011) and Guerra et al. (2011) noted that for Peruvian micro finance programmes the social (qualitative) goal assessment tended to use either external evaluators or quantitative proxy measures to assess the qualitative impacts. The practice of using quantitative proxies for social performance management is more than likely due to social impact assessment being complex, costly and involving deliberate methods of collecting and analysing impacts (Austin et al. 2006, Copestake 2007). This raises the issue of purpose; if the social impacts are considered important there should be some definition and measurement system implemented to assess them, rather than solely measuring the numerical financial or activity indicators (Austin et al. 2006, Binnendijk 2001, Copestake 2007).

Progress on capacity for undertaking performance management is developing. Donors and government have been advised to invest in staff (Alasino 2008) and NGO access to training through donor programmes and independent fee-based providers is occurring (Guerra et al. 2011). However, budget priorities and high staff turnover plague continuous human capital development within NGOs, with some facing the 'Catch 22' of not having the resources to train staff to apply for funds that would result in additional resources (Guerra et al. 2011). The organizations that overcome this dilemma can access resources to improve their capabilities and hence their accountability and their contractibility. Access to performance management information, through a programmed approach to training and development that is accessible and continuous, would assist with the spread of performance thinking across the sector (Guerra et al. 2011). Nonetheless, there are increasing compliance costs and as Peru's prosperity rises, so does the competition for already stretched aid flows.

In summary, performance systems in Peruvian ODA NGOs are probably best described as performance measurement; where specified processes are routinely measured and reported, but less integrated into the collection and assessment of outcome indicators (Austin et al. 2006). There seems to be a movement towards the use of data to assist with management planning and strategies; however, structural issues such as staff turnover, project-based capacity and infrequent training and development opportunities still hamper progress toward an integrated management system.

Even with these issues some organizations are finding pathways to achieve integrated performance-based management. Below is a brief case study that outlines one organization's structure and processes, identifying performance management at different levels within their network.

Case Study: SOS Faim – Peru

CASE BACKGROUND

SOS Faim[2] is a Belgian independent NGO for development created in 1964, with programmes and partners in 12 African and Latin American countries (SOS Faim 2011). Its mission is described as 'striving against hunger and rural poverty by supporting farmer agriculture and its actors in developing countries and by raising awareness in Northern populations' (SOS Faim 2011). SOS Faim Peru works with two sectors in the rural economy: (1) primary producers – farmers producing mainly coffee, cocoa and grains, organized as cooperatives or associations; and (2) micro credit agencies – savings and loan cooperatives, harnessing the synergy of providing credit services to the rural agrarian economy (SOS Faim 2005). SOS Faim provides loan finance through its donor funds.

While SOS Faim Peru has a direct relationship with the producer cooperatives and micro finance providers, during the 1990s due to economic uncertainties and structural reform an international guarantee fund, Fondo de Garantia Latinoamericana (FOGAL) was established in 2004. FOGAL provides guarantees and letters of credit for the rural producers/farmers and micro finance institutions when they require additional funds to meet growth (SOS Faim 2009). Further, SOS Faim has assisted small rural credit cooperatives to form Ciderural, an organization that aims to develop the rural regions

---

2   SOS Faim translates from French to SOS Hunger.

by being 'a solid cooperative institution' focusing on sustaining small rural entrepreneurs (Torres 2010), Both of these entities, FOGAL and Ciderural, have governance members sourced from stakeholder groups.

Results of these two initiatives are:

1. From the client perspective FOGAL provides access to letters of credit and guarantees and information on lending and financing, and Ciderural provides finance and business planning technical assistance to its members.

2. From SOS Faim Peru's perspective, an increase of capacity and reach without extending the size and costs of its operations while maximizing its mission, and reducing risks of SOS Faim's rural financing inputs relocating to the financial markets, should that occur.

Figure 12.1 maps the organizations and their relationships, communities of interest and service links.

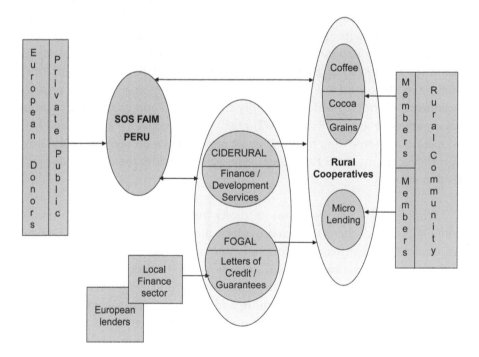

Figure 12.1   SOS Faim Peru system

DESCRIBING THE PERFORMANCE MANAGEMENT SYSTEM

At each level performance data is used to support the efficacy of the system, and to support the decision-making and the quality of relationships to promote quality management at the cooperative level.

First, performance is managed at the producer cooperative using standard accountability mechanisms. These organizations are operated under a constitution and they measure their performance through budgets and plans, reports to boards of directors and stakeholder communications. Managers are intuitive operators, working in traditional and informal ways – their knowledge is grounded in subsistence farming. The directors come from the membership base, with a president operating for a fixed period determined by the constitution – a situation that can lead to capture or other governance dysfunctions (SOS Faim 2005). The structured rollover provides for weakness in both skills and knowledge continuity and the redefinition of the important governance–management relationship between the chairperson and the employed manager. The member participation in directorship roles is a hallmark of cooperatives and it aims to involve members in all aspects of the cooperative's functioning and to build leadership potentials.[3]

Second, performance at the micro lending cooperatives or associations is more systematized, with formal plans developed using a *'marco lógico'* or logical framework using outcomes, specific objectives and their measures. This particular framework is introduced by SOS Faim and is based on a German planning module. The framework allows for economic, financial and social objectives and is measured by indicators. Social outcomes tend to be evaluated by quantitative proxies, with levels of gender participation and relative loan size representing changes in social capacity for the communities involved. This quantitative data is collated and received by SOS Faim as summary reports. The reports also represent part of a data chain and assisted by software. This software has been provided by SOS Faim through its international office, and is also used by FOGAL/Ciderural to support their roles.

Thirdly, at the FOGAL/Ciderural level, data is used to compare with international benchmarks for financing, such as profit and loss ratios, return on investment and other financial metrics, and micro lending statistics such as loan payment and default rates. These are used to inform and initiate the credit and

---

3   From http://www.ica.coop/coop/principles.html where more can be found on the principles
    and philosophies of the cooperative movement.

guarantee services provided. FOGAL has a social audit process to complement its financial reporting and undertook an impact study in 2005: however, this was confined to the FOGAL partners rather than their beneficiary communities, being limited to the outcome of having access to a loan guarantee. The study found that direct effects included increased capacity for business volumes and client range and improved terms of business. Indirect affects observed were improved relationships with the finance industry, the possibility of diversification and improved profitability and institutional development (SOS Faim 2009). Further, this information is augmented by data on training and capacity development activities, again against logframe or RBM (results-based management) framework objectives to observe development.

Finally, summaries of this data are utilized by SOS Faim to monitor the programme against the objectives, report to donors, seek to clarify and, if needed, provide for interventions to maintain the overall projects aims and operational goals.

CASE DISCUSSION

Most of the performance data is quantitative, probably because this is a finance-based intervention. There are criticalities for performance that lie outside the numerical data, especially those which concern relationships or social factors. This is where the SOS Faim country representative's judgement and industry experience is applied. The country representative has developed measures that are applied through observations to assess the quality of the cooperative's internal relationships. By applying rules of thumb, such as meetings attended by both the cooperative's president and manager, there are now evidentiary proxies for relationship quality. These measures allow for early intervention at cooperatives that may be exhibiting warning signs before any performance problems or conflicts become evident. The structural weaknesses of personnel turnover are mitigated through training and transparent communication. Moreover, relationship management is preferred to govern employee performances rather than strict contractual methods.

Whilst quantitative measures are useful for specific cases, the overall performance of SOS Faim's programme relies on quantitative measures. These measures provide decision-makers across the spectrum of interactions the opportunity to monitor and improve performance. Measures such as profits, production quotas and market volumes are used to quantify economic and organizational development outcomes. At a social level, the functionality of relationships that contribute to cooperatives' viability are measured through impression and objective indicators. Social outcomes are measured by proxy statistics and some external evaluations. However, cooperative meetings and stakeholder consultations provide narratives that may contain valuable qualitative and impact data. Data and process integrity relies as much on competency as it does on a shared vision of what the methods being applied are intended to achieve and are designed to do. All participants have a background in cooperative business and understand the cooperative culture and its purpose. By having a strong performance management framework, it is less likely that mission drift will occur (Copestake 2007) and bypass rural and agrarian business as some other micro lenders in Peru have (De Janvry et al. 2003).

CASE CONCLUSION

This case study exemplifies the importance of a performance framework and the coherence of its data as much as the group of people who must understand its limitations as well as its strengths. In this situation there is an attempt to maximize its use and provide access to data. There are also mechanisms to take advantage of that data to develop more 'entrepreneurial' ventures that can provide the returns desired by cooperative members. The SOS Faim country representative uses an intuitive frame of reference to value relationships that are key to the clients' business success – their intra-organizational relationships. A proxy measure has been devised providing an objective indicator reducing the reliance on the representative's judgement alone.

Conclusion

Sanborn et al. (1999) identified the lack of a publicly recognized third sector, and the political environment and historical factors that affect Peru's social cohesion, as problems which underlie this fragmented and varied sector. This is aptly demonstrated by the ODA sub-sector attempts to 'harmonize' aid in line with the Paris Declaration. Peru has found its historical problems, internal agendas and the sheer size of the task as barriers to generating sufficient momentum towards the Declaration's ideal. At the operational end of programme delivery, both donors and agents have capability and capacity issues that prevent a performance management culture from thriving. Structural and resource impediments are evident and these hinder organizations moving further than a performance measurement state. There is a norm of accountability for inputs and activities and appear to be few outcome-orientated assessments. However, as suggested by stakeholders and practitioners, Peruvian NGOs are not unfamiliar with the concepts of performance management and they are attracted to the benefits as they achieve further capacity, especially as the world is becoming one where outcomes matter.

References

Alasino, E. (2008). *Peru: The Kingdom of the NGO?* Madrid: FRIDE.

Austin, J., Gutiérrez, R., Ogliastri, E., and Reficco, E. 2006. *Effective Management of Social Enterprises: Lessons from Businesses and Civil Society Organizations in Iberoamerica – a Collaborative Research Project of the Social Enterprise Knowledge Network.* Cambridge MA: Harvard University, David Rockefeller Center for Latin American Studies and Inter-American Development Bank.

Binnendijk, A. 2001. *Results Based Management in the Development Co-operation Agencies: A Review of Experience – Background Report.* Paris: OECD.

Central Reserve Bank of Peru. 2010. *Inflation Report: Recent Trends and Macroeconomic Forecasts 2010–2012.* Lima: Government of Peru.

Copestake, J. 2007. Mainstreaming microfinance: social performance management or mission drift? *World Development*, 35(10), 1721–38.

Dávila, C., and Samper, H.G. 1994. Innovative management and organizational development in Latin America. *The International Executive*, 36(6), 671–88.

De Janvry, A., Sadoulet, E., McIntosh, C., Wydick, B., Luoto, J., Gordillo, G., et al. 2003. *Credit Bureaus and the Rural Microfinance Sector: Peru, Guatemala, and Bolivia.* San Francisco: University of California at Berkeley and The FAO Office for Latin America.

Guerra, N., Alvarado Vasquez, M., and Courrègues, S. 2011. Personal communication. Lima: Canadian Cooperation Services Support Unit.

INEI. 2009. Perú: Población y condición de pobreza, según departamento, provincia y distrito, 2007 [Online]. Available at: http://www.inei.gob.pe/biblioineipub/bancopub/Est/Lib0911/index.htm [accessed: 23 March 2011].

Luna, B.P. 2005. Transparency versus government supervision in Peru. *The International Journal of Not-for-Profit Law*, 7(2), 12–14.

Matzkin, D.S. 2008. Knowledge management in the Peruvian non-profit sector. *Journal of Knowledge Management*, 12(4), 147–59.

Necochea, W.T. 2011. Personal communication. Lima: SOS Faim.

OECD. 2005. *Paris Declaration on Aid Effectiveness* [Online]. Available at: www.oecd.org.

Peruvian Times. 2008. Peru poverty rate dropped last year 5.2 percentage points to 39.3 percent. *Andean Air Mail and Peruvian Times (online edition)*, 27 May [Online]. Available at: http://www.peruviantimes.com/27/peru-poverty-rate-dropped-52-percentage-points-to-393-percent/400/.

Sanborn, C., Cueva, H., Portocarrero, F., List, R., and Salamon, L.M. 1999. Peru, in *Global Civil Society*, edited by L.M. Salamon, S.W. Sokolowski and R. List. Baltimore: Center for Civil Society Studies, Institute for Policy Studies, The Johns Hopkins University.

SOS Faim. 2005. The savings-credit cooperatives in Peru and Ecuador and the development of rural financial services, in *Zoom Microfinance*, edited by SOS Faim, Action pour le développement, vol. 17. Brussels: SOS Faim Belgique asbl.

SOS Faim. 2009. Refinancing guarantees: calculated risks on behalf of small rural farmers, in *Zoom Microfinance*, edited by SOS Faim, Action pour le développement, vol. 28. Brussels: SOS Faim Belgique asbl.

SOS Faim. 2011. *About Us* [Online]. Available at: http://www.sosfaim.be/ong-developpement-EN-sosfaim_en-about_us.htm [accessed: 28 March 2011].

Torres, N. 2010. *Rural Cooperatives – The Experience of Ciderural* [Online]. Available at: http://www.institutodelperu.org.pe/index.php?option=com_co ntent&task=view&id=1188&Itemid=130 [accessed: 28 March 2011].

UNDP. 2010. *Regional Human Development Report for Latin America and the Caribbean 2010. Acting on the Future: Breaking the Intergenerational Transmission of Inequality*. New York: United Nations Development Programme.

World Bank. 2009. *Country Data, Peru* [Online]. Available at: http://data. worldbank.org/country/peru [accessed: 23 March 2011].

13

Nascent Journeys of Social Enterprise Measurements – A Reflection on Practitioners' Experiences

Ian Lucas and David Newton

Introduction

This is an informal review of a six-year collaborative effort to find and develop effective performance management tools for small and medium-sized social enterprises (SMSEs). It primarily involved two managing directors of two community development organizations based in Southampton: West Itchen Community Trust (WICT) and RISE Community Development Trust (RISE). It is worth noting that SMSEs make up the majority of social enterprises (SEs) (IFF 2005), and this finding concurred with our experience in the networks we are involved with, in that very few employ more than 10 full-time employees. Therefore, although not consciously at first, our performance tools concentrated on our own SMSE, which (inadvertently) matches the majority of SEs; that is, ranging from pre-start up to those employing 50 employees.

During this six-year period we have not had the luxury of sabbatical leave for academic study or funding for research. All that we have learned, trialled, experimented with and developed has been done during, or in many cases after, the day job. As we bent funding streams and stretched deadlines to try and make progress on performance management we were also trying to keep our SME-style social enterprises paying the wages, surviving another day and doing some good. In looking back over the past six years of experience and experimentation with performance measurement and management we have had to ask ourselves: 'Was it worth it? Did it make any difference?' Whilst we certainly do not claim any great revelations through this work, we do feel we are able to highlight a number of useful insights, understandings and conclusions from a practitioner perspective, and hope that our learning and the framework we have developed will help others navigate the complexities of social enterprise.

Top-Down Standards and Bottom-Up Community Audit

The origins of our work on and approach to managing performance within social enterprise stem from developing a process we named 'SO123 Community Audit'. SO123 is essentially an 'ideal' high-level process of defining, delivering, and managing social outcomes. Hence the 'SO' in the title refers to social outcomes (and the Southampton Postcode because that is where it was developed!) and the '123' refers to the three areas of activity within an organization which the process examines – planning, delivery and management. The Community Audit is a community-led and -delivered process of checking actual performance against the SO123 ideal standard. The SO123 Community Audit emerged from a convergence of two areas of work being developed independently by the authors.

The first strand related to Dave Newton's work on the Isle of Wight to explore the value of social audit for SMSEs. This lead to a paper on social auditing that looked at the methods of impact measurement being used by the private sector in the world of corporate social responsibility (CSR). The aim was to draw out parallel practical lessons for SMSEs. At the same time Iain Lucas was looking to provide an evaluation of RISE, and considering how we could most effectively understand and evaluate its social mission. It had become clear to him, that an over-reliance on the outside consultant providing the conclusions was not supporting the social mission. Any conclusions provided always found in favour of the client organization. Such terms as failure or even some constructive criticism was not evident. This may be what an organization requires – good PR – but good PR does not make a social mission successful. Iain was now seeking to find ways that an honest and forthright evaluation process could be designed to further progress the social mission of an organization.

During this time both areas of work were discussed at a Development Trust Association (DTA) regional conference which was considering the value of national indicators and standards. As a result of this discussion RISE Community Development Ltd and West Itchen Community Trust (which Dave had now joined) undertook a joint project to develop and test such an approach. In essence we devised a system that would enable the community of beneficiaries to carry out a social audit on local community-based organizations. Through an initial research phase we identified significant benefits from community-led audit. However, a major issue was the likely availability of 'audit-ready' members of the community to lead on such a project.

To address this issue the first live pilot was part appraisal, part training and a personal development programme. The development programme was designed to leave the community with the skills to carry out audits but also the wider knowledge and skills to run community organizations more effectively, so as to improve impact and accountability. Through this approach we sidestepped over-reliance on external consultants and top-down measurement set by funders. This put the community in control of evaluating projects undertaken on their behalf. This very fact of allowing the community the right to question was probably a bridge too far for some funders and external stakeholders but it did keep evaluation money in the community.

The SO123 Appraisal Process

The appraisal element of the pilot process examined three dimensions of an organization, as shown in Figure 13.1: (1) understanding of the community; (2) value of organizational activity; (3) effectiveness of management systems. This required:

- Checking standards of research and dialogue within the community. The outcome of such work should include the initial baseline data and identification of a community's needs and its expectations. This included a process of defining who the community was and so who the beneficiaries should be.
- Verifying the rationale of links from a community's needs to setting organizational objectives.
- Checking that the systems of management are appropriate to collate and report the information required to monitor progress towards organizational objectives.
- Verifying that the impact of any action taken is helping to achieve the organizational objectives.
- Ensuring that sufficient evidence is in place to 'prove' all of the above.

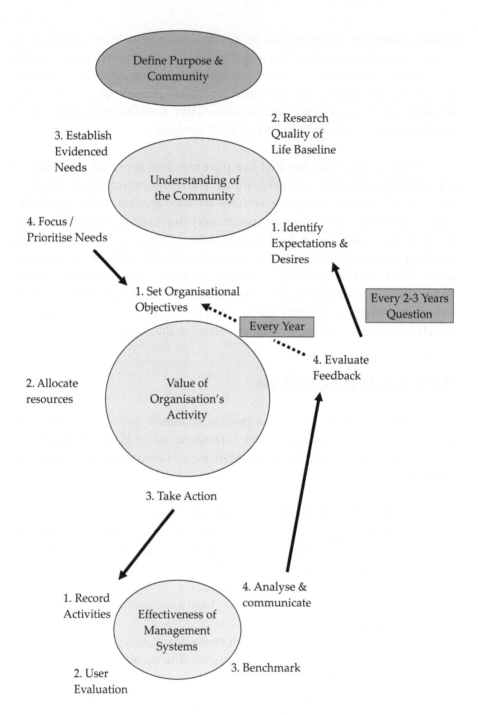

Figure 13.1   SO123 management model – benchmarking for excellence

The notion of capturing impact caused some issues and deliberation: what was an acceptable impact? How should it be quantified? Who should determine acceptable standards? Should impact improve year after year? As something of a compromise we decided that the Community Audit Team would simply have to have make a judgement on this. However, after some further work we realized we needed to build a cycle of continuous improvement into the fundamental assumptions that underpinned the system. But we felt it was important that this be linked to the general responsibility of a community-based organization to engage in community development, and as such we added a further requirement to evaluate whether the organization's community capacity-building raised expectations.

The trial of this process was in the RISE community, where individuals from that community were trained and then undertook an appraisal of RISE. What became clear was that the reality of what RISE had defined as a social mission was not the beneficiaries' reality. This forced us to question who should be setting the aims and the identity of a social mission or, as called by Austin et al. (2006), the social value purpose that should drive an organization forward. Indeed, what was required was not just about measurement but accountability. As Jezard and Master-Coles (2010) state: 'Accountability is not merely evaluation or impact measurement. Evaluation and impact measurement are one-dimensional. They look at what has happened and report on it. There is little meaningful stakeholder engagement, and measurement does little to support an organization to achieve its mission'. At this stage it should be mentioned that we met Cris Jezard, who influenced us enormously on our next steps and throughout the development of our measurement process and the resulting successor organization – the Social Enterprise Foundation (SEF), and a huge debt is owed to him. His greatest contribution was to encourage our desire to place social justice and the rights and responsibilities of communities at the forefront of our organizations. His concepts of inclusive governance ensured we focused not just on the process but how it could be developed by, and benefit, the communities we serve. He was dismissive of the fad for measuring the triple bottom line but passionate about putting an organization's social purpose at its heart. It was his view that by embedding the advancement of social justice within and throughout an organization its social purpose would then become a form of compass informing all action and thinking. Encouraged and inspired by such thinking we took our next challenge to be how to use a performance management system to bring an organization's social purpose to life rather than to simply pin down and quantify its performance. The practical requirement for this was to find ways of empowering and enabling members and other stakeholders to keep this purpose alive and act as its guardians into the future.

Accountability and Community Audit within Membership Organizations

With insight into the performance of RISE as an organization, community audit in practice, and our focus on social purpose, we were inspired to develop the SO123 process further. We explored how to take forward the concept of an identified community setting its own parameters in order to critically evaluate organizations and hold them to account. This is when we realized that a community audit approach and the SO123 process could easily be applied to communities of interest rather than just geographical communities. Equally the concept could be applied to a community of organizations rather than a community of individuals. At that time RISE and WICT were members of the Development Trust Association (DTA) and were experiencing some difficulty with our region's relationship with the organization's centre. As such, we saw this organization as an ideal test-bed for our new thinking and offered our services and this developmental process to the DTA. The offer involved us providing a pilot community audit but with the concept of a geographical community replaced by a 'community' of the organization's members. The offer of support was accepted and our second pilot project began. This work produced some notable insights into some of the potential benefits of a 'community' audit. The process was able to quickly identify that the problems stemmed from a relatively simple communication breakdown. This also highlighted how fragile the relationship between member and organization can be if simple traditional directive channels of communication are used. By having an informed discussion about these issues via an objective framework both members and organization felt able to take cooperative action to address the issues. It was also particularly informative for the community auditors who found out a great deal more about the organization and were able to work more productively within it as a result.

Why Measure Social Enterprise?

The understanding of the importance of engagement and communication developed through this second pilot began to inform our thinking about other umbrella organizations within the social enterprise (SE) sector. This was coupled with an increasing pressure to articulate the concept of SE to the public sector, private sector, the community and voluntary sector, and the wider public. This need for the clear communication of a sector's values became the major driver for a further evolution of our collaboration on performance measurement, management and accountability. This desire to apply our learning was fuelled further when we experienced organizations seeking an advantage in labelling themselves as an SE because it might be seen as legitimation (Dart 2004b). This culminated in a challenge to stem the process of institutionalization, where an organization is given credibility, shown it is trustworthy, ethical, doing good, yet at the same time has no identified social purpose. Further inspection would reveal that such organizations were often just departments or subsections of local authorities and other large human service organizations, as was discovered in recent research by Dart et al. (2010). On top of this issue it was our experience that much 'social enterprise' was taking place with little or no accountability to the communities of beneficiaries. What we felt we needed to do was expose some of this abuse and clarify and protect the use of the term 'SE'.

Throughout 2006 this issue was discussed at meetings of the Hampshire and Isle of Wight Social Enterprise Network (HIWSEN) and the South-East regional meeting of the DTA. There was a general consensus of opinion in all of these debates that as practitioners we wanted the term 'social enterprise' to be a brand that reflected the good practice that was evident and support those organizations who wanted to do better. However, before getting on our high horse we needed to check our own house was in order. This made us stop and think. Would measuring an SE be worth it, as we knew it was always going to be a lot harder to measure performance and be accountable to multiple stakeholders when what is being measured is not always tangible, like financial indicators or market share (Austin et al. 2006). This question forced us to debate further the purpose of managing measurement in an SE. The first conclusion we arrived at was we must measure that which was worthwhile for our organizations, not measure purely for someone else. Certainly the biggest mistake of our journey has been the adoption of a set of measurements that reflect the requirements of stakeholders originating outside our community. These people and organizations would be regarded and labelled by Kretzmann and McKnight's (1996) study of an asset-based community development programme as outsiders, who are not controlled by the people inside the community. So that was where our first change occurred, in that we decided we would not measure for every other organization when our *raison d'être* is our social purpose, not that of an outside agency. That was not a rejection of outside agencies' resources but an acknowledgement that the social purpose is owned by the community and its members have the power to address this purpose.

This rejection of external standards led inevitably to the need to measure progress against our social purpose. Our starting point was to look to the beneficiaries – those people who would benefit from our actions and the ultimate beneficiaries of the organizations' social purpose. It seemed obvious that the key stakeholders for our accountability would be the beneficiaries and as such the key areas of impact to focus on would be the particular benefits to be provided to this group. Therefore, if the identified group whom we said would benefit from our efforts were going to have increased well-being, then how would were we going to measure such an aspiration with limited resources whilst staying solvent? And what of our general duty to address inequality so as to work towards improved social justice? Would it be possible to use the assessment process as a further tool (as we had intended with SO123 Community Audit) to address inequality and increase access to wealth for that identified group? Could that risk the objectivity of an assessment if it was linked to wider objectives or income generation for either an organization or a community?

The Relationship between Enterprise and Social Purpose

These tensions highlighted another issue with SMSEs: how would we make a clear distinction between the social purpose of an SE and its business objectives? Our experience of advising, training and learning from other SMSEs had shown us what a vast range of organizational type and activity there was in the sector. The relationship between each organization's social purpose and its business model could vary widely. In order to make related learning more accessible we began to cluster these types of relationships under three headings characterized by the motive for undertaking social enterprise activity, which we called the three Ps.

The first headings for 'social enterprise type' were:

- *purpose* [later changed to '*product*' to avoid confusion with social purpose]
- *process*
- *profit*.

We defined *purpose/product*-driven social enterprises as being those that are seeking to create benefit through the delivery of the service or product that the enterprise operates. Such enterprises are not necessarily trying to grow income rapidly but instead often seek to simply sustain themselves and add value to beneficiaries where they can. Modern examples include community-owned village pubs and shops, some forms of health and social care delivery in the voluntary sector, and the classic volunteer-run community centre. Historically, much of the cooperative and mutual sector stems from a desire to sustain affordable services such as low-cost healthy food.

Alternatively to the above, we thought of *process*-driven social enterprises as those that created benefit not by what they did but *how* it was done. Examples would include social firms who seek to empower their workers and help them overcome disadvantage in the employment market; or The Big Issue, who work with their vendors to help them create a personal income while improving their self-esteem. Again, such a social enterprise may not always be seeking to maximize margin and profitability. In the above types the business model is entwined in the social purpose and further complicated by factors such as, in some instances, the customer being also the beneficiary. It may also be the case that workers' benefits, conditions and ways of working are an expensive way to do business but integral and effective means of advancing the social purpose.

Our third and final organizational type was the *profit*-driven social enterprise. This would be an SE that had effectively split its impact from its business and in many instances separate organizations would be responsible for each element of the wider aims. This is the approach that RISE Community undertook with their trading activity RISE Computers Ltd. Another classic example would be a registered charity with a wholly owned subsidiary trading company. There is an attractive simplicity to this model as the trading arm can focus on maximizing profit and then this activity finances the parent organization's work to assist its beneficiary group. However, no company operates in a vacuum and it is quite possible that the activities of a trading arm either reveal new opportunities to advance the social purpose or it becomes clear that its activities are having a detrimental impact on the work of the charity.

As we can see when running any type of SMSE, social objectives and business objectives can easily become confused. But it is critical to remember that they are not necessarily the same even if they appear so. These different kinds of objective should be looked at and measured differently. This is because, as with any business, a strategy must be flexible to meet the market needs, even if it is market failure. Additionally, social objectives also have a similar life cycle, and again may change. Here lies the danger: business objectives may need to change and the social objectives may need to change, yet if the methods of measurement or targets remain the same and inappropriately aligned, the processes of the organization will begin to exert more influence on the organization than its purpose. So by adopting dynamic management practices to measure business objectives and by separating the measurement of social purpose we able to begin developing a process to maximize beneficiaries' accountability and relevance over time.

Social Enterprise: Setting its Own Parameters for Success

That is when our experience played more of a role in shaping our methods of measuring the social purpose. Drawing upon past community capacity-building techniques and heavily on the SO123 Community Audit process we were able to focus our measurement of social purpose back on the community. This led us to question the very process and institutionalization of social enterprise. The term 'social enterprise' is always in debate (Defourny, 2001, Lyon and Sepulveda 2009, Jezard and Master-Coles 2010, Peattie and Morley 2008, Ridley-Duff and Bull 2010), but for ourselves we wanted to frame a debate for both experienced and new practitioners. This is where we decided that we would not leave the debate about definition, as this is important, but create an understanding based not on a pure definition, but on practice.

The central practice of SE is the desire to create social change towards social justice: this we called their *social purpose*. It is the *social purpose* that defines the fundamental difference between social and private enterprise: *social purpose* lies at the centre of social enterprise; it is the driver of the enterprise, its *raison d'être*. That is where we decided we could apply the same principles of the community audit to the development and support of social enterprise practitioners as they pursue their social purpose. Here was born the Social Enterprise Foundation.

Within that greater purpose our practice made us aware that decision-making processes and thus the measurement of any actions taken are not easy. This is where we decided to take the fundamental areas of decision-making in a social enterprise and focus those actions around the social purpose (see Figure 13.2). The following were the three fundamental values that should underpin the pursuit of the *social purpose* through enterprise: (1) sustainable enterprise; (2) inclusive governance; (3) social investment.

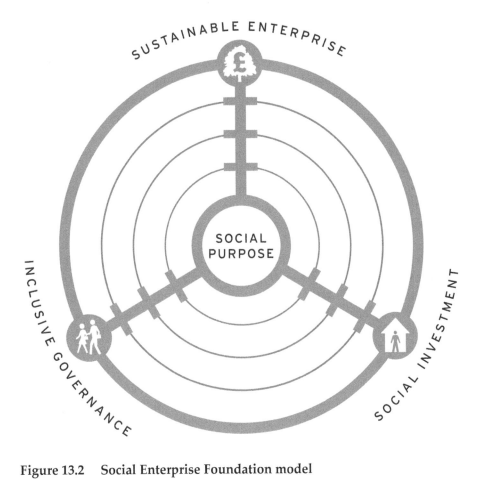

Figure 13.2   Social Enterprise Foundation model

Sustainable Enterprise

While its social purpose lies at the core of a social enterprise, it could not function if it was not running a successful business. This requires some form of trading but what seems like trading or enterprise can sometimes be misleading, such as the common practice of voluntary organizations undertaking to deliver work for a local authority under a contract. While this may seem like a commercial arrangement it is often more akin to a grant-funding relationship, with the voluntary organization doing what it has always done. So what is the definition of being 'enterprising'? We knew we meant something along the lines of 'operating in a business-like manner so as to sell an identifiable product or service to an identifiable market' (not just one council); however, even this definition created challenges. Eventually we set about using a series of indicators to give a sense of whether the undertaking was genuine and the organization was trying to be enterprising.

Included in the values of enterprise, the Social Enterprise Foundation uses the term *'sustainable enterprise'* because the term 'sustainable' has immediate and profound consequences for an SE compared to the effect on a standard enterprise. When we chose this term 'sustainability' we were aware that it was being used extensively – sustaining social value, economic sustainability, sustainable social change. It was if the holy grail were sustainability. However, when we explored this term we felt it was especially relevant, as the Foundation wanted to ensure that SEs have a heightened awareness of the competing goals, economic sustainability and sustaining social value.

It could be argued that economic sustainability strategies are about not decreasing assets whilst generating added value. In SEs this approach can create preoccupations with productivity, investment and profit (Reinhardt 2000). Yet an SE has to balance this goal with sustaining added social value. So to help such a process we felt that a closer examination and use of the term 'sustainability' could help. Sustainability as a formal concept was introduced onto the world stage in 1987 via a report by the World Commission on the Environment and Development, known as the Brundtland Report (WCED 1987). Although the term and associated metrics have been used previously and since by various organizations and research papers (Vos 2007), it is the 1987 report that set out to clearly define sustainable development as 'development that meets the needs of the present without compromising the ability of future generations to meet their own needs'. In analysing this statement some key components emerge. The first is that meeting the needs of the present raises the question of how we meet our needs, which is both an economic and societal issue. The second and most profound is how we ensure that future generations can meet their own needs, again posing the question of how they will meet their needs. This fundamentally changes the first question from not just a societal and economic issue into one that has to consider what the legacy of that action will be. Most notably it is a matter of how we use and exploit existing capital and what is left to bequeath the next generations. The concept of capital is used to cover many topics – economic, social, natural and entrepreneurial. This is what we wanted to consider in our own and others' practice, the impact of this generation's uses of capital upon the next. Such thinking was a recognition of the long-term nature of a social purpose. In other words we wanted to redefine the question to be not so much asking what sustainability is, but rather what it means to be an unsustainable enterprise (Vos 2007).

Inclusive Governance

If a social enterprise is to be sustainable and run for a social purpose, then its activities will benefit a group of people – its 'beneficiaries'. One of the key values in the organization's work with those beneficiaries is to do what is genuinely right for them. We felt that SE should help transform beneficiaries from passive participation to active involvement. Further, we felt that in doing so it should engage beneficiaries in the whole organization by providing a framework for discourse on trading activities and the acknowledgement of the need for wealth generation. As a result of our learning from community audit we also recognized that beneficiaries needed to be closely involved in developing the process to build empowerment rather than dependency.

Beneficiary involvement can be built into legal, governance and management structures. It can range from occasional consultation to full self-governance. As we explored different approaches to involvement within the sector we quickly identified a sliding scale of endeavour. This ranged from philanthropy to self-help with various forms of participation and cooperation occupying much of the middle ground. When we looked at the history of SE we found that many 'self-help' models are built on self-governance and we would argue that the modern social enterprise movement arose from such a philosophy. One such movement that adopted a social construction based on a self-help form of organization was that of the anarchists. The International took place in 1872 and anarchists left the coalition because of the arguments over class and state control. They wanted to advocate a pluralist form of organization that did not rely on the state; such an approach has remained through the Cooperative Movement's attachment to collective organization and community-based control (Ridley-Duff 2007).

This aim of achieving an inclusive governance approach was always about creating an SE phenomenon constructed by the people who benefit from the social purpose. In such an enterprise it is they who would dominate the dialogue and debates, laying down rules for their SE, rules that are aligned in their best interests. This process we have termed 'inclusive governance'. This process provides the platform through which the objectives of the social enterprise can now be set, together with the means of attaining those objectives. As such, governance will then monitor the performance of the organization against agreed objectives and means. This process should provide proper incentives for the management to pursue objectives that are in the interests of the social purpose. It should enable beneficiaries to monitor it effectively, so encouraging the social enterprise to use its resources effectively.

Social Investment

We believe that the resources generated by the social enterprise should be used to meet its social purpose. Those resources that go directly towards this purpose are known as the organization's *social investment*. A social investment is not necessarily a clearly identifiable lump sum, as many social enterprises invest in the running of the organization as the vehicle for achieving their purpose. For example, an organization that has been established to help the long-term unemployed in a certain area may spend a significant amount of time and money recruiting, training and supporting its beneficiaries as employees of the company. The costs associated with this (above the 'normal' costs of a commercial company) can be viewed as that organization's social investment. A social investment should be managed effectively, and in proportion to the costs of the core enterprise.

In order to effectively manage a programme of social investment an organization should be able to demonstrate an understanding of its impact, be seeking to improve its effectiveness, and be continuing to invest appropriate resources in its furtherance. The founders of the Social Enterprise Foundation and many of those we consulted felt it important that the degree of success and effectiveness remains a judgement for engaged beneficiaries rather than external observers. As such there is no requirement on any SMSE to quantify its impact by using any particular measuring tool or systems. However, an organization may find it useful to use such methods to communicate its impact to its beneficiaries as long as such measures do not evolve into being the de facto statement of success.

Communicating Impact to Key Stakeholders

Before measuring the impact of an organization, it is necessary to map out who and what it is wished to affect – the social purpose – and then consider what else and who else might be affected – externalities and stakeholders. This is where we referred back to the first section in the SO123 model to help a community identify its own social purpose, that is, understanding itself. The second area of the SO123 model looks at value of organizational activities and, in essence, the impact.

What is Impact?

Impact can be thought of as a change of state resulting from an action. Likewise, the impact on individuals or stakeholder groups can be assessed by considering what has changed for them. While a number of techniques can be used, the 'Five Capitals' model developed by Forum for the Future is a useful framework for a holistic view of impact. The Five Capitals model groups all things in the world into five categories of value:

1. natural capital – *natural resources and ecosystems*

2. human capital – *individual capability and well-being*

3. social capital – *the value of relationships and social networks*

4. financial capital – *money and other forms of monetized wealth*

5. manufactured capital – *materials and fixed assets produced within supply chains.*

At any given time all individuals and/or stakeholder groups in the world will have control of, influence over, or access to a mixed stock of these assets. The impact an organization has on a group or individual can be thought of as the net difference in this stock of capital and how that difference is valued. The Five Capitals model type of thinking could relate specifically to SMSEs as outlined below.

1. *Natural capital and the environment.* Any organization can look at its use of resources and the environmental impact of its day-to-day operations. Many social enterprises are also trying to bring about positive environmental change through raising awareness, changing behaviour and making improvements to the local environment.

2. *Human capital and individual capability and well-being.* Your enterprise has an effect on people as individuals – your employees, volunteers, beneficiaries and others who come into contact with your organization. There is much debate about how to define a person's 'well-being' but this is generally thought to mean the individual's level of satisfaction with their life, sense of personal development and social connectedness (through friends and community groups).

3. *Social capital and the community.* Social capital is about relationships, neighbourliness, social networks, support and civic engagement. You can measure how people feel about their local area, but you can also examine statistics about the community organizations in that area and the partnerships between them.

4.   *Financial capital and the economy.* There are many ways in which your enterprise can affect the economy. For example, if you employ people you have a direct economic impact on them and their families. Or you might address an economic disadvantage by providing an affordable service designed for people on low incomes.

5.   *Manufactured capital and organizational resources.* You may provide a product that would otherwise be missing from the local economy, or bring new materials, machinery and manufacturing capability to an area that had no such potential previously.

In-depth analysis of such interactions is beyond the resources of most SMSEs but as a guiding framework it can add great value to how one thinks about the impact of one's organization. It forces one to think 'What has changed?' 'What have our beneficiaries put into this process and what have they gained as a result of this investment?' If you are seeking to address disadvantage within your community, using such a framework as the basis for your needs analysis (as in the SO123 process) can create new insights and hopefully reveal new potential and opportunity.

Complexity and Value of Data

Armed with such insight and the resulting data it is arguably then possible to prove impact and value and therefore continue to improve performance. But such insight is wasted if it is not used or properly understood by key decision-makers. As an example, we recall a study of five years of WICT's performance against its original business plan so as to demonstrate the economic benefit it had had on the city of Southampton. This was undertaken at the request of the Regional Development Agency via their local accountable body – Southampton City Council. The resulting document ran to well over a hundred pages with forecasts of economic impact based on monetized outputs and a series of 25-year discounted cash-flow analyses. It soon became clear that the officers responsible for evaluating this document simply did not have the time to evaluate it in any detail and had not been given the time to develop a full understanding of the economic methodologies being applied. However, it did seem to benefit the officers' perception of our ability to deliver outcomes because we were able to deliver that document. For this external observer the complexity of management system had become an informal shorthand for effective management and positive impact almost regardless of the view of the community we served.

Final Reflections

This for us is where we began our story, why we wanted to challenge the notion that if someone uses a management performance system then they have a positive impact. If anything this journey has shown us that understanding that data must be for you to enable you to meet the standards set by your community. As discussed earlier, any fundamental change is by the community; they constitute the primary building blocks of capacity-building. We hope this story of ours has shown how we came to realize that a balanced performance and accountability are key to improving the impact of SMSEs. We needed to remember that to be accountable you need honest communication of impact to members and/or beneficiary groups. They do not need to rely on external auditors to confirm honesty. *They* can appoint and/or elect auditors from among their own number and demand the use of language and indicators they understand and value.

The models that have been created and the underlying understanding of the measurement have been used extensively in both RISE and WICT. Due to its inclusive approach it has been possible to engage with the public sector, the private sector and the third sector. It has helped stakeholders and the wider community understand what we are trying to achieve and how they can provide support. In addition the model has been applied when supporting other local SMSEs and has had a strong impact on their focus of social purpose and how they will achieve their purpose. The underlying feedback is often along the lines of 'I can now see what I need to do and how I am going to get there'. So in answer to our original questions 'Was it worth it? Did it make any difference?', I can only suggest that the communities we have worked with can be the judge of that and that is how we like it!

References

Austin, J., Stevenson, H., and Wei-Skillern, J. 2006. Social and commercial entrepreneurship: same, different, or both? *Entrepreneurship Theory and Practice*, 30(1), 1–22.

Dart, R. 2004a. Being 'business-like' in a nonprofit organization: a grounded and inductive typology. *Nonprofit and Voluntary Sector Quarterly*, 33(2), 290–310.

Dart, R. 2004b. The legitimacy of social enterprise. *Non-Profit Management and Leadership*, 13(4), 411–424.

Dart, R., Clow, E., and Armstrong, A. 2010. Meaningful difficulties in the mapping of social enterprises. *Social Enterprise Journal*, 6(3), 186–93.

Dees, G. 1998. *The Meaning of Social Entrepreneurship*. Paper funded by Kauffman Centre for Entrepreneurial Leadership.

Defourney, J. 2001. Introduction: from third sector to social enterprise, in *The Emergence of Social Enterprise*, edited by C. Bourgaza and J. Defourny. London: Routledge, 1–28.

IFF Research Ltd. 2005. *A Survey of Social Enterprises across the UK, Small Business Service* [Online]. Available at: http://webarchive.nationalarchives.gov.uk/+/http://www.cabinetoffice.gov.uk/media/cabinetoffice/third_sector/assets/survey_social_enterprise_across_uk.pdf [accessed: September 2012].

Jezard, C., and Master-Coles, R. 2010. *Your Guide to Spotting a Social Enterprise*. Southampton: Natty Platy.

Kretzmann, J., and McKnight, J.P. (1996). Assets-based community development. *National Civic Review*, 85(4), 23–9.

Lyon, F., and Sepulveda, L. 2009. Mapping social enterprises: past approaches, challenges and future directions. *Social Enterprise Journal*, 5(1), 83–94.

Peattie, K., and Morley, A. 2008. Eight paradoxes of the social enterprise research agenda. *Social Enterprise Journal*, 4(2), 91–107.

Reinhardt, F. 2000. Sustainability and the firm. *Interfaces*, 30(3), 26–41.

Ridley-Duff, R. 2007. Communitarian perspectives on social enterprise. *Corporate Governance: An International Review*, 15(2), 382–92.

Ridley-Duff, R., and Bull, M. 2010. *Understanding Social Enterprise: Theory and Practice*. London: Sage.

Vos, R.O. 2007. Defining sustainability: a conceptual orientation. *Journal of Chemical Technology and Biotechnology*, 82(4), 334–9.

WCED (World Commission on Environment and Development). 1987. *Our Common Future*. Oxford: Oxford University Press, Oxford.

Conclusion

This book has provided a much-needed focus on contextual factors influencing change, ethical stance and sustainability of third sector organizations. The layout of the book has been designed to provide a perspective almost as broad as the third sector itself. As such, it covers three broad areas: third sector financial services, third sector academic work, and finally a section on reflective practitioner accounts. Together these have provided a body of knowledge which can be built upon with subsequent research into these areas.

The value of all the contributions to this book is to reflect the breadth and diversity of the third sector in their social, financial, economic and international dimensions. Furthermore, the academic performance measurement and management contributions provide an indication of breadth of research opportunities available in this area.

Undoubtedly, the latent potential within the third sectors of national economies is vast, and as yet largely untapped. There are signs that successive governments are waking up to this potential, and intend to reposition such organizations centrally with the socioeconomic aspect as a much more integrated and participative element of society. The challenge for third sector organizations is therefore ultimately to retain their innate philanthropic stance, whilst adopting a more business-like organizational position regarding the way they manage their resources and offer their services to the local community or central government. This is a huge and immanent challenge for a sector which has traditionally been left to do its own thing.

As this book goes to print, there are more academics engaging in third sector research, particularly from a performance management and sustainability standpoint. In the UK the philosophy underpinning the Big Society could mean that more imaginative ways of delivering public services may be devised. The Big Society may be interpreted in different ways depending on the individual or stakeholder group's political ideological stance. An interpretation with neo-liberal leanings may view this philosophy as an opportunity to decentralize and empower localism to free up social enterprise to deliver public services in more imaginative and efficient ways without the inertia of the dead hand of the state. On the other hand, a more left-wing interpretation could conclude that it is a cynical ploy to fulfil a free market dogmatic agenda of a small state provision, which would have been unthinkable prior to the financial crisis of 2008.

There is no doubt that the changes to public service delivery will bring both opportunities and challenges to the third sector. With respect to opportunities, it could result in services being delivered by the third sector which were previously delivered by the state. Alternatively it could involve a tripartite approach involving public, private and third sector organizations. The challenges may emerge in the form of funding cuts to those services that were previously commissioned by public sector bodies to third sector organizations either being withdrawn or appreciably scaled down. The next few years will be critical for the members of the third sector as they position themselves to maximize the opportunities that may be presented to their sector.

Index

Page numbers in *italics* refer to figures.

For Product Safety Concerns and Information please contact our
EU representative GPSR@taylorandfrancis.com Taylor & Francis
Verlag GmbH, Kaufingerstraße 24, 80331 München, Germany